Macroeconomic Analysis

an intermediate text

Macroeconomic Analysis
an intermediate text

Second Edition

David Cobham

LONGMAN
London and New York

Addison Wesley Longman Limited
Edinburgh Gate
Harlow
Essex CM20 2JE
United Kingdom
and Associated Companies throughout the world

Published in the United States of America
by Addison Wesley Longman, New York

First published 1987
Fourth impression 1991
Second edition 1998

ISBN 0582 27452 4

British Library Cataloguing-in-Publication Data

A catalogue record for this book is available from the
British Library

Library of Congress Cataloging-in-Publication Data
Cobham, David P.
  Macroeconomics analysis: an intermediate text/
  David Cobham. – 2nd ed.
     p. cm.
  Includes bibliographical references and index.
  ISBN 0-582-27452-4 (paper)
     1. Macroeconomics.   I. Title.
  HB172.5.C63   1998
  339-dc21   97-51476
Typeset by 57
Printed in Malaysia, PP

for Mollie, Jean and Pat

Contents

Preface to the first edition

This book was written mainly for second-year university and polytechnic students, though others may also find it useful. It assumes some familiarity with elementary Keynesian macroeconomics, and it assumes that students have mastered all they need to know at this level about the national income accounts and the construction of price indices.

It is intended to give students a grounding in the techniques of macroeconomic analysis (although it does not use calculus or sophisticated mathematics). It therefore pays particular attention to the three key macro models – the Keynesian cross, the IS–LM and aggregate demand/aggregate supply models. At the same time it aims to cover all the main subject areas of modern macroeconomics, from consumption and investment to inflation and open economy issues. It is therefore selective *within* rather than *between* subjects, and avoids lengthy discussions of the empirical evidence and case-study material. However, a small number of additional readings covering both analytical and empirical material are suggested at the end of each chapter.

Above all, the book is designed to give a coherent and structured outline of macroeconomics in a simple but clear historical perspective which goes from classical via Keynesian and monetarist to New Classical macroeconomics. This inevitably involves some simplification, but at this level of economics some sacrifice of complexity to clarity is well justified, and the key qualifications to the arguments developed in the text are mentioned in the concluding sections of the chapters.

I am grateful to students and colleagues at St Andrews University on whom this text was first tried out; to Bill Lynch and Alex Pratt who read preliminary drafts of some chapters at an early and crucial stage; to Chris Adam who gave me a number of useful comments on the book; and, most of all, to Mike Sumner and George Zis who commented in detail on the first draft. Nevertheless, full responsibility for this final version rests with me.

Preface to second edition

In preparing this new edition I have tried to retain the strengths of the previous edition but at the same time to extend significantly the range of material covered. The thirteen chapters of the first edition have therefore become Part 1 of this, and six further chapters have been added in a new Part 2.

The chapters of Part 1 have been revised to take account of new developments in macroeconomics since the mid-1980s and to remedy some previous omissions. In particular, the history of schools of thought given in Chapters 1 and 13 has been extended, and now includes the emergence of New Keynesian economics, the difficulties experienced by New Classical Macro, and the revival of what I have called Mainstream economics, an eclectic grouping that has absorbed ideas from both of the former schools within a framework which is identifiably descended from non-traditional Keynesians, non-New Classical monetarists and the Keynesian–monetarist convergence of which much was made in the first edition. At the same time relevant chapters now include more material on, among other things, rational expectations and consumption, Tobin's q theory of investment, later Keynesian and buffer-stock theories of the demand for money, and the flow of funds derivation of the credit counterparts/money supply relationship.

Part 2 covers more advanced material, at the level of macro systems rather than single sectors, ranging from the IS–LM with a government budget constraint through policy ineffectiveness, time inconsistency, and debt and deficits, to the overshooting exchange rate model, and concludes with a more detailed look at elements of New Keynesian and New Classical economics not covered elsewhere. It operates at a higher technical level, with more maths including some calculus (the only point at which calculus is used in Part 1 is for the Baumol–Tobin transactions demand in Chapter 5). However, the intuition underlying the various models is always elucidated, and mathematical derivations are carefully explained.

Part 2, in particular, contains many more references and suggestions for further reading, while nearly every chapter now includes some exercises at the end.

I am grateful to students at St Andrews who have heard some of the new material in lecture form, to my macroeconomics colleagues at St Andrews for discussion on various issues, and to Alexander Cobham for his comments and encouragement on some of the new chapters and for constructing the index.

PART 1

Chapter 1

Introduction

The aim of this chapter is to introduce some of the key debates in macroeconomics and to revise or introduce the three most important models of the determination of national income. It gives a simple and schematic account of the history of macroeconomics, concentrating on the answers given by the various schools of thought to two questions: (1) is a market economy self-equilibrating, in particular can a sustained situation of unemployment exist? and (2) if the economy is not self-equilibrating can the government do anything to improve it, in particular can the government reduce and/or prevent sustained states of unemployment? The three models of national income determination are introduced at appropriate points in this historical account.

Classical macroeconomics

The starting point of any history of macroeconomics must be 'classical' macroeconomics, but the term 'classical' is not unambiguous. In other areas of economics, especially that of value and distribution, 'classical' refers to writers such as Adam Smith, David Ricardo and Karl Marx who used largely non-marginalist methods of analysis (the so-called 'surplus approach'), as opposed to the 'neoclassical' writers who used the marginalist methods and propounded marginalist theories of value and distribution, from Stanley Jevons, Karl Menger and Léon Walras onwards. In macroeconomics, however, conventional practice has been strongly influenced by Keynes's definition of the word 'classical' in the first chapter of his *General Theory* (1936) to include more or less all macroeconomics before him. This was a considerable oversimplification (though the marginalist revolution had less obvious importance for macro- than for microeconomics); however, the usage is now so widespread that it will be employed here without further question.

The answer given by classical macroeconomics in this sense to the first of the two questions posed above was unequivocal: a market economy is self-equilibrating, it adjusts so that the supply of and demand for labour are equated, and sustained states of *involuntary* unemployment – where people wish to work at the existing wage rate but cannot find a job – cannot occur. In essence, macroeconomic relationships were regarded by classical economics as simple aggregations from microeconomic relationships, and wages and prices were assumed to be flexible at the aggregate macro as well as the disaggregated micro level. This can be seen most clearly in the work of Walras, which can best be thought of as a substantial contribution to the development of general equilibrium theory. It can also be seen in Say's law (after the economist J.-B. Say), the idea that the aggregate demand for goods and services must always be equal to the aggregate supply of goods and services, on the grounds that economic agents (firms and households) will supply goods and services only if, and because, they demand other goods and services.

Classical macroeconomics was thus hardly a separate branch of the subject. In particular, as Keynes remarked, it had no theory of the demand for (or supply of) output as a whole. It had a theory of the determination of the price level, the Quantity Theory of Money (see Chapter 5 below), and a theory of the determination of real wages in the labour market (Chapter 8). But it had very little to say about aggregate demand, it perceived no problem of unemployment and it envisaged no role for any form of macro policy other than control of the money supply to prevent inflation. The essential reason for all this was that classical economics concentrated, at least in its more formal and rigorous analysis, on the long-term development of the economy, and it produced no clear-cut agreed explanation of short-run fluctuations in economic activity.

Keynes

John Maynard Keynes was an economist in Cambridge (England) whose *The General Theory of Employment, Interest and Money* is commonly thought to have produced a revolution in macroeconomics. At the very least Keynes's work can be regarded as the *sine qua non* of modern macroeconomics, and his writings and ideas still provide a background to the thinking even of those economists who oppose them most strongly.

The answers Keynes gave to the two questions posed above are clear: (1) the economy is *not* self-equilibrating, and sustained states of involuntary unemployment may occur; and (2) the government *can* do something to reduce and/or prevent unemployment, by making appropriate use of monetary and fiscal policy. Keynes therefore provided a justification for a policy of macroeconomic intervention, in contrast to the *laissez-faire* of the classical economists who preceded him.

Exactly how Keynes arrived at these answers is, however, less clear, for his writings are open to a number of interpretations. Exactly what is the 'correct' interpretation of Keynes is not a subject discussed in this book, although occasional reference is made to it; the term 'Keynesian' is used here primarily to refer to the work of economists who *saw themselves* as following in Keynes's footsteps, whether they 'really were' or not. One thing that is clear, however, is that in contrast to classical economics Keynes was very concerned to develop a theory of the demand for output as a whole and hence a model of the (short-run) determination of national income. The simplest model of this kind is that referred to as the Keynesian cross model, though Keynes himself never expressed his ideas in quite this way.

The Keynesian cross model: revision

It is commonplace in economic models for equilibrium to occur where supply equals demand; for a model of the determination of national income this means that equilibrium occurs where aggregate supply, that is the output of all goods and services, is equal to the aggregate demand for goods and services. The key characteristic of the Keynesian cross model is that aggregate supply responds passively to aggregate demand and national income is therefore determined by the latter. On the other hand, aggregate demand, which in the simplest case in the sum of consumption and investment, is partly autonomous and partly positively related to income, with a marginal propensity to spend (on all forms of demand) less than unity. This means that aggregate demand depends on income as follows: at low levels of income aggregate demand is greater than income, and at high levels of income it is less. On the other hand, aggregate supply or output is simply equal to national income, as a result of the way both aggregates are defined and measured in terms of the *value added* in production which corresponds to the factor incomes (wages, profit, interest and rent) generated. Equilibrium, that is the position from which there is no endogenous tendency for the economy to move, occurs at the (unique) level of income where (*ex ante* or planned) aggregate demand is equal to income and therefore output. Moreover, it can be argued that this is a *stable* equilibrium, for if demand is greater than output, firms will find their sales exceed their output and will therefore expand it; while if demand is less than output, firms will find their output exceeds their sales and will contract it.

In diagrammatic terms an aggregate demand curve AD can be constructed as in Figure 1.1 which has demand on the vertical axis and income (or output) on the horizontal axis. AD is the vertical sum of consumption *C*, which varies positively with income *Y* and may (as in Figure 1.1) or may not have a positive intercept on the vertical axis (i.e. an autonomous component), *plus* investment *I* which is assumed to be autonomous: AD is constructed by adding together the amounts of *C* and *I* at each level of income. Figure 1.1 also shows a 45° line through the origin: it is a geometric property of such a line that at any point along it, the level of income (e.g. at point X the distance OA = BX) is equal to the level of demand (the distance OB = AX); thus the 45° line is a representation in the diagram of the condition for equilibrium that aggregate demand, measured on the vertical axis, must be equal to aggregate supply

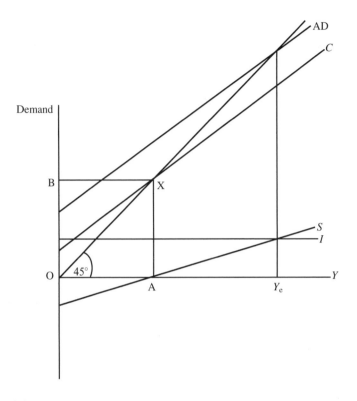

Figure 1.1

or output (which equals income), measured on the horizontal axis. It is also a property of the 45° line that its slope is equal to one (unity), for the slope of a straight line is given by the ratio of the length of the vertical side to that of the horizontal side of any right-angled triangle drawn underneath the line with the line as the third side, such as OAX; the slopes of the *C* or **AD** curves, on the other hand, are less than one. Equilibrium occurs in this model where aggregate demand is equal to income and output, that is where the **AD** curve and the 45° line intersect or *cross* (hence the name of the model), which is at income Y_e in Figure 1.1. Changes in aggregate demand, that is shifts of the **AD** curves caused by shifts of the *C* or *I* curves, cause changes in income, with equilibrium income occurring where the new **AD** curve intersects the 45° line.

The same analysis can be carried out in algebraic terms as follows. The elements of aggregate demand are given by

$$C = a + bY \tag{1.1}$$

$$I = \bar{I} \tag{1.2}$$

where *a* and *b* are constants representing the autonomous component of consumption and the marginal propensity to consume respectively, and the bar over the I indicates that investment is autonomous. The equilibrium condition is

$$Y = C + I \qquad [1.3]$$

that is, output or income Y is equal to total aggregate demand $C + I$. Substituting from [1.1] and [1.2] into [1.3] gives

$$Y = a + bY + \bar{I} \qquad [1.4]$$

In order to express Y in terms of autonomous elements and parameters only (i.e. in terms which do not include any Y element), equation [1.4] needs to be manipulated as follows:

$$Y - bY = a + \bar{I}$$

$$Y(1 - b) = a + \bar{I}$$

$$Y = \frac{a + \bar{I}}{1 - b} = \frac{1}{1 - b} \cdot (a + \bar{I}) \qquad [1.5]$$

Here $(a + \bar{I})$ is total autonomous expenditure and $1/(1 - b)$ is the multiplier, that is the amount by which total autonomous expenditure must be multiplied to obtain the equilibrium level of income. Similarly, the *change* in income which results from a *change* in total autonomous expenditure is equal to the latter multiplied by $1/(1 - b)$:

$$\Delta Y = \frac{1}{1 - b} \cdot \Delta(a + \bar{I}), \text{or}$$

$$\frac{\Delta Y}{\Delta(a + \bar{I})} = \frac{1}{1 - b} \qquad [1.6]$$

where Δ means 'the change in'. It is useful to call this multiplier the 'basic multiplier' to distinguish it from the multipliers for (changes in) particular components of autonomous expenditure which may or may not be the same (for example, the multipliers for government expenditure or taxes – a negative component – which are considered in Chapter 4).

The above analysis can also be carried out in terms of an alternative form of the equilibrium condition: aggregate demand is equal to consumption *plus* investment, but income is equal by definition to consumption *plus* saving, therefore the equality of aggregate demand and output or income can be expressed as the equality of saving and investment, where saving can be thought of as the (only) withdrawal from the circular flow of income, and investment as the (only) injection into the flow. Diagrammatically this can be shown as in Figure 1.1 by the intersection of saving and investment at Y_e, where the saving curve S is constructed by subtracting C vertically from Y (i.e. from the 45° line along which the vertical distance from the horizontal axis is equal to Y). The S curve must have an intercept on the vertical axis equal in magnitude but of the opposite sign to that of the C curve, and it must cut the horizontal axis at the level of income where consumption equals income and the C curve cuts the 45° line; if the diagram is drawn correctly the S curve will intersect the I curve at the same level of income as that at which the AD curve intersects the 45° line. In terms of the algebra,

$$S = Y - C = Y - a - bY = -a + (1 - b)Y$$

$$I = \bar{I}$$

Equilibrium occurs where $S = I$:

$$-a + (1 - b)Y = \bar{I}$$

$$(1 - b)Y = a + \bar{I}$$

$$Y = \frac{a + \bar{I}}{1 - b}$$

as before.

Finally the above analysis can be extended to incorporate government expenditure on goods and services G together with tax revenue T, where consumption is now related to disposable income $Y_d = Y - T$; and to incorporate exports X and imports F. Aggregate demand is now equal to $C + I + G + X - F$, which must be equal to output or income Y for equilibrium. Since Y is now equal to $Y_d + T = C + S + T$, the alternative form of the equilibrium condition is obtained as follows:

$$Y = C + S + T = C + I + G + X - F$$

$$S + T = I + G + X - F$$

$$S + T + F = I + G + X \qquad [1.7]$$

where the left-hand side of [1.7] is withdrawals from the circular flow of income and the right-hand side is injections into it. This more comprehensive version of the Keynesian cross model is discussed in Chapter 4.

The Keynesian cross model is a very simplified model and it suffers from at least three obvious defects: (a) it includes no money and no interest rate, or more technically no 'monetary sector'; (b) it implicitly assumes an exogenously fixed price level, which does not vary when output and income vary; and (c) it incorporates no analysis of the labour market and implicitly assumes an exogenously fixed wage level. However, it produces two key results related to the two questions posed at the beginning of the chapter and Keynes's answers to them. Firstly, income can in principle be at any level, depending on aggregate demand, and there is nothing that makes it tend towards the full employment level of income (which was not even specified in the above exposition). Secondly, in principle the government can do something to bring this level of income closer to the full employment level, by varying its own expenditure G (which directly affects aggregate demand) or by varying tax revenue T (which affects aggregate demand indirectly via its influence on disposable income and hence consumption). Thus the Keynesian cross model is consistent with the rationale Keynes provided for an active macroeconomic policy.

Keynesians versus neoclassicals

Keynes's *General Theory* led to a lively debate in the 1940s and 1950s between those economists who saw themselves as his followers and other economists who felt closer to the instincts and policy recommendations of pre-Keynesian classical economics but were prepared to use Keynes's analytical framework with its emphasis on aggregate demand in arguing against him and his followers. These economists are commonly referred to in macroeconomics as *neoclassical economists* or neoclassicals. The answers they gave to the two questions posed at the beginning of this chapter were as follows: (1) yes, a market economy is self-equilibrating and it will automatically tend to full employment, provided wages and prices are flexible; and (2) in theory there is therefore no need for the government to intervene in the economy, but in practice the automatic mechanisms may take so long to work that some limited intervention may be justified. Much of the argument between the Keynesians and the neoclassicals was conducted in terms of the second of the three models of national income determination, the IS–LM model.

The IS–LM model: introduction

This model involves adding a monetary sector to the Keynesian cross model; it therefore corrects for the first of the three defects of that model listed above (in fact historically the IS–LM model preceded the Keynesian cross model and the latter originated as a simplification of the former).

The condition for equilibrium in the money market is that the supply of money equals the demand for it; the supply is generally assumed to be fixed exogenously by the government or central bank and the demand to depend positively on income and negatively on the interest rate. The money market therefore interacts with the market for goods and services where aggregate demand depends on income as before and now on the interest rate too, since investment is assumed to depend partly on the latter. The effect is that both income and the interest rate are determined simultaneously by the interaction of the money and goods and services markets. Figure 1.2 gives the most common, diagrammatic, representation of the model. With the interest rate on the vertical axis and income on the horizontal axis the IS curve shows all the combinations of income and interest rate at which the goods and services market is in equilibrium, while the LM curve shows all the combinations at which the money market is in equilibrium: the only combination where both markets are in equilibrium, that is the unique point of overall equilibrium, occurs where the two curves intersect.

The construction and use of this model are described in detail in Chapter 7. For present purposes what should be noted is that the IS–LM model is a more comprehensive model than the Keynesian cross model of the *determination of aggregate demand*: it includes a monetary sector, and this allows a wider range of relationships and effects to be discussed. For example, the government can

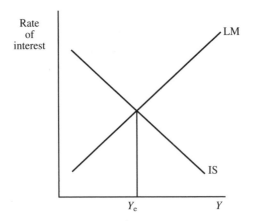

Figure 1.2

influence income in this model by manipulating the supply of money, as well as by varying government expenditure or taxes. However, prices and wages remain exogenous to the IS–LM model and it includes no labour market.

The Keynesian–neoclassical synthesis

Keynes had emphasised aggregate demand in a way that classical economics had not; the neoclassicals were prepared to argue within Keynes's framework but the way in which they used it was different. Essentially they argued that provided wages and prices were flexible then if there was (temporarily) less than full employment wages and prices would fall, and this would lead to increases in real aggregate demand which would restore full employment. In terms of the IS–LM model a fall in prices shifts the LM curve and, more controversially, the IS curve to the right, so increasing aggregate demand and the equilibrium level of income (as in the Keynesian cross model, aggregate supply responds passively to aggregate demand). What this means is that if wages and prices are flexible there cannot be a shortage or deficiency of aggregate demand, so that there cannot be an equilibrium with less than full employment. This conclusion was strongly resisted by the Keynesians (the debate is surveyed in Chapter 8), but in the end they were forced to concede it. However, the neoclassicals were also obliged to concede that in practice wages and prices did not seem to be very flexible, so that there *was* a justification for the kind of macroeconomic policy supported by the Keynesians.

A 'truce' of this sort between Keynesians and neoclassicals, often referred to as the 'Keynesian–neoclassical synthesis', was reached in the mid-1950s. It involved in effect an agreement that different conclusions were appropriate in theory and in practice; alternatively it could be understood as giving different conclusions for different time periods, on the grounds that wages and prices were inflexible in the short run but flexible in the long run.

Keynesians versus monetarists

This synthesis allowed Keynesian economists to continue their work on short-run macro policy much as before, but in the 1960s they came under attack from a different group of economists who later became known as monetarists. There was some overlap between monetarists and neoclassicals, but the overlap was always limited and there are notable examples of economists who were neoclassical in one debate but Keynesian in the other, or Keynesian in one debate but monetarist in the other, so that it is better to keep the categories distinct.

The first main strand of the Keynesian–monetarist controversy centred on the determinants of aggregate demand; it related in other words more to the second than to the first of the two questions posed above. The monetarists were concerned primarily to argue that monetary factors (mainly the growth of the money supply, which they treated as under the exogenous control of the monetary authorities) rather than autonomous expenditures (such as investment or government expenditure) were the dominant influence on aggregate demand. By this time the Keynesians on the other hand were arguing much more strongly than Keynes himself had argued that monetary factors were of very little importance but autonomous expenditures were all-important. Much of the debate can be summarised in terms of the IS–LM model (which was shown to be an extremely versatile analytical apparatus): essentially Keynesians argued that the IS curve was relatively steep and the LM curve relatively flat, in which case (as is explained in Chapter 7) aggregate demand was dominated by autonomous expenditure; while monetarists argued that the IS curve was relatively flat and the LM curve relatively steep, in which case aggregate demand was dominated by monetary factors. In turn, the slope of the IS curve depended mainly on the interest-elasticity of investment (Chapter 3) and that of the LM curve on the interest-elasticity of the demand for money (Chapter 5) together with the behaviour of the monetary authorities in operating on the money supply and/or the interest rate (Chapter 6).

The second main strand of the debate between Keynesians and monetarists centred on the causes of inflation: while Keynesians argued that inflation was essentially caused by increases in costs, especially in labour costs, monetarists viewed it as a monetary phenomenon caused by excessive growth of the money supply leading to excess demand for goods and services, together with the influence of economic agents' expectations about the rate of inflation. Monetarist arguments here were presented in the framework of the 'expectations-augmented Phillips curve' (Chapter 9) where long-run equilibrium occurred only at the so-called 'natural rate of unemployment'; in other words, there *was* a tendency for the economy to move towards something very like the Keynesian concept of full employment. Thus in this strand monetarist thinking was more obviously neoclassical than in the first strand of the debate; with respect to macro policy there was no longer any role for demand management or stabilisation policy in the long run though there remained a minor short-run role for it. Keynesian thinking on the other hand continued to envisage a major role for stabilisation policy, together with a need for an incomes policy to control labour costs and hence inflation.

Subsequent developments

In the second half of the 1960s and the first half of the 1970s the division between Keynesians and monetarists lay at the heart of nearly all of the major debates in macroeconomics. However, between the mid-1970s and the early 1980s there were some important changes and differences of view within as well as between those schools of thought, so that the Keynesian–monetarist classification ceased to be of such value or importance.

On the one hand, two elements of the second strand of monetarist thinking were taken up and developed into what came to be called New Classical macroeconomics. The first element was the more neoclassical emphasis on the economy's own self-equilibrating mechanisms, closely associated with the assumption of price and wage flexibility. The second was the emphasis on expectations of inflation. This idea was originally articulated by monetarists such as Friedman in terms of 'adaptive expectations' in which economic agents are thought to adapt or adjust their expectations in response to the errors they find they have made in their previous expectations. However, certain problems with this hypothesis led to the introduction of the 'rational expectations' hypothesis according to which agents form their expectations as if they were making forecasts on the basis of a correct model of the economy and of all the latest available information (see Chapters 2 and 9 for further discussion). With price and wage flexibility and rational expectations it turned out that stabilisation policy lost all its power to influence the levels of economic activity and unemployment, and the New Classical macroeconomics ended up by giving essentially the same answers to the two questions posed at the beginning of the chapter as the classical economists of the nineteenth and early twentieth centuries – although the way in which they derived their results was much more sophisticated, both theoretically and technically, and their underlying vision of how the economy works was somewhat different. However, other monetarists were reluctant to adopt the assumption of perfect price and wage flexibility, or rather of perfect market clearing as it is generally called, with its corollary that all unemployment is voluntary.

On the other hand, while some Keynesians reiterated their commitment to the Keynesianism of earlier years a significant number moved away from those views on a range of issues. Indeed, there was an important process of convergence between this second group of Keynesians and the non-New Classical monetarists mentioned above.

These developments are discussed in more detail in Chapter 13, but their effect was that macroeconomics could be analysed most clearly in terms of three schools of thought: traditional Keynesianism, the Keynesian–monetarist convergence, and New Classical macroeconomics. Their answers to the two questions with which the chapter started can be expressed most conveniently in terms of the third and final model of national income determination, the aggregate demand/aggregate supply (AD/AS) model (which is examined in further detail in Chapters 8 and 13).

The aggregate demand/aggregate supply model: introduction

This model allows for the simultaneous determination of national income and the price level by the interaction of aggregate demand (determined largely as in the IS–LM model) and aggregate supply; the latter therefore no longer just responds passively to the former. Moreover, the aggregate supply curves are based explicitly on analyses of the labour market, so that the model corrects for both the second and the third as well as the first of the defects of the Keynesian cross model. The AD/AS model involves the construction of a curve which shows how aggregate demand, measured on the horizontal axis in terms of Y, varies with the price level, shown on the vertical axis, and of a corresponding curve which relates aggregate supply to the price level. This sort of model is not of recent origin, indeed such models were used in the Keynesian–neoclassical debate, but they were less commonly used in the 1960s and have only recently returned to popularity.

There is little difference between the three schools of thought regarding the aggregate demand curve: it is regarded as sloping downwards from left to right. There are a number of possible mechanisms underlying this relationship but at this point it is probably easiest to think of it in the following terms: when the price level is lower, the real value of the money supply is higher, and this leads economic agents to spend more. The AD curve can in principle be shifted by fiscal policy, monetary policy, changes in autonomous expenditure, and so on. However, the AS curves differ sharply between the three schools.

For traditional Keynesians the AS curve is horizontal up to the full employment level of national income (Y_f), and then vertical, as in Figure 1.3. The rationale for this form of AS curve is discussed in Chapters 8 and 13; here what is important is its implications: shifts of the AD curve (typically caused for traditional Keynesians by autonomous expenditure changes or by fiscal policy) cause fluctuations in income and therefore in (involuntary) unemployment without (so long as Y remains less than Y_f) any effect on the price level. Thus the economy is not self-equilibrating; equilibrium positions with significant amounts of unemployment can occur, but the government can act to prevent or reduce unemployment by expanding aggregate demand by means of fiscal policy. Moreover, inflation here is entirely a cost-push phenomenon, with increases in costs causing increases in prices which shift the AS curve upwards.

For New Classical macroeconomists the primary AS curve (a secondary curve is introduced in Chapter 13) is vertical as in Figure 1.4, vertical at the 'natural rate of output' which corresponds to the 'natural rate of unemployment'. Thus the economy is strongly self-equilibrating; in particular, involuntary unemployment never occurs, and there is no place for active macroeconomic policy because policy-induced shifts in AD have no effect on output or employment and only change the price level. Inflation here is essentially a monetary phenomenon, for prices are determined by aggregate demand which is dominated by monetary factors.

Finally for the economists of the convergence school it is necessary to distinguish between the long-run AS curve (AS^{LR}) which is vertical as in the New Classical case, and the short-run AS curve (AS^{SR}) which slopes upwards from left to right, as in Figure 1.5. Shifts in aggregate demand cause movements along the short-run AS curve in the first instance, so that output and employment can depart from the natural rate; prices will also adjust to some extent. In the long run, however, wages adjust and prices adjust more fully so that the short-run AS curve shifts and long-run equilibrium always occurs where the AD curve intersects the long-run AS curve, with the appropriate short-run AS curve also passing through this point. For this school then there are self-equilibrating tendencies in the long run, but in the short run there can be involuntary unemployment and there is some justification for an active stabilisation policy. Inflation is largely a monetary phenomenon in the long run but cost-push pressures can shift the AS^{SR} curve up and affect prices in the short run.

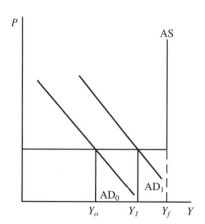

Figure 1.3

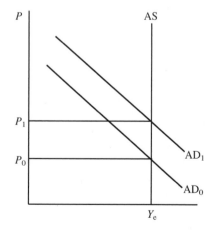

Figure 1.4

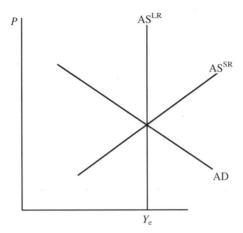

Figure 1.5

Conclusions

This chapter is essentially introductory and much of the material is examined in more detail later. However, it is still appropriate to draw some conclusions at this stage, to identify the broad characteristics of the different schools of thought to which reference is made later in the book. Thus classical economics had little specifically *macroeconomic* theory but it assumed that the price mechanism operated efficiently, that is prices and wages were flexible and economic agents' behaviour was responsive to them. This efficient operation of the price mechanism excluded both the possibility of involuntary unemployment and the need for stabilisation policy. Keynes and the Keynesian economists concentrated on the analysis of aggregate demand, partly at least because they did not think the price mechanism operated efficiently at the macro level, and they advocated the use of stabilisation policy to compensate for its defects. Neoclassical economists emphasised the potential efficiency of the price mechanism but conceded that it did not always operate at its full potential. Monetarists were originally concerned to argue the importance of monetary rather than expenditure factors for aggregate demand, but later analysed inflation in a way that accepted at least the long-term efficiency of the price mechanism. Later Keynesians of all kinds – 'traditional', 'Post-Keynesian' and 'New Keynesian' – have tended to emphasise in different ways the failings of the price mechanism, and therefore to argue that involuntary unemployment is possible even though they do not always agree on the possibility of controlling it by stabilisation policy. New Classical economists have assumed perfect market clearing along with rational expectations, and this means that stabilisation policy is unnecessary as well as ineffective. The Keynesian–monetarist convergence regarded market economies as largely self-equilibrating in the long run but envisaged some role for stabilisation policy in the short run. This convergence has now been largely superseded by a 'Mainstream' school which developed more generally out of non-traditional Keynesian and non-New Classical monetarist thinking but has absorbed significant elements of New Classical macroeconomics (notably rational expectations) and sometimes draws on the partial-equilibrium microfoundations analyses offered by New Keynesian economics. According to this school involuntary unemployment can exist, and for quite significant periods, and the government may be able to do something about it at least in some cases: stabilisation policies may be needed and may be effective, but must be handled with considerable caution.

The plan of the book

Subsequent chapters in Part I follow the logical order in which the three models of national income determination were developed here. Chapters 2 and 3 analyse the two primary components of aggregate demand, consumption and investment. Chapter 4 integrates a government sector and a foreign trade sector into the Keynesian cross model. Chapter 5 and 6 analyse the demand for and supply of money. Chapter 7 develops the IS–LM model. Chapter 8 takes a preliminary and partly historical look at the labour market and the AD/AS model. Chapters 9 and 10 analyse inflation, the first examining the various forms of Phillips curve and the second taking a broader perspective on theories of inflation. Chapters 11 and 12 examine the implications and effects of the openness of an economy, under fixed and flexible exchange rates respectively. Finally Chapter 13 draws the threads together again, returning to the AD/AS model and bringing the history up to date.

Part 2 of the book examines in further detail and at a higher technical level some of the key issues of macroeconomic debates in the last two decades. Chapter 14 looks at the effects of including in the IS–LM model a government budget constraint, an important factor in the development of Mainstream thought. Chapter 15 discusses the New Classical 'policy ineffectiveness proposition'. Chapter 16 examines the time-inconsistency argument against discretionary monetary policy, an argument which has largely been absorbed by Mainstream thinking. Chapter 17 looks at the relationship between fiscal deficits and monetary policy over the longer term, another element of New Classical thinking which has been at least partly absorbed in the Mainstream. Chapter 18 discusses models of the exchange rate, particularly the influential Dornbusch model which incorporates both rational expectations and price stickiness, and is therefore a good example of Mainstream macroeconomics. Finally Chapter 19 looks in more detail first at the New Keynesian school and then at aspects of New Classical macroeconomics which have not been considered elsewhere.

Exercises

Suppose that there is a sudden downturn in investment. Analyse the effects of this first in a Keynesian cross model, then in an IS–LM model, and finally (distinguishing carefully between short-term and long-term effects) in the different versions of the AD/AS model presented in this chapter.

Further reading

The work of classical economists such as Walras and Say is discussed in Harris (1981, Chapters 4 and 6). Other topics covered in this chapter are examined in more detail in the following chapters; further references are given there.

Chapter 2

Consumption

This chapter considers the determinants of consumption. It looks mainly at the early Keynesian 'absolute income hypothesis' of consumption and at Milton Friedman's 'permanent income hypothesis', exploring the consistency of the hypotheses with the evidence and the significance of the difference between them for wider macroeconomic issues. These hypotheses can in principle refer to either individual households or a community of households; the main concern in macroeconomics is with community or aggregate relationships but some of the analysis refers to household behaviour and the 'aggregation problem' involved is explained towards the end of the chapter, in the context of a brief discussion of variables other than income which may affect consumption.

The absolute income hypothesis (AIH)

This hypothesis derives from the analysis of Keynes in his *General Theory*, according to which 'The fundamental psychological law . . . is that men are disposed, as a rule and on the average, to increase their consumption as their income increases, but not by as much as the increase in their income' (J. M. Keynes, *The General Theory of Employment, Interest and Money*, Macmillan 1936 p. 96).

More specifically, consumption is assumed in the AIH to be partly autonomous and partly related to current (disposable) income, with a marginal propensity to consume out of current income which is positive but less than unity. In diagrammatic terms the hypothesis is depicted by the C line in Figure 2.1; the intercept on the vertical axis shows the amount of autonomous consumption and the line is flatter than (and therefore intersects at some point) the 45° line drawn through the origin, which has a slope of unity. In algebraic terms the AIH says that

$$C = a + bY, \quad 0 < b < 1, \tag{2.1}$$

where C and Y are real consumption and real income, a is the autonomous component of consumption and b is the marginal propensity to consume

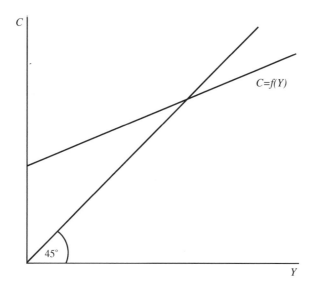

Figure 2.1

(MPC) which is assumed to be less than 1. The algebraic representation of the hypothesis can easily be related to the diagrammatic representation: a is the intercept on the vertical axis and b is the slope of the line.

Notice that in the AIH the average propensity to consume (APC) gets smaller as income rises. This results from the existence of the autonomous component, which does not change as income rises. It can be seen algebraically from the definition of the APC as C/Y:

$$\frac{C}{Y} = \frac{a+bY}{Y} = \frac{a}{Y} + b,$$ [2.2]

where a/Y falls as Y rises. Geometrically the same thing can be seen by noting

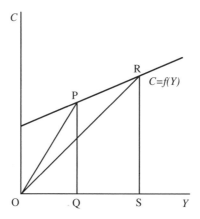

Figure 2.2

that at any point on the C line the APC = C/Y is the slope of a ray from the origin to that point such as OP (slope PQ/OQ) or OR (slope RS/OS) in Figure 2.2: for points on the C line further to the right (when Y is higher) the ray from the origin is flatter so that the APC is smaller.

The key points to note about the AIH are that it relates consumption to actual (later referred to as 'absolute' or 'measured') income with a constant MPC and a declining APC. As stated above, the AIH is derived from the work of Keynes; it differs in that Keynes thought the MPC would decline at higher levels of income whereas the MPC in the AIH is constant.

The stylised facts

At this point it is convenient to introduce the 'stylised facts' on the relation between income and consumption, that is the typical results of evidence on a variety of different countries over a variety of different time periods. This evidence comes in three forms: short-run aggregate time series data on national consumption and national income over relatively short time periods (say 30 to 40 quarters); cross-sectional data on consumption and income of different households in a community at a particular time; and long-run aggregate times series data on national consumption and income over long periods (say several decades).

The stylised facts on the relation between consumption and income in terms of both short-run aggregate time series data and cross-sectional data broadly conform to the predictions of the AIH, that is, the 'average' estimated relationship derived by econometric methods looks like the short-run consumption line in Figure 2.3 (where C and Y are measured in aggregate terms for the former and in terms of households for the latter), with constant MPC and declining APC. Evidence of this type, when it was first obtained in the 1940s, was taken as confirmation of the AIH. However, evidence on the long-run aggregate time series relationship, which first became available

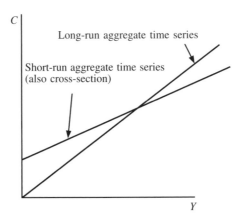

Figure 2.3

slightly later, did not conform to this pattern: it showed a constant, rather than a declining, APC equal to the MPC and a relationship such as the long-run consumption line in Figure 2.3. This finding, together with the failure of consumption functions derived from pre-Second World War data to predict accurately post-war consumption (they seriously underestimated it), led to a search for alternative theories of consumption. The most important group of such theories is the 'normal income hypotheses' and the most prominent of the latter in subsequent macroeconomic debates is the 'permanent income hypothesis' originally due to Friedman (1957).

The permanent income hypothesis (PIH)

The basic idea of the permanent income hypothesis is that people's consumption depends in a proportional manner, not on the income they actually receive in the current period, which is often referred to as 'absolute' or 'measured' income (measured in the official statistics), but to their 'permanent' or 'normal' income, the income which they expect to receive on a continuing basis. Friedman thus distinguishes between permanent income (Y^p), measured income (Y^m) and transitory income (Y^t), the latter defined as the difference between permanent and measured income, such that

$$Y^m = Y^p + Y^t, \quad Y^t \gtrless 0 \qquad [2.3]$$

He also distinguishes similarly between permanent, measured and transitory consumption; this distinction is less important for it is assumed that in the aggregate with some people spending more than normal and some less over any given period, overall transitory consumption will be zero so that consumption is simply C and no subscripts are needed. With income on the other hand, although some elements of transitory income will cancel in the aggregate (for example, if temporary illness reduces one worker's earnings but enables another's to increase), other elements will not, particularly those related to cyclical movements in economic activity. In a boom consumers as a group are likely to earn more than normal through higher overtime and higher employment (so that for most individuals and in aggregate Y^t is >0 and $Y^m > Y^p$), while in a recession consumers as a group are likely to earn less than normal ($Y^t < 0$ and $Y^m < Y^p$).

Given these distinctions, the PIH can be formally stated as the proposition that consumption is proportional to permanent income:

$$C = kY^p, \quad 0 < k < 1 \qquad [2.4]$$

This relationship has the property that the marginal propensity to consume out of permanent income is equal to the average propensity to consume out of permanent income, and neither MPC nor APC varies with income.

It may be noted that the PIH is consistent with conventional microeconomic theory in the form of utility maximisation by individual consumers, while the AIH is not. Some claims of superiority for the PIH have been made on this basis, but it is possible to provide some microeconomic support for the AIH by appealing to imperfections in information and/or in capital markets: in effect the PIH assumes people can borrow without difficulty against expected future incomes, but if they cannot do so, consumption may be constrained by current measured income and the AIH may be more relevant.

One particular implication of the PIH is that transitory or windfall additions to income do not lead directly to increases in consumption. Since this may appear counter-intuitive, two points are worth making. Firstly, the PIH refers to *consumption* rather than to *consumers' expenditure*, where consumption is defined to include the value of the flow of services received by consumers from their consumer durables but not the purchase of those durables themselves, while consumers' expenditure includes the latter. Thus if a windfall leads a consumer to purchase a car, her consumption as defined for the PIH rises only by the amount of the value of the services provided to her by the car over the period concerned. The AIH by contrast refers to consumers' expenditure; since for empirical macroeconomic analysis this is the more important aggregate (and that to which the official statistics refer) the PIH needs to be supplemented by a theory of spending on consumer durables. In practice such theories have much in common with theories of investment by firms and they are not specifically considered in this book. Secondly, if windfalls are saved rather than consumed they will obviously increase permanent income by the amount of the return expected on them; thus some small increase in consumption in response to windfalls is compatible with the PIH.

Is the PIH consistent with the stylised facts given above? The answer to this depends heavily on the relationship assumed to exist between permanent and measured income, since the data used to obtain the stylised facts refer to measured income: briefly, it can be argued that on plausible assumptions each of the stylised facts is consistent with the PIH. In the case of the long-run aggregate time series data, for example, it seems reasonable to assume that in the long run, that is over periods of several years which encompass both booms and recessions, the transitory income elements cancel each other out so that permanent income is equal to measured income. In this case the PIH is clearly consistent with the stylised fact since both have constant (and equal) APC and MPC.

In the case of short-run aggregate time series data, in which booms and recessions show up strongly, it seems reasonable to assume that with transitory income being positive in booms and negative in recessions, measured income fluctuates more widely than permanent income. Consumption depends on permanent income, and $C/Y^p = k$ is constant. However, with Y^m fluctuating more widely than Y^p in both directions, C/Y^m, the observed APC, will not be constant. The argument is shown diagrammatically in Figure 2.4. Here Y^p fluctuates between Y^p_1 and Y^p_2, and consumption varies accordingly between C_1 and C_2 as shown by the $C = kY^p$ line. However, Y^m fluctuates more widely so that Y^p_2 for example, is associated with positive transitory income in a boom and measured income Y^m (giving point (C_2, Y^m_2) on the graph), while Y^p_1 is associated with negative transitory income in a recession and measured income

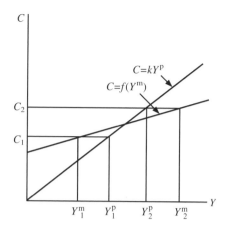

Figure 2.4

Y_1^m (point (C_1, Y_1^m)). The effect of this is to generate a short-run relationship between consumption and measured income such as that given by the $C = f(Y^m)$ line in the graph, where there is a positive intercept on the vertical axis, declining APC and a smaller slope (MPC) than that of the $C = kY^p$ line; in other words a relationship comparable to that of the stylised fact. Given the assumption about Y^m and Y^p then, the PIH is consistent with the stylised fact.

Another explanation of the last point is given below. For the moment turn to the cross-sectional data. Here the assumption is that at any moment in time (such as the moment for which the data were obtained) some households will have measured income above their permanent income, some will have measured income below their permanent income, and some will have the two in line. It is helpful to use a simple numerical example here. Suppose the community consists of nine households, of which three have permanent income of 4 000, three of 5 000, and three of 6 000. Within each of these groups one household has measured income 20% above its permanent income, one has it 20% below, and one has its measured income equal to its permanent income. For all households the marginal and average propensity to consume out of permanent income is 0.9. The income and consumption of each household is set out in Table 2.1, and the nine consumption/measured income combinations are plotted in Figure 2.5.

From those combinations an attempt to work out the 'average' relationship of C to Y either by the naked eye or by econometric methods will produce a line such as that shown in the diagram: this line has a slope less than 0.9 and has a positive intercept on the vertical axis. Thus on the basis of the PIH and a particular assumption about the measured and permanent income of different households it is possible to generate a relationship between C and Y comparable to the stylised fact on cross-sectional data: given the assumption then the PIH is consistent with the stylised fact. Moreover, the general argument here would be strengthened if measured consumption were assumed

Table 2.1

Household	Permanent income	Measured income	Consumption
1	4 000	4 800	3 600
2	4 000	3 200	3 600
3	4 000	4 000	3 600
4	5 000	6 000	4 500
5	5 000	4 000	4 500
6	5 000	5 000	4 500
7	6 000	7 200	5 400
8	6 000	4 800	5 400
9	6 000	6 000	5 400

to vary around permanent consumption (provided these divergences were not correlated with the divergences between measure and permanent income).

The measurement of permanent income

In the last section it was shown that on certain plausible assumptions the PIH can be reconciled with each of the stylised facts on the relation between consumption and income. It is now convenient to introduce a further and more precise assumption about the relationship between measured and permanent income which will both clarify the consistency of the PIH with short-run aggregate time series evidence and lay the basis for the examination of short-run multipliers in the next section.

Permanent income is essentially a theoretical concept. It refers to the income

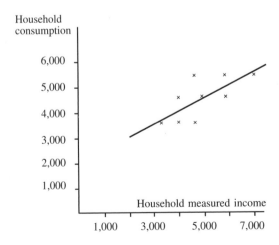

Figure 2.5

which people expect to receive over some long-run future time period, and it is therefore not directly observable. The question therefore arises, how can Y^p be calculated? Friedman's answer to this, which has been widely used since, was to introduce the further hypothesis that permanent income is determined by current and past levels of measured income, with greater importance attached to the measured income of more recent periods. Intuitively the idea is that consumers' perceptions of their permanent income depend on their actual experience, with the most recent experience affecting their perceptions most strongly. In specific algebraic form,

$$Y_t^p = \lambda Y_t^m + \lambda(1-\lambda)Y_{t-1}^m + \lambda(1-\lambda)^2 Y_{t-2}^m$$
$$+ \lambda(1-\lambda)^3 Y_{t-3}^m + \dots, 0 < \lambda < 1.$$
[2.5]

This formula is less complicated than it looks. Each of the terms on the right-hand side consists of: (a) a Y_{t-i}^m term referring to measured income in a specific time period (indicated by the subscript), the period becoming successively further away in the past as i grows larger; and (b) a weighting factor which has the basic form $\lambda(1-\lambda)^i$ where i is the same number as in the Y_{t-i}^m term to which it is attached (anything to the power of zero equals 1, so that $\lambda(1-\lambda)^0 = \lambda$). These weighting factors or weights have two important properties. First, they get successively smaller as i rises, so that the weight on measured income in less recent periods is smaller than that for more recent periods. Suppose, for example, that $\lambda = 1/3$; the weights are then as follows:

$\lambda = 1/3$

$\lambda(1-\lambda) = 1/3 \times 2/3 = 2/9 < 3/9 = 1/3$

$\lambda(1-\lambda)^2 = 1/3 \times 2/3 \times 2/3 = 4/27 < 6/27 = 2/9$

$\lambda(1-\lambda)^3 = 1/3 \times 2/3 \times 2/3 \times 2/3 = 8/81 < 12/81 = 4/27$

etc.

The second property of these weights, which are a geometric expansion, is that they sum to 1. This is important to the intuitive plausibility of equation [2.5] as a formula for permanent income: suppose measured income is now and always has been exactly 5 000, i.e. $Y_t^m = Y_{t-1}^m = Y_{t-2}^m = \dots = 5\,000$. In this case equation [2.5] reduces to

$$Y_t^p = 5,000 \cdot \{\lambda + \lambda(1-\lambda) + \lambda(1-\lambda)^2 + \dots\}$$
[2.6]

and if the sum of the weights, which is the contents of the curly brackets in [2.6], is equal to 1 then $Y_t^p = 5\,000$. The point is that this would not be so if the weights did not sum to 1 but any other value for Y_t^p would be intuitively unacceptable: it must be the case that, if income is and always has been 5 000, people will expect it to go on being 5 000.

There is a useful manipulation which can be performed with equation [2.5]. First, consider what permanent income of the previous period, that is permanent income lagged one period, would be: it involves rewriting equation

[2.5] with all the terms on both sides of the equation lagged one (more) period, as follows:

$$Y_{t-1}^{p} = \lambda Y_{t-1}^{m} + \lambda(1-\lambda)Y_{t-2}^{m} + \lambda(1-\lambda)^{2}Y_{t-3}^{m} + \ldots \qquad [2.7]$$

Next rewrite the original equation [2.5], factorising out $(1-\lambda)$ from the second and all subsequent terms on the right-hand side:

$$Y_{t}^{p} = \lambda Y_{t}^{m} + (1-\lambda)\{\lambda Y_{t-1}^{m} + \lambda(1-\lambda)Y_{t-2}^{m} + \lambda(1-\lambda)^{2}Y_{t-3}^{m} + \ldots\} \qquad [2.8]$$

Now compare the contents of the curly brackets on the right-hand side of equation [2.8] with the right-hand side of equation [2.7]: they are the same, so that equation [2.8] can be rewritten as

$$Y_{t}^{p} = \lambda Y_{t}^{m} + (1-\lambda)Y_{t-1}^{p} \qquad [2.9]$$

Thus the original formula of equation [2.5] with a large (in principle an infinite) number of terms on the right-hand side can be reduced to a much simpler formula with only current measured income and previous period permanent income on the right-hand side, appropriately weighted.

It is worth noting that equation [2.9] can also be derived, not from equation [2.5], but from the hypothesis that permanent income changes between one period and the next by a fraction of the difference between permanent and measured income. The idea is that when people find they have been mistaken in their expectations they modify their expectations by a proportion of the mistake they have made. In algebraic terms,

$$Y_{t}^{p} - Y_{t-1}^{p} = \lambda(Y_{t}^{m} - Y_{t-1}^{p}) \qquad [2.10]$$

Adding Y_{t-1}^{p} to both sides of [2.10] and rearranging produces equation [2.9]. This particular derivation is almost the same as that used in some work on expectations of inflation (see Chapter 9), and the term 'adaptive expectations' is used in both cases to refer to the adjustment of expectations in response to previous errors.

The formula of equation [2.9] turns out to be very useful in theoretical work. Substituting it into the basic PIH proposition (equation [2.4]) gives

$$C_{t} = kY_{t}^{p} = k\lambda Y_{t}^{m} + k(1-\lambda)Y_{t-1}^{p} \qquad [2.11]$$

Now in the current period the previous period's permanent income is something fixed, unchangeable, constant. In equation [2.11] the second term on the right-hand side, $k(1-\lambda)Y_{t-1}^{p}$, can therefore be interpreted as a constant in analytical exercises in which alternative positions for the current period are considered. Thus in the short run the PIH together with the hypothesis of equation [2.5] produces a relationship between consumption and measured income which has declining APC (because of the constant term) and an MPC of $k\lambda$ which is less than the long-run APC and MPC of k. Equation [2.5] thus provides a second way of explaining the consistency of the PIH with the stylised fact of short-run aggregate time series data.

The short-run multipliers

The significance of the differences between the AIH and PIH lies in their contrasting implications for wider macroeconomic issues, and can be seen most clearly by a comparison of the multipliers associated with each hypothesis.

Consider the Keynesian cross model of Chapter 1 for a simple economy in which there is no government sector (and so no government expenditure or taxes), no foreign sector (so no exports or imports), and no monetary sector (so no changes in or effects from the money supply or interest rates). Investment (I) is exogenous. The equilibrium condition for national income is that income equals consumption plus investment. In the AIH case,

$$C = a + bY$$

$$I = \bar{I}$$

$$Y = C + I$$

Hence, as in Chapter 1,

$$Y = a + bY + \bar{I}$$

$$Y - bY = a + \bar{I}$$

$$Y(1 - b) = a + \bar{I}$$

$$Y = \frac{a + \bar{I}}{1 - b} = \frac{1}{1 - b} \cdot (a + \bar{I})$$

where the basic multiplier is $1/(1 - b)$. Typical estimates of the MPC using the AIH are in the range 0.5–0.8; if $b = 0.6$, the multiplier is $1/0.4 = 2.5$.

In the case of the PIH the first point to note is that the size of the multiplier depends on the period considered. For the long run in which permanent income is fully adjusted the multiplier can be derived using the long-run $C = kY^p$ function. However, it is the short run rather than the long run which is important for policy purposes, and for the short run in which permanent income is not fully adjusted the multiplier needs to be derived on the basis of equation [2.11], as follows:

$$C = k\lambda Y + z, \quad \text{where } z = k(1 - \lambda)Y^p_{t-1} \text{ is constant}$$

$$I = \bar{I}$$

$$Y = C + I$$

Hence,

$$Y = k\lambda Y + z + \bar{I}$$

$$Y - k\lambda Y = z + \bar{I}$$

$$Y(1 - k\lambda) = z + \bar{I}$$

$$Y = \frac{z + \bar{I}}{1 - k\lambda} = \frac{1}{1 - k\lambda} \cdot (z + \bar{I})$$

where the basic multiplier is $1/(1 - k\lambda)$. Typical estimates of k and λ using the PIH (on annual data), such as Friedman's own estimates, are $k = 0.9$ and

$\lambda = 0.33$. On these figures the multiplier is $1/0.7 = 1.43$. This is considerably smaller than the multiplier associated with the AIH. The intuitive explanation is that under the PIH when say investment rises and income rises, people interpret the increase in Y largely as a transitory phenomenon rather than an increase in Y^p; they therefore do not increase their consumption by as much as in the AIH case and they increase their saving instead; since the new equilibrium level of income is that at which saving has risen by the amount of the initial rise in investment, this (short-run) equilibrium is reached at a lower level of income under the PIH than under the AIH.

What does this mean in terms of wider macroeconomic issues? First, fluctuations in the exogenous elements of expenditure such as investment cause smaller fluctuations in income under the PIH than under the AIH; that is, under the PIH the economy is more stable. Secondly, variations in government expenditure (thought of as part of I, or considered separately in a model with a government sector) have less effect on income under the PIH than under the AIH; that is, under the PIH fiscal policy is less powerful.

The PIH with rational expectations

The discussion of the last two sections has been based on what has since come to be called 'adaptive expectations', where consumers are thought of as forming expectations of their permanent income on the basis of current and past experience. The hypothesis of adaptive expectations was also used by Friedman with respect to expectations about inflation in his analysis of the relationship between inflation and unemployment, which is considered below in Chapter 9. However, in that context the hypothesis was challenged and largely displaced by that of 'rational expectations', and the idea of rational expectations was then applied also to the formation of expectations by consumers about their income. The fundamental idea of rational expectations is that economic agents form their expectations as if they were making predictions on the basis of a correct model of the economy, which includes the systematic behaviour of the government as well as that of other economic agents. Thus expectations are 'forward-looking' rather than 'backward-looking'.

Since the PIH itself is essentially a theory about the relationship between expected or permanent income and consumption, there is in principle no problem in incorporating rational expectations. The PIH is still represented by equation [2.4] but Y^p now stands for the rational expectation of future income.

According to the idea of rational expectations, which is examined in more detail in Chapter 9, expected income is the best prediction that can be made on the basis of all currently available information. The expectation can therefore change only if new information becomes available which could not have been predicted. Such new information must be essentially random or arbitrary, for otherwise it could have been predicted. But this implies in the context of the PIH a striking result: consumption in one period must be equal to consumption in the previous period plus some random element which reflects the impact on expectations of newly available information. In technical jargon consumption should 'follow a random walk' which means that it should have no systematic trend (or cyclical movement) in any direction.

A second striking result concerns the size of the short-run multiplier. In the adaptive expectations version of the PIH the multiplier is relatively small, because people adjust their idea of their permanent income only slowly in response to the mistakes they find they have made. But in the rational expectations version of the PIH if, for example, government policy brings about a change in expectations, that will have a large and immediate impact on consumption because expected income is adjusted rapidly and fully.

Empirically this version of the PIH has had mixed success; in particular, while consumption appears to be strongly influenced by previous period consumption, it also seems to be related in a systematic way to previous levels of income. One possible explanation for these findings is that some consumers are 'liquidity-constrained', that is, they cannot borrow without difficulty against future income so that recent (and current) income affects their actual consumption by allowing them to spend more than they otherwise could.

Other variables which might affect consumption

There is no doubt that income (in whatever form) is much the most important determinant of consumption, but there are a number of other variables which should be mentioned here. First, if there are important differences in the marginal propensities to consume of different groups in the community, a transfer of incomes from one group to another will affect the level of consumption for an unchanged level of community income. So far the analysis of this chapter has switched freely between the individual household and the community, but it should be noted that, as with all macroeconomic relationships, there is an 'aggregation problem', that is to say a serious question as to whether aggregating from individuals to community is justified: can we be sure either that the distribution of income does not change or that any changes which occur do not matter, so that stable relationships for individual households necessarily produce a stable aggregate relationship? In practice changes in the distribution of income large enough to have significant effects on aggregate consumption are probably infrequent, and most macroeconomic analysis has therefore tended to ignore this problem.

A second variable which might affect consumption is wealth. It is commonly suggested that of two households (or two communities) which have equal incomes but different wealth holdings, the richer household (or community) will spend more. It should be noted that in principle the PIH takes care of this point, since permanent income is in one place defined by Friedman as the return on wealth where wealth includes human capital (that is the value of a person's skills), but this is not the case for the AIH. In wider macroeconomic analysis the most important wealth effect is the 'real balance effect', that is the increase in consumption caused by an increase in the real money balances component of wealth, which rises if the quantity of nominal money balances (the nominal money supply) rises or if the price level falls. One particular form of real balance effect, the 'Pigou effect', is discussed in Chapter 8.

However, one other form of wealth effect needs to be mentioned here. Many countries experienced significant increases during the 1970s in the personal savings ratio, that is the average propensity to save (equal to $1 - $ APC), followed by significant decreases in the 1980s. Economists have attempted to explain these variations in terms of the effect on liquid assets of inflation, which was much higher in the 1970s than in the 1960s and then lower in the 1980s than in the 1970s. Liquid assets are financial assets whose value is fixed in nominal terms and which can be easily turned into cash; bank deposits, deposits at building societies, National Savings deposits and bonds, and so on. The point about inflation is that higher inflation erodes more quickly the real value of a given stock of liquid assets. If people then increase their rate of saving in order to compensate for the inflation and maintain or restore the real value of their liquid assets, saving will be higher and consumption lower. On the other hand, lower inflation will allow people to consume more while keeping the real value of their liquid assets unchanged. There are several specific hypotheses from which this mechanism can be derived; their common point (which is borne out by some empirical evidence) is that consumption varies positively with the real value of consumers' liquid assets.

A final variable which might affect consumption is the interest rate. In principle an increase in the interest rate will have two opposing effects on an individual's consumption: on the one hand it raises the rate of return on saving and thereby produces a substitution effect in favour of more saving and less consumption; on the other hand it makes it easier to accumulate a given sum of money (e.g. for retirement purposes) and thereby produces an income effect in favour of less saving and more consumption. The direction of the net effect is unclear at the individual level, and even more so at the aggregate level. As with wealth, it should be noted that in principle this factor is taken account of in the PIH since the microeconomic analysis from which the PIH can be derived covers the choice between consumption and saving, and a change in the interest rate may lead to a change in k, the marginal propensity to consume out of permanent income. However, in practice the magnitude of the effects on consumption of likely changes in the interest rate is small, partly because it is the *real* interest rate which is relevant here. The latter is the nominal interest rate minus the change in the price level which is expected to occur over the period concerned, and variations in the real interest rate are typically smaller than those in the nominal rate.

Conclusions and qualifications

The main focus of the chapter has been the contrast between the original Keynesian absolute income hypothesis and the adaptive expectations version of Friedman's permanent income hypothesis. If the latter is correct, the implication is that the economy is more stable and fiscal policy is less powerful. As the chapter has shown, this version of the PIH is indeed more consistent with the stylised facts than the AIH (which is inconsistent with the long-run aggregate time series evidence). It also performs better than the simple AIH in many econometric tests. On the other hand, the rational expectations version of the PIH implies that consumption is more stable in 'normal' times, but could change more sharply in response to unexpected factors (which might on some occasions include fiscal or monetary policy).

However, a number of qualifications should be made here. Firstly, there are other normal income hypotheses such as Franco Modigliani's life-cycle hypothesis. This views consumption as determined by households maximising their utility from the flow of consumption over their lifetimes subject to the constraint of their lifetime resources. At the micro level it emphasises the varying pattern of saving and dissaving over the lifetime, but its basic macroeconomic implications are similar to those of the PIH. It can also be combined like the PIH with rational expectations of future income. The superiority of the PIH over these other hypotheses is much less clear-cut.

Secondly, much of the econometric evidence in favour of the PIH has also been consistent with revised versions of the AIH which supplement it by including either lagged (measured) income or lagged consumption on the right-hand side. It should be obvious that such formulations have much in common with formulations of the PIH which use equation [2.5]. The main practical implication of the PIH, that consumption responds relatively slowly to changes in current income, therefore, came to be widely accepted even by economists who did not support Friedman's concept of permanent income or his wider views on macroeconomics, although the AIH continued to be used in analytical work, such as in the IS–LM model discussed in Chapter 7, largely for reasons of simplicity. The introduction of rational expectations and its integration into the PIH seemed likely to transform the theory of consumption, but the empirical evidence of persistent effects of lagged income (which is consistent with previous evidence) has limited its impact.

Thirdly, it was shown that in a simple model the short-run multiplier associated with the adaptive expectations version of the PIH is smaller than the AIH multiplier. However, this result does not necessarily hold in more complex models which include a monetary sector. Nor, as already indicated, does the result hold in the rational expectations version of the PIH for cases where forward-looking expectations of income are significantly changed.

Exercises

(i) Calculate the short-run multipliers in a simple macro model with no foreign trade or government sector; (a) for the AIH where $C = 6\,000 + 0.75Y$ and (b) for the adaptive expectations version of the PIH where $C = 0.75Y^p$ and Y^p is determined as in equation [2.5] with $\lambda = 0.33$.

(ii) How would permanent income and therefore consumption be affected under the two versions of the PIH if the government announced and then introduced (a) a temporary rise and (b) a permanent rise in personal income taxation?

Further reading

The microeconomic aspects of consumption and the choice between consumption and saving are discussed in most microeconomic theory texts, e.g. Estrin and Laidler (1995, Chapters 6 and 7), Varian (1993, Chapter 10). Thomas (1993, Chapter 10) provides a survey of empirical work on the consumption function. The rational expectations version of the PIH is discussed in Attfield *et al.* (1991, Chapter 9).

Chapter 3

Investment

The second major element of aggregate demand after consumption is investment. This chapter examines a number of approaches to the question of what determines investment, ranging from the Keynesian marginal efficiency of capital analysis via the accelerator hypothesis, to the neoclassical emphasis on relative factor prices, and identifying the interest rate, income and expectations as the key determinants of investment.

By 'investment' economists mean physical rather than financial investment, that is the purchase of physical rather than financial assets. Investment includes capital expenditure by the government, private residential construction and (a relatively volatile item) changes in inventories, that is firms' stocks of raw materials, work in progress and finished goods. Consumers' expenditure on durable goods should also be thought of as a form of investment. However, this chapter, like the more interesting parts of the economic literature, concentrates on the purchase by firms of plant, machinery and other durable capital goods. A further useful distinction is that between gross investment and net investment: gross investment is total expenditure on capital goods, whereas net investment is equal to the change in the capital stock, or to gross investment *minus* physical depreciation (the decay of the existing capital stock due to wear and tear, including the scrapping of old machinery, etc.). The amount of physical depreciation is usually assumed to be proportional to the size of the existing capital stock, but it will not be discussed here and the focus of the chapter is the determinants of net industrial investment in fixed capital.

Discounting and the marginal efficiency of capital

The marginal efficiency of capital (MEC) approach to investment is essentially a formalisation by Keynes in his *General Theory* of the approach taken by classical economists before him. In simple terms it involves calculating whether it is profitable for a firm to make a certain investment, but this requires some means of comparing the costs of the investment with its prospective benefits (in the form of profits) in the future.

The technique of 'discounting' is the standard way of translating values at different time periods into a common time period (usually the present) so that they can be directly compared. Before considering the present value of some future profit, it is useful to think of the future value of some sum of money held in the present. If a firm has £1 m. now and this sum could be lent out (by depositing it in a bank or using it to buy a bond) at a rate of interest of say 10%, then at the end of the year the sum inclusive of the interest would be £1 m. + 10% of £1 m. = £1 m. $(1 + 0.1) = £1.1$ m. If the money is lent for another year its value at the end would be £1.1 m. $(1.1) = £1.21$ m. Thus A_{t+i}, the future value in year $t + i$ of A_t, a sum of money in year t, is $A_t(1 + r)^i$ where r is the interest rate. This process can be reversed: instead of asking what is the future value of a sum in the present, consider what is the present value of a future sum. Since finding the future value involves multiplying the sum by $(1 + r)$ for each year, finding the present value of a future sum involves dividing the sum by $(1 + r)$ for each year. In symbols, since

$$A_{t+i} = A_t(1 + r)^i,$$

$$A_t = \frac{1}{(1 + r)^i} \cdot A_{t+i} \qquad [3.1]$$

Equation [3.1] is a general formula which can be applied to obtain the present value of any sum of money at any time in the future.

The MEC approach involves using the technique of discounting to compare the initial outlay cost of a particular investment, O_t; the future running costs (labour, raw materials, etc), $C_t, C_{t+1}, C_{t+2}, \ldots$; and the future sales revenues of the product which is to be made, $R_t, R_{t+1}, R_{t+2}, \ldots$ The net returns from the investment can be calculated, using equation [3.1] separately for the costs and revenues in each time period, as

$$(R_t - C_t) + \frac{(R_{t+1} - C_{t+1})}{1 + r} + \frac{(R_{t+2} - C_{t+2})}{(1 + r)^2} + \ldots + \frac{(R_{t+n} - C_{t+n})}{1 + r)^n} \qquad [3.2]$$

where n is the last period over which the investment is expected to produce any output, and where R_t and C_t may be zero if production does not begin immediately. The expression [3.2] can be rewritten, using the summation sign $\sum$, as

$$\sum_{i=0}^{i=n} \frac{(R_{t+i} - C_{t+i})}{(1 + r)^i} \qquad [3.3]$$

(remember that $(1 + r)^0 = 1$). One way of presenting the investment decision is to say that the investment will be profitable if

$$O_t \leqslant \sum_{i=0}^{i=n} \frac{(R_{t+i} - C_{t+i})}{(1 + r)^i}, \qquad [3.4]$$

and this is sometimes referred to as the 'present value' approach. An alternative approach to the investment decision involves replacing the market interest rate in [3.3] by the unknown m, and turning the inequality into an equality:

$$O_t = \sum_{i=0}^{i=n} \frac{R_{t+i} - C_{t+i})}{(1 + m)^i} \qquad\qquad [3.5]$$

This equation is then solved to find m. This m can be thought of as that interest rate which, if it were used to discount the net returns on an investment, would make that investment neither profitable nor unprofitable: it is therefore the yield on the investment, which Keynes called the *marginal efficiency of capital* (MEC), and the investment will be profitable if

$$m \geqslant r \qquad\qquad [3.6]$$

Condition [3.6], which involves comparing the yield on an investment with the current interest rate (regarded here as the opportunity cost of capital), is *broadly* equivalent to condition [3.4], which involves comparing the present value of net returns, calculated using the current interest rate, with the outlay cost. There are certain cases where the present value and 'internal rate of return' (MEC) approaches give different indications and in some areas of economics this phenomenon is of great importance; however, it has little relevance for macroeconomics.

Given the above technique for calculating the MEC of a particular investment project, a firm can work out the MEC for all the investments open to it, and it could then arrange these projects in descending order of the MECs as in Figure 3.1. Aggregating horizontally across firms, that is taking all the investment projects open to all the firms in the economy at each level of m, and arranging them in descending order, would produce the aggregate MEC schedule of Figure 3.2 (where the scale on the horizontal axis is much smaller than that in Figure 3.1). Superimposing on the diagram a market rate of interest r_0 is equivalent to applying condition [3.6] on an aggregate basis: in this case investment projects to a total value of O a have a yield or MEC greater than or equal to the interest rate, and would therefore be profitable for the firms concerned.

However, it is important to emphasise that so far all that has been calculated is the amount of investment that would be profitable: the concepts and information used to derive Figure 3.2 do *not* indicate how fast firms will actually undertake the investment projects concerned and therefore do not provide a theory of the demand for investment in the current period, which is what is required to build a macroeconomic model. In the early days of the MEC approach some economists tended to jump directly from the MEC to investment without any consideration of the speed at which the capital stock is likely to adjust. Now, however, it is clearly recognised that the MEC schedule shows the demand for (additional) capital, which is the (unsatisfied) demand for a *stock*; it does not show the flow demand for investment per period.

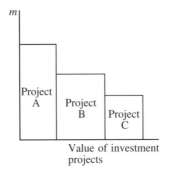

Figure 3.1

The marginal efficiency of investment

One attempt to get from the MEC to a theory of investment is the marginal efficiency of investment analysis. This involves making the speed of adjustment from the existing level of the capital stock to some new level (as determined by the MEC) dependent on the behaviour of the firms which produce capital goods: the idea is that firms undertaking investment projects (purchasers of capital goods) would prefer to undertake them immediately, but if there is a high demand for capital goods the producers of capital goods may experience capacity constraints which prevent them from supplying all the orders at once, so that they raise their prices. Similarly, when the demand for capital goods is low, producers might lower their prices. These alterations in capital goods prices mean changes in the outlay cost of investment projects to capital goods

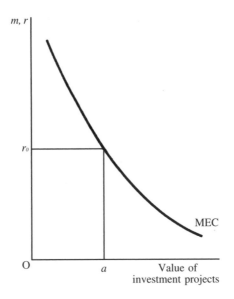

Figure 3.2

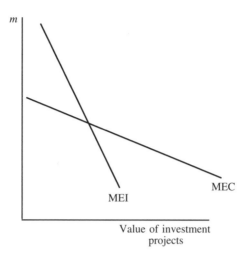

Figure 3.3

purchasers, such that firms have to recalculate the yield on their investments projects, by setting

$$O'_t = \sum_{i=0}^{i=n} \frac{(R_{t+i} - C_{t+i})}{(1 + m')^i} \qquad [3.7]$$

where O'_t is the new outlay cost and m' is the new yield. Repeating this exercise for all different levels of demand for capital goods (and for the prices associated with them) and then aggregating in the usual way across firms produces a revised MEC schedule incorporating the variation in capital goods prices. This new schedule is called the *marginal efficiency of investment* (MEI) schedule and is steeper than the MEC schedule, as in Figure 3.3: when the interest rate is high (low) investment demand is higher (lower) than on the MEC because capital goods prices are lower (higher).

If it is assumed that firms undertake in the current period all projects for which the MEI is greater than or equal to the interest rate, the MEI schedule can be interpreted as showing the flow demand for investment. However, this assumption is essentially arbitrary (what, for example, is the length of this 'current period'?) and the assumed variation in capital goods prices is inconsistent with the general framework of fixed prices, so that the MEI analysis cannot be accepted as a proper answer to the problem of how to get from a theory of the demand for capital to a theory of the demand for investment.

A better answer to this problem is given below, but since the MEC/MEI analysis constitutes a large part of received Keynesian theory on investment, it is worth pausing to highlight the variables identified in the analysis as determinants of investment. One such variable is the interest rate, which figures in this analysis as a measure of the opportunity cost of capital. If firms are to make investments they must borrow or use internal funds which could otherwise have been lent. In practice the interest rates for borrowing and lending are not the same, but that is of limited importance here. The key point is that the lower the interest rate, the larger the level of investment predicted. A second determinant of investment in the MEI analysis is firms' expectations of future sales revenues, which determine the R_{t+i} terms; at the macroeconomic level future sales revenues clearly depend primarily on the state of aggregate demand, and higher expected demand will lead to higher investment. And a third variable which comes into the analysis but is not usually emphasised in Keynesian expositions is firms' expectations of future running costs (C_{t+i}): these depend on the quantity of sales or output expected but also on the prices of labour and raw material inputs with higher input prices making investment less profitable and therefore lower.

Expectations and the accelerator

Keynes himself put great emphasis on firms' expectations of future demand, which he regarded as a matter partly of what he called 'animal spirits', that is non-rational confidence factors. Changes in business confidence or animal spirits cause changes in expected future sales revenues and hence changes in the likely profitability of investments, and they therefore shift the MEI schedule to the left (in the case of an increase in pessimism) or the right (for increased optimism), as in Figure 3.4. Some of Keynes's followers continued to stress animal spirits, but others tried to develop the emphasis on expectations in a more systematic way through the 'accelerator hypothesis' (which has its roots in pre-Keynesian writing).

The simplest view of the accelerator starts from the assumption of a fixed ratio relating output to the amount of capital normally required to produce it, that is a fixed capital–output ratio:

$$K_t^* = \alpha Y_t \qquad [3.8]$$

where K^* is the desired capital stock, Y is output and α is the fixed capital–output ratio. It is assumed that firms always adjust their capital to their output, so that the capital stock of the previous period must be in the same ratio to the output of the previous period:

$$K_{t-1} = \alpha Y_{t-1} \qquad [3.9]$$

Net investment is the growth in the capital stock between periods:

$$\begin{aligned} I_t = K_t^* - K_{t-1} &= \alpha Y_t - \alpha Y_{t-1} \\ &= \alpha(Y_t - Y_{t-1}) = \alpha \Delta Y_t \end{aligned} \qquad [3.10]$$

Thus net investment is proportional to the growth of output, rather than its level (it is for this reason that the term 'accelerator' is used): rising output brings about positive net investment; constant output brings about zero net

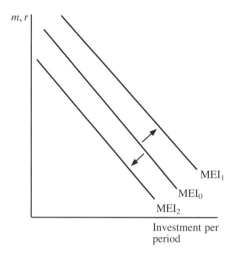

Figure 3.4

investment; and falling output brings about negative net investment, i.e. not all worn-out capital is replaced (but aggregate gross investment cannot be negative). Moreover, an increase in investment requires an increase in the rate of growth of output.

A more sophisticated view of the accelerator hypothesis is that it attempts to formalise the role of expectations as the key determinant of investment together with the assumption that expectations of future demand are determined by current demand. On the simple view an increase in current sales leads firms to increase their capital stock as a result of the technical requirements for increasing output, but on this more sophisticated view firms interpret the current level of sales as indicating the likely future level and increase their capital in order to maintain the most efficient mix of the factors of production: if production functions are homogeneous and there are constant returns to scale, the most efficient mix and the consequent capital–output ratio remains constant so long as relative factor prices are unchanged.

On either view, however, the accelerator has been widely criticised. Firstly, it omits the interest rate which featured importantly in the MEC/MEI analysis above. Secondly, the simple view is open to the criticism that capital–output ratios are not necessarily fixed, particularly in the short run. Thirdly, the more sophisticated view is open to the criticism that it views firms as forming their expectations in a mechanical way from current sales, and apparently taking no account of other factors which might affect future sales such as the government's macroeconomic policy or developments in world trade. Fourthly, the hypothesis takes no account of the existing level of capacity utilisation or of firms' ability to meet demand changes by means of changes in their stocks and/or variations in their capital–output ratios: firms may in fact have much more flexibility, particularly in some situations, than the hypothesis allows since it assumes that capital was fully adjusted to output in the previous period (equation [3.9]). And fifthly, the hypothesis takes no account of the possible supply constraints in the capital goods producing industries which underlie the MEI analysis.

The capital stock adjustment principle

So far the MEI analysis has been shown to suffer from a flaw regarding the movement from a theory of desired capital to a theory of investment demand, while the accelerator hypothesis is open to a number of criticisms, most of which amount to the charge that it is too mechanical and rigid. However, it turns out that both the flaw in the MEI and at least some of the problems with the accelerator can be overcome by the use of a simple technical device, the 'capital stock adjustment principle'.

This principle makes it possible to separate out two questions: (a) what determines the optimal or desired capital stock?; and (b) how does the actual capital stock adjust towards the desired level? Question (a) is the question to which the MEC analysis is properly directed; the accelerator hypothesis, particularly on the more sophisticated view, can also be seen in this light. The capital stock adjustment principle provides an answer to question (b) in the very simple form of an assumption that net investment per period is some fraction of the difference between actual and desired capital stock:

$$I_t = \gamma(K_t^* - K_{t-1}), \quad 0 < \gamma < 1 \tag{3.11}$$

This is a partial adjustment mechanism of the sort used in Chapter 2 to relate permanent income to measured income, and in a number of other places in macroeconomics; in this case it is being used to relate a flow to a stock.

According to the MEC analysis, the aggregate desired capital stock is a function primarily of the interest rate and expected aggregate demand. Such a function can be substituted in equation [3.11], to give an equation which relates investment, via a partial adjustment mechanism, to the interest rate, expected aggregate demand and the existing level of the capital stock. The algebraic presentation becomes complicated and at this level offers no new insight, so it will not be given here, but the arguments of this investment function should be noted together with the direction of their effects on investment: current investment is predicted to be higher as the interest rate is lower, as expected aggregate demand is higher, as the existing capital stock is smaller, and as the partial adjustment parameter is larger.

In the case of the accelerator, equation [3.11] can be used to derive the 'flexible accelerator' model of investment by substituting in [3.11] the accelerator relation for the desired capital stock [3.8], to give

$$I_t = \gamma(\alpha Y_t - K_{t-1}) \tag{3.12}$$

In this model investment is predicted to be higher as current output/demand is higher, and as the partial adjustment parameter is larger. This formulation of the accelerator is clearly not vulnerable to the fourth of the criticisms listed above, since it does not assume that the existing capital stock is always fully adjusted (so that capacity utilisation is always at some optimal level). And it can be made less vulnerable to some of the other criticisms by appropriate treatment of the partial adjustment parameter.

In empirical work it is possible to allow γ simply to be determined by the data, at least if it turns out to be stable over time. At an analytical level, however, it is preferable to consider what determines γ. The natural approach is to regard γ as dependent on the costs of adjustment: *ceteris paribus* the larger the costs of adjusting their capital stocks, the more slowly firms will adjust them. This has led to an emphasis on three factors as determinants of γ: (a) the size of the capital stock change concerned, on the assumption that larger changes are more disruptive to current production; (b) the situation of the capital goods producing industries, on the assumption that a higher demand for capital goods (associated with a higher level of investment) will encounter capacity constraints and/or rising capital goods prices; and (c) the interest rate, which is required to discount future adjustment costs and benefits to obtain their present value. If the capital stock adjustment parameter in the flexible accelerator is viewed in this light, it should be clear that the flexible accelerator model is less vulnerable to the fifth and first of the criticisms listed above.

Profits and retained earnings

One other variable which is stressed in some theories of investments is profits. On the one hand the desired capital stock has been seen as a function of profits or expected profits rather than output. On the other hand it has been suggested that firms have a strong preference for internal rather than external financing of investment, so that non-distributed profits or retained earnings become the key determinant of investment. In either case the emphasis on profits has brought financial factors into an essentially Keynesian perspective, though in the form of quantity constraints rather than opportunity costs or relative prices.

Tobin's q model

An alternative approach to investment, which takes its inspiration from a different aspect of Keynes's work, is that of the q-ratio proposed by Tobin (1969). The essential idea is that movements in share prices relative to the cost of investment affect the level of investment. For an individual firm q is defined as the ratio of the average value of the firm's stock of capital to the cost of a unit of capital:

$$q = \frac{V/K}{p_k} = \frac{V}{p_k K}$$

where the average value of the capital stock is the market capitalisation of the firm V (the share price times the number of shares) divided by the number of (physical) units of capital K, and the cost of a unit of capital is p_k. This ratio can then be aggregated across firms to produce an economy-wide q.

The crucial issue for investment is whether q is greater than or less than 1. If q is greater than 1, that suggests that if the firm makes an investment its value on the stock market will increase by more than the cost of the investment. On the other hand if q is less than 1, an investment will increase the firm's market value by less than its cost, in which case the investment is not sensible from the firm's point of view.

Much effort has been devoted to the development and testing of the q model, with an important distinction being made between average and marginal q and some emphasis on adjustment costs. While this effort has not been entirely successful (see below), the model has continued to be influential as a theory which relates investment directly to the state of the stock market. Indeed, the market valuation of a firm should in principle incorporate in a single objective statistic a wide variety of information about the past performance and future prospects of the firm.

The neoclassical approach to investment

All the approaches to investment discussed so far in this chapter can be situated within the (broadly defined) Keynesian tradition: they all try to answer the question 'how much investment will occur in the current period?' in terms of firms' desires to *increase* their capacity and the impact of these desires on the demand for and output of capital goods and hence on aggregate demand as a whole. The neoclassical approach starts from a very different perspective. It asks 'with what combination of factors will firms choose to produce given levels of output?' and it emphasises changes in the mix of factors in response to changes in their relative prices.

In this approach profit-maximising firms are assumed to choose the optimal path of accumulation of capital on the basis of certain knowledge about current and future factor prices, output prices and technology; moreover the capital stock is continually adjusted to its optimal level and is always fully utilised. These assumptions enable the approach to focus on the cost of using capital relative to other prices as the key determinant of the optimal path of capital accumulation, and hence of investment. The optimal capital stock (relative to output) is regarded as a function of the price level P, the wage rate W, and the 'rental price of capital services' or 'user cost of capital' c:

$$K^*/Y = f(P, W, c) \qquad [3.13]$$

Alternatively the optimal capital stock can be presented as a function of the real rental price of capital services and the real wage:

$$K^*/Y = g(c/P, W/P)$$

The rental price of capital services is the price of using one unit of capital per period (analogous to the real wage rate which is the price of using one unit of labour per period). Since firms typically buy capital goods rather than hiring or renting them, it can best be thought of as the net cost to a firm of purchasing a capital good, using it for one period, and then selling it. More precisely it is composed of the opportunity cost of purchasing capital goods (equal to the interest rate r times the price of capital goods per unit q) *plus* the cost of (physical) depreciation (a proportion δ of the price of capital goods) *minus* any increase in the price of capital goods over the period (that is the proportional growth rate of q, $\Delta q/q = \dot{q}$):

$$c = qr + \delta q - \dot{q} \qquad [3.14]$$

Under the assumptions above, firms maximise their profits (or rather their 'net present value' which includes all future profits) by choosing their capital/labour ratios such that the marginal physical product of capital is equal to the rental price of capital services, c/P. The essence of the approach can be presented in terms of an isoquant diagram as in Figure 3.5, where a higher price of labour L relative to that of capital K involves the use of more capital-intensive techniques (the comparison between points B and A in the diagram) which require additional investment.

Thus the principal contribution of the neoclassical approach is its emphasis on relative factor prices as a determinant of investment, where the price of capital includes the interest rate as one element. However, the neoclassical approach also puts emphasis on output as a determinant of investment. In

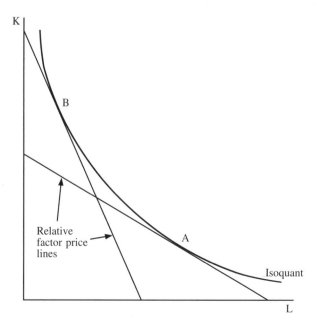

Figure 3.5

addition, modified versions of the neoclassical approach which have been used in empirical work relax the assumption of instantaneous adjustment by introducing some form of capital stock adjustment process similar to that of equation [3.11] above. It is also possible to take account in this framework of the effect of corporation and other taxes on firms' net profits and hence on their investment decisions.

Summary

Six different approaches to investment have been considered in this chapter: the MEC/MEI analysis; 'animal spirits'; the accelerator; the profits approach; Tobin's q model; and the neoclassical approach. The first four of these represent different strands of Keynesian thinking, the sixth represents the more sharply contrasting neoclassical approach, and the fifth stands somewhere in between. How far do these approaches differ in the variables they identify as the main determinants of investment?

Expected aggregate demand or output is emphasised in the MEC/MEI analysis as the underlying determinant of expected net revenues and hence one of the main determinants of investment. In the animal spirits approach expected demand is presumably the driving force behind the fluctuations in confidence which determine investment, while in the accelerator model this idea is developed more systematically: current output, featuring as a proxy for expectations of future output, plays the key role via the normal capital–output ratio. In the profits approach, current or expected demand is likely to be a key determinant of current or expected profits, and hence of investments. Expected demand also features in principle in Tobin's q model, since stock market valuations of firms should reflect expectations about future demand and therefore profitability. And in the neoclassical approach while the capital–labour mix depends on relative factor prices, the absolute amount of capital depends on output. From different perspectives there is therefore considerable agreement on the importance of aggregate demand or output, either current or expected.

The interest rate comes into the MEC/MEI analysis as a measure of the opportunity cost of capital which determines the profitability of investment projects. It also features as a determinant of the partial adjustment parameter in the capital stock adjustment mechanism. Tobin's q model incorporates a broader view of financial factors with its emphasis on share prices (which are strongly affected by interest rates). And the interest rate constitutes a large element of the real rental price of capital services which is the key determinant of the capital–labour intensity of production, and hence of investment in the neoclassical approach. On the other hand, the interest rate plays no role in the animal spirits approach or the basic (as opposed to the flexible) accelerator model and the kind of financial factors emphasised in the other strand of Keynesian thinking – profits – is very different. Thus there is considerable disagreement about the importance for investment of the interest rate or of financial factors more generally.

It should also be noted that the impact of the demand for capital goods on capital goods prices plays a role in the MEI analysis, comes into some discussions of the determinants of the capital stock adjustment parameter, and in practice could perhaps be taken into account in the neoclassical approach (at the theoretical level, however, this approach assumes that all prices are known in advance with certainty).

Empirical evidence

What light does the empirical evidence throw on these agreements and disagreements? A large amount of empirical testing of investment functions has been carried out but the results are less clear-cut than economists would have liked; the main results appear to have been the following. Firstly, there is little doubt that output or demand in some form is a major determinant of investment, though in what form is less clear; in particular the basic accelerator model does not fit the data well, and the failure of empirical work to establish clear-cut systematic relationships might be taken as indicating that animal spirits are important (i.e. that investment decisions are partly arbitrary and non-rational). Secondly, the importance of the interest rate is far from clear. Early studies of this question which took the form of questionnaires to businessmen were originally interpreted as implying that the interest rate was not a significant consideration in their decisions, and this evidence was one of the factors which led Keynesian thinking to shift towards either the animal spirits view or the basic accelerator model; however, this interpretation of the questionnaire evidence has been strongly disputed. Later econometric evidence found some influence from the interest rate on investment in the USA, but less such effect in the UK or Canada. Thirdly, the q ratio has proved unable to explain investment satisfactorily unless supplemented by additional explanatory variables such as output, liquidity and capacity utilisation (whose presence is difficult to explain in theoretical terms); in addition, econometric results have implied implausibly large lags in adjustment. And fourthly, while econometric work has generally found considerable lags in the adjustment of the capital stock, that is lags in the response of investment to changes in its determinants, there is also considerable support for some sort of accelerator mechanism in the sense that a given change in output or demand is associated over time with a larger change in the capital stock.

Significance: stability and the transmission mechanism

The significance of these unresolved differences between the approaches to investment lies in their contrasting implications for two questions. The first is 'how stable or unstable is the economy?'. The key point here is that the more slowly the capital stock adjusts, that is the longer the lags in the investment function, the less likely it is that violent fluctuations in investment will cause national income to fluctuate widely; but in so far as some sort of accelerator mechanism or animal spirits effect exists, investment can be a source of instability because it can magnify over time a given fluctuation in income originating elsewhere or be an independent cause of fluctuations. Apart from this the contribution of investment to the stability of national income will depend on the stability of its determinants such as the interest rate.

The second question is that of the 'transmission mechanism'. This term is used in macroeconomics to refer to the mechanism by which increases in the money supply are transmitted into increases in national income. The existence or otherwise of a transmission mechanism was at one stage crucial to the disputes between Keynesians and monetarists, with the former arguing that there was little or no such mechanism and the latter asserting that there was a strong one. In the 1960s in particular, the existence or otherwise of a transmission mechanism was understood almost entirely in terms of the interest-elasticity of investment together with the interest-elasticity of the demand for money: the idea was that increases in the money supply would (if the demand for money was less than perfectly interest-elastic) bring about reductions in the interest rate which (if investment was interest-elastic) would lead to increases in investment. As will be seen later in Chapter 7, the controversy on these points led within the IS–LM model to sharply differing policy implications. By the 1980s, however, a number of other transmission mechanisms had been recognised – notably real balance effects, expectations of inflation and the exchange rate – so that this controversy had been largely defused.

Exercises

(i)   If an investment project has an outlay cost of 10 000 and is expected to produce net revenues of 1 000 a year for the rest of time, use equation [3.5] to work out the marginal efficiency of capital. (Think of $1/(1+m)$ as equal to α and use the property that, if $0 < \alpha < 1$, then $\alpha + \alpha^2 + \alpha^3 + \alpha^4 + \cdots = \alpha/(1 - \alpha)$.)

(ii) Suggest a variety of channels by which a loosening of monetary policy might lead to an increase in investment.

(iii) Suggest a variety of channels by which increased confidence about the future among firms might lead to an increase in investment.

Further reading

An up-to-date, but technically quite advanced, survey of theoretical and empirical work on investment can be found in Chirinko (1993).

Chapter 4

The government and foreign trade sectors

This chapter introduces the government sector and the foreign trade sector, and derives and discusses some results from a simple model of the economy with fixed prices and no monetary sector.

The government sector

It is conventional to assume that government expenditure on goods and services G is exogenous – determined by the government and invariant with respect to income; and to aggregate together tax revenue *minus* government expenditures on transfer payments (which are treated as a sort of negative tax) and assume the aggregate to be partly autonomous ('lump sum') and partly dependent on income. In symbols,

$$G = \overline{G}$$

$$T = \overline{T} + tY, \ 0 < t < 1.$$

Consumption now becomes a function of disposable income Y_d, and the equilibrium condition for national income now requires income (output) to equal the sum of consumption, investment and government expenditure on goods and services. Using a simple AIH consumption function and assuming investment to be entirely exogenous in this simple model,

$$C = a + bY_d, \ 0 < b < 1.$$

$$Y_d = Y - \overline{T} - tY$$

$$I = \overline{I}$$

$$Y = C + I + G$$

Equilibrium income can now be found as follows:

$$Y = a + b(Y - \overline{T} - tY) + \overline{I} + \overline{G}$$

$$Y - bY + btY = Y(1 - b + bt) = a - b\overline{T} + \overline{I} + \overline{G}$$

$$Y = \frac{1}{1 - b + bt} \cdot (a - b\overline{T} + \overline{I} + \overline{G}) \tag{4.1}$$

where the basic multiplier is $1/(1 - b + bt)$.

The balanced budget multiplier

In the development of macroeconomics some importance has been attached to the 'balanced budget multiplier', that is the multiplier for an equal increase in government expenditure and taxes. It is helpful to analyse this first in a model where all taxes are lump sum, that is $t = 0$: equation [4.1] becomes

$$Y = \frac{1}{1 - b} \cdot (a - b\overline{T} + \overline{I} + \overline{G}) \tag{4.2}$$

and the basic multiplier is $1/(1 - b)$. The effect on income of an increase in government expenditure, $\Delta Y'$, can be calculated from knowledge of the multiplier as

$$\Delta Y' = \frac{1}{1 - b} \cdot \Delta \overline{G}$$

Alternatively, the level of income Y_0 associated with the level of government expenditure $\overline{G}_0$ can be subtracted from the level of income Y_1 associated with government expenditure $\overline{G}_1$ as follows (readers familiar with calculus will realise that the result [4.3] can be obtained more quickly by the appropriate differentiation of [4.2]):

$$Y_0 = \frac{1}{1 - b} \cdot (a - b\overline{T} + \overline{I} + \overline{G}_0)$$

$$Y_1 = \frac{1}{1 - b} \cdot (a - b\overline{T} + \overline{I} + \overline{G}_1)$$

$$Y_1 - Y_0 = \frac{1}{1 - b} \{(a - b\overline{T} + \overline{I} + \overline{G}_1) - (a - b\overline{T} + \overline{I} + \overline{G}_0)\}$$

$$Y_1 - Y_0 = \frac{1}{1 - b} \cdot \{\overline{G}_1 - \overline{G}_0\}$$

$$\Delta Y' = \frac{1}{1 - b} \cdot \Delta \overline{G} \tag{4.3}$$

Similarly, the effect on income of an increase in taxes, $\Delta Y'$, can be calculated as follows:

$$Y_0 = \frac{1}{1 - b} \cdot (a - b\overline{T}_0 + \overline{I} + \overline{G})$$

$$Y_1 = \frac{1}{1 - b} \cdot (a - b\overline{T}_1 + \overline{I} + \overline{G})$$

$$Y_1 - Y_0 = \frac{1}{1 - b} \cdot \{-b\overline{T}_1 + b\overline{T}_0\}$$

$$= -\frac{b}{1 - b} \cdot \{\overline{T}_1 - \overline{T}_0\}$$

$$\Delta Y'' = -\frac{b}{1-b} \cdot \Delta \overline{T} \tag{4.4}$$

The total effect on income of an equal increase in government expenditure and autonomous taxes, ΔY, is obtained by adding $\Delta Y'$ and $\Delta Y'$ and setting

$\Delta \overline{G} = \Delta \overline{T}$:

$$\begin{aligned} \Delta Y &= \Delta Y' + \Delta Y'' \\ &= \frac{1}{1-b} \cdot \Delta \overline{G} - \frac{b}{1-b} \cdot \Delta \overline{T} \\ &= \frac{1}{1-b} \cdot \Delta \overline{G} - \frac{b}{1-b} \cdot \Delta \overline{G} \\ &= \frac{(1-b)}{1-b} \cdot \Delta \overline{G} \end{aligned}$$

$$\frac{\Delta Y}{\Delta \overline{G}} = 1$$

Thus the effect on income of equal increases in government expenditure and taxes is that income increases by the same amount. Moreover, this result is independent of the size of the marginal propensity to consume.

What is the intuitive explanation of this result? The increase in government expenditure results in a 'first-round' addition to aggregate demand of $\Delta \overline{G}$, which is then multiplied by the multiplier process in the usual way. The increase in taxes results in a reduction in aggregate demand, again multiplied in the usual way, but because taxes affect aggregate demand only via their effect on disposable income and hence on consumption, the first-round reduction in aggregate demand is not $\Delta \overline{T}$ but $b\Delta \overline{T}$. (Some of the first-round effect of the tax increase falls on saving rather than consumption.) The net first-round impact is therefore $\Delta \overline{G} - b\Delta \overline{T}$ or (for a balanced budget increase) $\Delta \overline{G} - b\Delta \overline{G} = \Delta \overline{G} \cdot (1-b)$. Thus the first-round impact is positive and non-zero (given $b < 1$) and such that the ultimate, multiplied, effect on income is equal to the original increase in each of government expenditure and taxes.

The derivation of the balanced budget multiplier in a model where taxes are partly autonomous but partly income-related is more complicated. In this book changes in lump-sum taxes when the marginal tax rate is non-zero, but not changes in the marginal tax rate itself, will be considered. The equilibrium condition is now equation [4.1] and the basic multiplier is $1/(1-b+bt)$. The effects on income of increases in government expenditure and (autonomous) taxes are now

$$\Delta Y' = \frac{1}{1-b+bt} \cdot \Delta \overline{G}, \tag{4.5}$$

and

$$\Delta Y'' = -\frac{b}{1-b+bt} \cdot \Delta \overline{T} \tag{4.6}$$

However, when income rises, income-related taxes rise; to obtain the balanced budget multiplier the increase in government expenditure needs to be equal to the sum of the increase in lump-sum taxes and the increase in income-related taxes. If the marginal tax rate remains constant this means that

$$\Delta T = \Delta\overline{T} + t\Delta Y = \Delta\overline{G} \qquad [4.7]$$

From [4.5] and [4.6],

$$\Delta Y = \Delta Y' + \Delta Y'' = \frac{1}{1-b+bt} \cdot \Delta\overline{G} - \frac{b}{1-b+bt} \cdot \Delta\overline{T} \qquad [4.8]$$

Substituting from [4.8] into [4.7] and rearranging gives

$$\Delta\overline{T} + \frac{t\Delta\overline{G}}{1-b+bt} - \frac{tb\Delta\overline{T}}{1-b+bt} = \Delta\overline{G}$$

$$\frac{\Delta\overline{T}(1-b+bt-tb)}{1-b+bt} = \frac{\Delta\overline{G}(1-b+bt-t)}{1-b+bt}$$

$$\frac{\Delta\overline{T}(1-b)}{1-b+bt} = \frac{\Delta\overline{G}(1-b)(1-t)}{1-b+bt}$$

$$\Delta\overline{T} \cdot (1-b) = \Delta\overline{G} \cdot (1-b)(1-t)$$

$$\Delta\overline{T} = \Delta\overline{G}(1-t) \qquad [4.9]$$

Equation [4.9] identifies the size of the change in autonomous taxes required to produce a change in total (autonomous and income-related) taxes equal to the change in government expenditure. Substituting from [4.9] into [4.8] gives the total effect on income of a balanced budget increase in expenditure and taxes:

$$\Delta Y = \Delta Y' + \Delta Y''$$

$$= \frac{1}{1-b+bt} \cdot \Delta\overline{G} - \frac{b}{1-b+bt} \cdot \Delta\overline{T}$$

$$= \frac{1}{1-b+bt} \cdot \Delta\overline{G} - \frac{b}{1-b+bt} \cdot (1-t)\Delta\overline{G}$$

$$= \frac{\Delta\overline{G}(1-b+bt)}{1-b+bt} = \Delta\overline{G}$$

$$\frac{\Delta Y}{\Delta\overline{G}} = 1.$$

Thus the original result that the balanced budget multiplier is unity also holds when taxes are partly income-related.

The foreign trade sector

It is conventional to assume that exports X are exogenous and autonomous whereas imports F are partly autonomous and partly income-related:

$$X = \overline{X}$$

$$F = \overline{F} + fY, \quad 0 < f < 1.$$

These assumptions are not contradictory or asymmetric; in principle exports depend on the incomes of other countries just as imports depend on the home country's income, but other countries' incomes are held constant for the purpose of analysing alternative states of the home country. The equilibrium condition for national income now needs to incorporate the foreign trade balance $X - F$, as an additional element of demand. Using the same functions as before for other elements of demand, equilibrium income is found as follows:

$$Y = C + I + G + X - F$$

$$Y = a + b(Y - \overline{T} - tY) + \overline{I} + \overline{G} + \overline{X} - \overline{F} - fY$$

$$Y(1 - b + bt + f) = a - b\overline{T} + \overline{I} + \overline{G} + \overline{X} - \overline{F}$$

$$Y = \frac{1}{1 - b + bt + f} \cdot (a - b\overline{T} + \overline{I} + \overline{G} + \overline{X} - \overline{F}) \qquad [4.10]$$

The basic multiplier is now $1/(1 - b + bt + f)$, and the following results can be obtained in the usual way for the effects on income of changes in the components of autonomous expenditure:

$$\frac{\Delta Y}{\Delta \overline{G}} = \frac{\Delta Y}{\Delta \overline{I}} = \frac{\Delta Y}{\Delta \overline{X}} = \frac{1}{1 - b + bt + f}$$

$$\frac{\Delta Y}{\Delta \overline{F}} = \frac{-1}{1 - b + bt + f}$$

$$\frac{\Delta Y}{\Delta \overline{T}} = \frac{-b}{1 - b + bt + f}$$

The basic multiplier in the full Keynesian cross model

The basic multiplier in the full model with government and foreign trade sectors, that is

$$\frac{1}{1 - b + bt + f}, \qquad [4.11]$$

can now be compared with the multipliers for models with no foreign trade sector $(f = 0)$ and no income-related taxes $(t = 0)$. More generally, since the larger the denominator of expression [4.11] the smaller is the value of the expression as a whole, the following relationships hold:

(i)   the larger t, the smaller the multiplier;
(ii) the larger f, the smaller the multiplier; and
(iii) the larger b, the larger the multiplier.

The last point, which can be seen more easily if the multiplier is rewritten as $1/\{1 - b(1 - t) + f\}$, is already familiar from Chapter 2 where it was shown that since the marginal propensity to consume out of current income in the permanent income hypothesis is lower than the MPC in the absolute income hypothesis, the short-run multiplier associated with the PIH is smaller than that associated with the AIH.

Point (i) is often made in the form of the statement that income-related taxes are an 'automatic' or 'built-in stabiliser'; the larger t, the smaller the multiplier, so that the smaller the effect on income of given changes in the exogenous elements of demand. The economy is therefore more stable in the presence of exogenous fluctuations in investment or exports. It will also, however, be less responsive to fiscal policy in the form of a given change in government expenditure.

According to point (ii) a larger marginal propensity to import f also reduces the multiplier through what is commonly known as the 'import leakage'. The effect is exactly the same in qualitative terms as that of the tax rate in point (i). Thus foreign trade could be regarded as an automatic stabiliser. It has not usually been regarded in this way, however, and it is interesting to consider why.

Income-related taxes have a stabilising influence because they displace some of the effect of exogenous fluctuations in expenditure away from income and on to tax revenue and the government's budget: the stabilisation of income is therefore obtained at the price of greater instability in the budget deficit. From a traditional Keynesian point of view this price was insignificant because the size of the budget deficit was not important in itself. On the other hand the stabilising effect of foreign trade involves a displacement of the effect of exogenous fluctuations in expenditure on to imports and the balance of trade, and the latter was regarded as of importance in itself.

The automatic stabiliser characteristic of income-related taxes means that the budget deficit varies in response to changes in any autonomous expenditure element (or exogenous parameter), and not only in response to changes in government expenditure or taxes. This in turn means that the budget deficit does not provide a clear measure of the 'stance' of fiscal policy – how expansionary or contractionary policy is. Instead, fiscal stance is sometimes measured by the 'full employment budget deficit', that is the deficit that would exist for the given levels of government expenditure $\overline{G}$, lump sum taxes $\overline{T}$ and the tax rate t, if income were at the full employment level. However, there are a number of other issues involved here which go beyond the scope of this book.

Conclusions and qualifications

In this chapter a government sector and a foreign trade sector have been added to the simple income–expenditure model. The balanced budget multiplier of unity was derived in the cases of only lump-sum and of lump-sum and income-related taxes, but without a foreign trade sector. And the role in the full multiplier of the marginal tax rate and the marginal propensity to import were analysed.

Several qualifications are in order. Firstly, consideration of the full multiplier in equation [4.11] should make clear that in a model with a foreign trade sector the balanced budget multiplier will be less than one, because some of an expansionary stimulus will be dissipated on imports. Secondly, even with a government sector and a foreign trade sector the model analysed here is seriously defective: in particular it includes no monetary sector and it assumes a fixed price level (with no capacity constraint, that is there are always unemployed resources available for use). The next two chapters lay the basis for the construction in Chapter 7 of a model with a monetary sector; a full model with endogenous prices is reached in Chapter 13. One of the effects of adding a monetary sector and also of allowing prices to be endogenously determined is that both the basic multiplier (corresponding to [4.11]) and the balanced budget multiplier are further reduced in size. Thirdly, few economists would now regard the size of the budget deficit, or the stock of government debt outstanding which deficits generate, as of no importance; some of the issues involved are discussed in Chapters 14 and 17.

Fourthly, although the model developed here includes a foreign trade sector it is a very poor picture of a country's international economic relationships: it includes no capital flows and no monetary interdependence, it implicitly assumes fixed exchange rates and it ignores anything connected with the *price* of imports and exports. These matters are dealt with in Chapters 11 and 12.

Exercises

Students should ensure that they thoroughly understand the models deployed in this chapter by working through the following questions:

(i) Show that the balanced budget multiplier is less than unity in a model where the tax rate is zero but the marginal propensity to import is positive.

(ii) Explain intuitively why the multiplier for equal increases in government expenditure and lump sum taxes is less than unity, in a model where the marginal propensity to import is zero and the tax rate is positive.

In a model where the tax rate and the marginal propensity to import are both positive,

(iii) Taking account of any change in income, analyse the effect on the government budget deficit $(\overline{G} - \overline{T} - tY)$ of: (a) an increase in government expenditure; and (b) an increase in investment.

(iv) Taking account of any change in income, analyse the effect on the balance of trade surplus $(\overline{X} - \overline{F} - fY)$ of: (a) an increase in exports; and (b) an increase in investment.

(v) Analyse the effect on (a) income, (b) the budget deficit and (c) the balance of trade surplus of an equal increase in government expenditure and autonomous imports, such as might result from an increase in government purchases of foreign defence equipment.

Further reading

Different measures of the budget deficit are discussed in Buiter (1985).

Chapter 5

The demand for money

A number of approaches to the demand for money can be found in the literature; this chapter discusses the basic forms of the most important, including the classical quantity theory of money, the Keynesian theory of the demand for money and the modern quantity theory of the demand for money. The emphasis is on the variables which the various theories identify as determinants of the demand for money, and on the extent to which they predict the demand to be stable. First, however, something should be said about money itself.

There is no universally agreed theoretical definition of 'money'. Most attempts to produce such a definition start from the three 'functions' of money – as medium of exchange, store of value and unit of account – but this does not solve the problem because some assets fulfil one of these functions but not others. There is agreement on the idea of money as 'notes and coin in circulation *plus* bank deposits', but this leaves open the question of exactly what sorts of deposits at which institutions should be counted: for example, should building society deposits which function as store of value but not (at least until recently) medium of exchange, be counted as money? Thus there has been a long and interesting but unresolved debate in the theoretical literature, while at the same time official agencies produce statistics on a range of different measures of the money supply which are commonly used in empirical work. This chapter proceeds on the assumption that these difficulties and differences of definition are of secondary importance: that is, that the demand functions for different definitions of money are essentially the same. Some further comments on the subject are made in the concluding sections.

The classical quantity theory

The roots of the classical quantity theory go back at least to David Hume, the Scottish philosopher and political economist of the eighteenth century, and the theory was taken for granted by nearly all economic thinkers before Keynes.

The central proposition derived from it was the idea that increases in the money supply lead to increases in prices.

The classical quantity theory is not strictly a theory of the demand for money, but it can reasonably be interpreted as being derived from a demand function, a supply function which has the money supply fixed exogenously by the government, and an equilibrium condition which requires the supply of money to equal the demand for it. A relationship derived like this from several more basic – 'structural' – relationships is called a 'reduced form' relationship.

There are two precise formulations of the theory, that due to the American economist Irving Fisher and that associated with Cambridge economists such as A.C. Pigou, both dating from the second decade of the twentieth century, and these will be examined in turn.

Fisher's version of the quantity theory is usually presented in terms of an equation which relates the money supply M times the velocity of circulation of money V to the price level P times an index T of the volume of transactions carried on in the economy:

$$MV = PT \qquad [5.1]$$

Of the four variables in equation [5.1], three (M, P and T) are defined and measured outside the equation, but what about V, the velocity of circulation? If V is simply PT/M the equation [5.1] is a tautology or an identity (substituting $V = PT/M$ into [5.1] reveals merely that $PT = PT$) rather than a behavioural equation which incorporates some non-trivial hypothesis about the behaviour of economic agents. However, Fisher assumed that V was fixed, that is $V = \overline{V}$. He also assumed that T is fixed, that is $T = \overline{T}$, since T is closely related to the level of output and the latter is assumed to be fixed at the level corresponding to the full employment of available resources. The identity of equation [5.1] therefore becomes the behavioural equation [5.2]:

$$M\overline{V} = P\overline{T} \qquad [5.2]$$

If it is further assumed, as it was by Fisher and other classical economists, that the money supply is controlled by the government, and is exogenous, the price level becomes determined endogenously by M: with V and T fixed, an $x\%$ increase in M leads to an $x\%$ increase in P.

In discussing the velocity of circulation Fisher emphasised institutional factors and the aggregate relationship: he focused on the question 'how much money does the community need to carry on its economic existence?', and he answered it by reference to factors such as the frequency of wage payments (and hence the size of the average money balances held by workers). However, the other specific version of the quantity theory, the Cambridge version, started from a very different point of view: it considered the aggregate relationship as derived from individual preferences and focused on the question 'how much money does the individual wish to hold?'. The Cambridge economists then answered this question in terms of factors such as the liquidity services of money to its individual holders – that is, the convenience of money as a form of wealth which can readily be exchanged for goods and services of all kinds – the services provided by other assets (which are generally less liquid but carry a higher rate of return), and the overall wealth or income constraints on the individual's holdings of money and other assets.

For operational purposes their analysis was simplified into the proposition that an individual's demand for money is proportional to his or her nominal income; when this is aggregated and put in reduced form terms it becomes the proposition that the money supply is proportional to nominal national income:

$$M = kPY, \quad k > 0 \qquad \text{[5.3]}$$

This formulation has real income Y in place of the transactions index T of equation [5.2], and the parameter k in place of the V of [5.2]. Here k is in principle a function of the interest rate and other variables (which measure the rates of return on money and other assets), but for simplicity it is assumed to be constant, just as V is assumed constant in the Fisher version. Similarly, Y is assumed to be fixed at, or at least to gravitate strongly towards, the full employment level of income. Thus equation [5.3] becomes the (non-tautological) proposition

$$M = \bar{k}P\bar{Y} \qquad \text{[5.4]}$$

with the implication that increases in the money supply lead to increases in prices in the same proportion.

Since k appears on the right-hand side of equation [5.4] while V is on the left-hand side of [5.2], and since [5.4] has Y rather than T, k is the reciprocal of the income velocity of circulation while V is the transactions velocity of circulation. Y and T are obviously strongly related, so the Cambridge formulation of the quantity theory [5.4] is very close to the Fisher formulation of [5.2]. However, it should be emphasised that the thinking underlying these two formulations is very different. Moreover, the full employment assumption is more of a *long-run* tendency in the Cambridge version than in the Fisher case. And since for Fisher the velocity of circulation was determined by technological and institutional factors which change only very slowly, his constant-velocity assumption refers to the short run, while the constant-velocity assumption in the Cambridge version refers more to some sort of long-run equilibrium.

Keynes's theory of the demand for money

Keynes was a Cambridge economist and the Keynesian theory of the demand for money is clearly a development out of the Cambridge tradition. But Keynes felt himself to be rebelling against that tradition, and the theory which he put forward in his later works (e.g. 1936) differed from the Cambridge version of the quantity theory in several respects. Keynes was more careful to separate the demand for and the supply of money instead of working with a reduced form relationship such as equation [5.4]. While the Cambridge tradition was concerned largely with the analysis of long-run equilibria where some sort of full employment might be held to be the norm, Keynes was concerned above all with the short run in which income could be expected often to be below the full employment level and in which variations in the velocity of circulation were of great importance. And Keynes laid much more emphasis on the individual economic agent's *motives* for holding money.

The first motive he identified was the *transactions* motive: individuals hold money in order to make transactions (that is, to buy and sell). The amount they wish to hold for this purpose depends primarily on the value of the transactions they expect to make, and the latter depends on their income, as in the Cambridge version of the quantity theory. The second motive for holding money was the *precautionary* motive: individuals hold money as a precaution against unforeseen payments or expenditures. The precautionary demand for money is also regarded as varying primarily with income, and is usually aggregated together with the transactions demand. Keynes himself thought the transactions and precautionary demand for money would also vary with the interest rate (the latter reflecting the opportunity cost of holding money rather than other assets), but his followers dropped this and simply set demand proportional to nominal income:

$$M_{T+P} = mPY, \quad m > 0,$$

[5.5]

where M_{T+P} is the transactions and precautionary demand for money. Equation [5.5] can also be written in terms of the *real* transactions and precautionary demand which is proportional to real income:

$$\frac{M_{T+P}}{P} = mY$$

[5.6]

The third motive for holding money identified by Keynes was the *speculative* motive, and this is the part of Keynesian theory that marks it out most strongly from other theories of the demand for money. According to Keynes, individuals also hold money as an alternative to holding bonds when they expect to make a loss from holding bonds and therefore a (relative) gain from holding money; and the amount of money held for this purpose varies primarily with interest rates. Individual economic agents (firms and households) are regarded as choosing whether to hold their wealth in the form of money or bonds, on the basis of the relative rates of return. Bonds are a form of debt issued by governments and companies (most economic analysis here refers to government bonds) on which the holder is paid a fixed 'coupon' each year and which are usually redeemed (bought back) by the issuer at a specified date in the future. The return on holding a bond (which is foregone by agents who hold money) consists of the fixed coupon and any capital loss or gain from movements in the market price of the bond; agents must therefore try to predict this movement.

The market price of a bond varies inversely with the rate of interest. Market forces ensure that the stock of bonds will be willingly held only if the equilibrium yield on them varies in line with interest rates in general. The yield on a bond is the coupon C divided by the price of the bond P_b, *plus* any change in the price of the bond over the period up to its redemption (again divided by the price of the bond); and since the coupon is fixed the yield can vary only by a variation in the price of the bond. In the simplest case (that of a non-redeemable bond or 'perpetuity') the yield on a bond is equal to the coupon divided by the price of the bond and this must be equal to the interest rate r,

$$\frac{C}{P_b} = r, \qquad\qquad [5.7]$$

such that when r rises or falls P_b must fall or rise.

If bond prices vary inversely with interest rates then predicting the movement of the former is tantamount to predicting the movement of the latter. In Keynesian theory these predictions are discussed in terms of speculators having some idea of the 'normal' level of interest rates, to which they expect interest rates to return if they are currently out of line. If current interest rates are above the normal level, speculators expect them to fall, which means that they expect bond prices to rise: in this situation capital gains as well as the coupon can be made from holding bonds, and speculators choose to hold bonds rather than money. On the other hand, if current interest rates are below the normal level, speculators expect them to rise, which means that they expect capital losses from holding bonds: if these losses are large enough to outweigh the coupon element of the return on bonds, speculators hold money instead of bonds.

If an individual's idea of the normal level of the interest rate is r^* in Figure 5.1, then there is some critical level of the interest rate $\hat{r}$ at which she believes that the capital loss resulting from the expected interest rate rise will exactly offset the coupon payment: the return on holding bonds or money is zero, and the speculator will be indifferent between them. However, if the actual interest rate is above (below) $\hat{r}$ the individual will believe she can make a net gain (loss) from holding bonds and she will accordingly hold her entire portfolio OP in bonds (money). Thus her speculative demand for money would have the shape of the curve in Figure 5.1.

If all speculators had identical ideas of the normal interest rate they would all hold bonds when the interest rate was above some critical level, they would all hold money when the interest rate was below it, and they would hold bonds or money when the interest rate was at the critical level. This would give a sharply discontinuous relationship between the interest rate and the speculative demand for money. However, it is usually assumed that speculators' ideas of the normal level vary (within some range), so that the higher the interest rate the more speculators expect capital gains and hold bonds, while the lower the interest rate the more speculators expect capital losses outweighing the coupon and hold money. This assumption generates the typical continuous speculative demand for money function M_{SPEC} in Figure 5.2.

This function is non-linear, but for some purposes it is convenient to represent the basic idea in linear terms by the approximation of the M'_{SPEC} curve in Figure 5.3 and by the following equation:

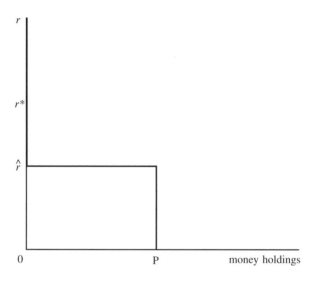

Figure 5.1

$$\frac{M'_{\text{SPEC}}}{P} = d - lr, \quad l > 0 \tag{5.8}$$

where M'_{SPEC} is the speculative demand for money, d is simply a constant corresponding to the intercept on the horizontal axis of the M'_{SPEC} line in Figure 5.3, and l indicates the sensitivity of the demand for money to the interest rate and is the reciprocal of the slope of the M'_{SPEC} line (it is the reciprocal because the equation expresses the variable on the horizontal axis as a function of the variable on the vertical axis – cf. the discussion of $C = a + bY$ in Chapter 2, pp. 18–19).

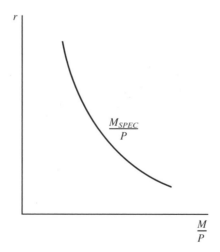

Figure 5.2

The speculative demand for money can now be added to the transactions and precautionary demand to obtain the total demand for money. In symbols, from equations [5.6] and [5.8],

$$\frac{Md}{P} = \frac{M_{T+P}}{P} + \frac{M'_{SPEC}}{P} = d + mY - lr \tag{5.9}$$

According to Keynesian theory then, the <u>real demand for money varies</u> <u>positively with real income and inversely with the interest rate</u>. The introduction of the interest rate into the equation (compare equations [5.9] and [5.4]) means that the proportional relationship of the classical quantity theory between money demand and nominal income or between real money demand and real income has disappeared.

Two further points should also be noted. Firstly, Keynesian theory predicts that the speculative demand and hence the total demand for money, or in Keynes's words 'liquidity preference', is unstable. Fluctuations in the financial markets' confidence about future interest rates and about the future in general, regarded (like animal spirits) as largely non-rational in character, bring about fluctuations in the normal level of interest rates expected by speculators and may therefore move the M_{SPEC} curve in Figure 5.2 to the left or to the right. This is represented in equation [5.8] and in Figure 5.3 by shifts of the intercept term d.

Secondly, there is a Keynesian 'special case' – not, it seems, necessarily believed by Keynes himself to be relevant, but at one time widely upheld by Keynesian economists – in which the speculative demand for money becomes infinite at some level of the interest rate r^* as in Figure 5.4. At r^* <u>all</u> <u>speculators expect the interest rate to rise and bond prices to fall by an</u> <u>amount that exceeds the coupon return</u>, so all speculators want to hold money rather than bonds. From the point of view of the monetary authorities, usually if they want to increase the amount of money held they can do so by buying bonds, but this raises the price of bonds. However, in

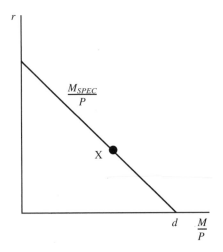

Figure 5.3

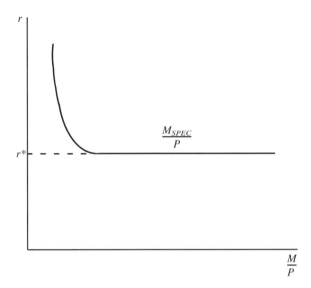

Figure 5.4

this special case they can buy all the bonds in the market without raising the price because no one else wants to hold them. The authorities cannot therefore reduce the interest rate, and any increase in the money supply arising from their purchase of bonds is simply held as additional speculative balances. It is for this reason that the special case is called the 'liquidity trap': additional money (liquidity) is trapped in the financial markets and has no wider effect on the economy. In terms of Figure 5.3, suppose the curve M'_{SPEC} is pivoted around the point X so that the curve becomes flatter: as it gets flatter l gets larger (the slope, $1/l$, gets smaller) and the interest elasticity of the demand for money, which is $\{\Delta(M_d/P)/\Delta r\} \cdot \{r/(M_d/P)\} = l \cdot \{r/(M_d/P)\}$, becomes larger; in the limit when the curve is horizontal, l is equal to infinity (and so also is the intercept term d), the slope of the line is zero, and the interest elasticity is infinite. Thus the liquidity trap occurs when $l = \infty$ and when the demand for money is infinitely or perfectly interest-elastic.

Later developments of the Keynesian theory of the demand for money

The 1950s saw two crucial developments or extensions of Keynesian thinking on money demand. First, Baumol (1952) and Tobin (1956) produced similar models of the transactions demand for money by households, focusing on the situation where the household receives a regular 'monthly' payment and spends all of that money gradually over the 'month', giving a sawtooth pattern to its money holdings like that shown by the outer line in Figure 5.5. Suppose the household has the possibility of investing the payment in an interest-bearing asset (e.g. in a savings account in a bank or other intermediary, and then withdrawing funds from that account at intervals, so that its actual money holdings would resemble the inner dashed-line sawtooth pattern in the figure. How often should it withdraw funds and how much should it withdraw each time?

The household must be concerned to minimise the costs of managing its financial assets, where those costs consist of two elements: first, the cost of making a withdrawal times the number of withdrawals, and second, the interest which is forgone by not holding bonds to the extent that the household holds cash instead. In symbols

$$C = b \cdot \frac{T}{K} + r \cdot \frac{K}{2} \qquad\qquad [5.10]$$

where C is the overall cost, b is the brokerage fee (cost of withdrawal), T is the regular 'monthly' payment (equal here to the total 'monthly' expenditure), K is the amount withdrawn on each occasion, and r is the interest rate per 'month'. Thus T/K is the number of withdrawals, and $K/2$ is the average amount of money held at each time (corresponding to the horizontal line in Figure 5.5).

It can be shown (by setting the derivative of expression [5.10] with respect to K equal to zero – but students who do not know calculus can simply take this result as given) that the optimal level for K is

$$K = \sqrt{\frac{2bT}{r}}$$

which implies that the household's average money holding is

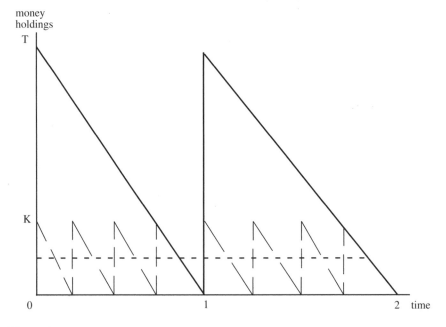

Figure 5.5

$$\frac{M_d}{P} = \frac{K}{2} = \frac{1}{2}\sqrt{\frac{2bT}{r}} \qquad\qquad [5.11]$$

Thus the household's money demand varies with the square root of the brokerage fee and the square root of income/expenditure, and varies negatively with the square root of the interest rate. The brokerage fee should be understood here not just as a fee that has to be paid to make a withdrawal but as the cost to the household of making the withdrawal, which includes the time and trouble involved in going to the bank; notice that if the fee is zero the household will never hold cash (instead it will withdraw cash only at the moment at which it is making a payment).

The fact that money demand varies with the square root of income/expenditure means that there are economies of scale in money holding: as a household's income rises from, say, 100 to 121, its money holdings will rise only from $10x$ to $11x$ where $x = 1/2 \cdot \sqrt{2b/r}$, so that a 21% increase in income gives rise to a 10% increase in money demand. This last point leads to two significant predictions at the aggregate level (when all households are taken together). First, a change in money supply will have a larger effect in the short run (*ceteris paribus*) because (with prices and interest rates unchanged) the money market can clear only if there is a proportionally larger change in income/expenditure. Secondly, the distribution of income among households will affect the overall demand for money: the economies of scale mean that a redistribution towards those with higher incomes will increase their money demand by less than the decrease in the money demand of those with lower incomes.

The second important development of Keynes's work was Tobin's (1958) theory of liquidity preference. Keynes's speculative demand for money was unsatisfactory because it required agents to have different views of the normal interest rate in order to generate a smooth relationship between the demand for money and the interest rate, and because even casual evidence suggests that individual investors do not hold their portfolios either all in money or all in bonds. Tobin produced an alternative analysis of this overall relationship which made no use of the concept of a normal interest rate and predicted that an individual would hold a diversified portfolio.

Tobin assumed that the investor is uncertain about the future and risk-averse, and her utility depends positively on the mean of the expected return on the portfolio μ and negatively on the standard deviation of the expected return σ (i.e. the risk of the portfolio). If the financial assets open to the investor consist of a safe but low-earning asset and a high-earning but more risky asset, the investor's wealth constraint can be depicted as the line r_sA in Figure 5.6, where the vertical axis in the upper part of the diagram measures return and the horizontal axis risk, r_s is the return on the safe asset (which could be zero) and r_r is the return on the risky asset: the investor can, by choosing the right combination of the two assets, reach any point on r_sA. The curve in the lower part of the diagram shows the proportion of the investor's portfolio which is invested in the risky asset for each level of σ for the portfolio as a whole. The investor's indifference curves such as I_0 slope upwards from left to right because μ is 'good' and σ is 'bad', and are convex downwards because of risk-aversion (the investor needs more and more return to compensate for additional risk). The investor's utility is then maximised at the point on the wealth constraint where she is on the highest possible indifference curve, i.e. at the point of tangency with the indifference curve.

Suppose now that the return on the risky asset rises, so that the wealth constraint pivots to $r_s B$. As with a change in price for a consumer good there are substitution and income effects. The substitution effect must lead the investor to increase her holding of the risky asset, whereas the income (or rather, wealth) effect for a risk-averse investor will tend to reduce her holding of the risky asset. It is normally assumed that the former will outweigh the latter in this case, so that the net effect of a rise in the interest rate is to increase the holding of the risky asset, which can be thought of as bonds, and reduce holding of the safe asset, money. This analysis therefore provides a rationale both for an individual investor to hold a diversified portfolio (some

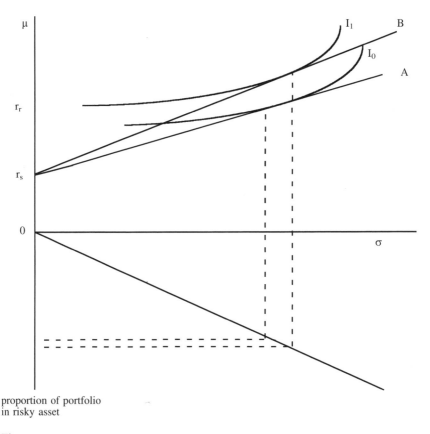

Figure 5.6

combination of bonds and money) and for her demand for money (and the aggregate demand also) to vary negatively with respect to the rate of interest.

Overall, if the Baumol–Tobin transactions demand for money analysis is combined with the Tobin liquidity preference analysis, the aggregate demand for money varies positively with income (but with economies of scale) and negatively with the interest rate (from both parts of the analysis). But in each case the underlying behaviour has been examined in more detail and in ways that are more consistent with the optimising behaviour assumed in most microeconomic work.

The modern quantity theory of the demand for money

After Keynes the classical quantity theory was widely discredited, not least because of its assumption of full employment. However, Friedman (1956) presented a 'restatement' of the quantity theory explicitly as a theory of the demand for money and without any assumption of full employment. It is in fact a moot point whether Friedman's theory is closer to the classical quantity theory or to Keynesian theory; it can be argued that Friedman was developing ideas present in the Cambridge tradition but not emphasised by Keynes, but it can also be argued that he was mainly restating (particularly later) Keynesian theory in a different conceptual and terminological context.

The starting point of Friedman's approach is the rejection of the Keynesian concern with the motives for holding money and the Keynesian view of money as something unique and deserving of special treatment. Friedman set out to analyse what determines not why but how much money is demanded and to analyse the demand for money in the same way as the demand for any other asset. It is helpful to begin, however, by considering how economists approach the demand for a good such as pens: they do not ask 'what do people want pens for?', they simply analyse the factors on which the amount of pens people want depends, and the standard approach would be to regard the demand for pens as a function of the price of pens, the prices of substitutes such as pencils, the prices of complements such as paper, income, and tastes.

To apply this approach to the demand for an asset, two modifications are necessary: first, the budget constraint which is relevant for decisions on how much of which assets to hold is not income (as in the case of pens) but wealth; and second, the key variable affecting the choice between alternative assets is not their relative prices but their relative rates of return. With these modifications the demand for an asset is predicted to be a function of the rate of return on the asset concerned, the rates of return on substitute assets, the rates of return on complementary assets (if they exist), wealth, and tastes. This is the basis of Friedman's approach to the demand for money, and the arguments in this sort of demand function will now be considered in turn.

On most definitions some part of 'money' consists of interest-bearing deposits, and the rate of interest on such deposits is an important element of the 'own' rate of return, that is the rate of return on money itself. However, a large part of money is non-interest bearing, but that does not mean the own rate of return on money is zero. A few studies have tried to estimate the value of the services provided by banks against non-interest bearing deposits, as a sort of implicit interest payment, but the most important element of the own rate of return on non-interest bearing money (and an important element for interest-bearing money) is the rate of inflation. In so far as prices rise, the real value of money falls and this represents a negative return to its holders; it is, however, the *expected* rate of inflation which is relevant to decisions on asset holdings and this is not easy to observe or measure.

The rate of return on substitute assets is more straightforward: in principle all sorts of assets, from bonds through equity to housing and durable goods, are relevant but the closest substitutes to money are obviously financial assets such as bonds or equity, and their rates of return are the coupon or dividend payment *plus* any expected capital gain. There appear to be no assets complementary to money.

Wealth is the appropriate budget constraint variable, as argued above, but not all forms of wealth can be readily transformed into money so that wealth holders whose wealth is partly in this form cannot easily hold money instead. In particular, human capital, that is skills which enable their owners to earn income in the future, cannot always be so transformed (the skills themselves, rather than the labour services they provide, cannot be sold, and there are limits to the extent to which they can be used as security for loans). Friedman therefore argued that the demand for money function should include the ratio of human to non-human capital. It should also be noted that since permanent income is in principle the return on wealth and must therefore vary closely with wealth, permanent income can be and has been used instead of wealth as the budget constraint variable.

The last three paragraphs should have given some idea of the careful analytical approach which Friedman applies, in much greater detail and complexity, to the demand for money. In empirical work, however, Friedman's theory has been simplified even further than in the above exposition. Firstly, the expected rate of inflation is frequently omitted in studies of countries and periods or of hypothetical situations where inflation is relatively low or stable. Secondly, the theoretical specification of the yields on an array of financial (and non-financial) assets is replaced by the use of a single yield variable, usually an interest rate, on the grounds that all yields tend to move together. Thirdly, the ratio of human to non-human capital, which probably varies little and is difficult to measure, has been universally omitted.

These simplifications reduce Friedman's modern quantity theory to the proposition that the real demand for money is a function of wealth or permanent income and the interest rate. This brings the theory much closer to the Keynesian theory of the demand for money, and indeed it is possible and convenient at this level to interpret equation [5.9],

$$\frac{M_d}{P} = d + mY - lr,$$

in either Keynesian or modern quantity theory terms, with the following differences in the variables and the expected values of the parameters: (a) the income variable Y refers to measured income in the Keynesian case, but to permanent income in the modern quantity case; (b) l is expected in Keynesian theory to be large, and in the special case of the liquidity trap infinite, while in modern quantity theory it is expected to be low or even (as in Friedman's own original empirical work) zero; and (c) d is predicted by Keynesians to fluctuate as the speculative demand for money shifts, while in modern quantity theory no such fluctuations are expected.

Buffer-stock money

The Baumol–Tobin transactions demand considered above is unsatisfactory for several reasons: it is not clear that it is efficient for the household to transfer its money payment into bonds at the start of the 'month', it is not obvious why households should spend their income at a constant rate through the 'month' (there may be economic incentives to rearrange outgoings, e.g. towards the first few days after the payment), and in any case actual money holdings appear to be much larger than this analysis would suggest, given the frequency of wage and salary payments. However, the analysis had considerable influence on later research.

Miller and Orr (1966) considered the individual firm, rather than the household, and assumed the firm has random cash inflows and outflows instead of a certain sawtooth pattern of receipts and expenditure, so that its actual cash balance varies as inflows or outflows predominate. The questions they ask are; (a) at what level of its cash balance should the firm replenish its cash holdings by selling bonds; (b) at what level should it transfer excess cash into bonds, and (c) in each case to what level should it restore its cash balance? In their model it turns out that the lower limit of the firm's cash balance should be zero, its upper limit varies positively with the brokerage fee and the size of the random inflow or outflow, and negatively with the interest rate on bonds, and it should restore its cash balances to a level which is one third of the upper limit, as in Figure 5.7. The reason why this 'return level' is a third rather than a half of the upper limit is that, although the brokerage fee is the same in both cases, more interest is foregone when the firm is nearer the upper limit than when it is nearer the lower, so that it is efficient to be on average nearer the lower limit.

While the influence of this theory has been restricted by the fact that it is not possible to test it (because firms and banks are not willing to release the kind of data required), the basic ideas were taken up in the 1980s and applied at a macroeconomic level under the name of 'buffer-stock money', mainly by economists of the Keynesian–monetarist convergence. The basic idea was that firms and households treat their cash balances as buffers or cushions, which they allow to vary, within certain limits, in response to unforeseen expenditures or receipts. Only when they find that their cash balances have reached significantly different levels (and perhaps sustained those levels for a period) do economic agents take action by changing their expenditures or their holdings of non-money financial assets.

What this means is that the demand for money should be thought of as a long-run phenomenon. In the short run economic agents can be pushed off their long-run demand function, and they will return it only slowly. In macroeconomic terms the result is that a change in the money supply may not have any effect on economic behaviour at least in the short run, for it may be simply absorbed in agents' money holdings. This contrasts both with the conventional Keynesian view that the money market must adjust to a change in money supply through some combination of a change in the interest rate and a change in income (as in the IS–LM analysis examined in Chapter 7), and with the New Classical view that the money market adjusts through an (immediate) change in prices (as in the New Classical AD/AS model discussed in Chapters 9 and 13). Instead, on this buffer-stock view, only sharp and/or sustained changes in money supply will lead to changes in behaviour. In addition, these changes will typically include significant real balance effects, as agents whose money holdings have risen or fallen beyond the normal limits adjust their expenditures in response.

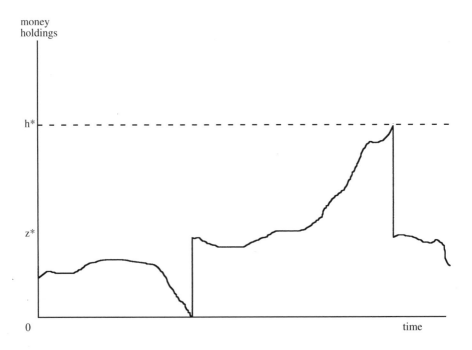

Figure 5.7

Summary

It is now possible to summarise the theories considered in terms of their predictions about the velocity of circulation. In both precise formulations of the classical quantity theory the velocity, equal to $\overline{V}$ in Fisher's version and to $1/\overline{k}$ in the Cambridge version, is constant. In the Fisher case the constancy is the result of the slow pace of change in the technological/institutional factors that determine velocity, while in the Cambridge case the constancy of velocity is a characteristic of long-run equilibrium.

Velocity in the Keynesian or modern quantity theories can be derived by rearranging equation [5.9] in the reduced form context of classical theory where the demand is equal to the supply of money M_s which is fixed exogenously $(M_s = \overline{M})$:

$$\frac{M_d}{P} = d + mY - lr$$

$$M_d = M_s = \overline{M}$$

$$\frac{\overline{M}}{P} = d + mY - lr$$

$$\overline{M} = P(d + mY - lr)$$

$$mPY = \overline{M} - P(d - lr)$$

$$PY = \frac{\overline{M}}{m} - \frac{P}{m} \cdot (d - lr)$$

$$V = \frac{PY}{\overline{M}} = \frac{1}{m} - \frac{P}{m\overline{M}} \cdot (d - lr) \tag{5.12}$$

If the variables and parameters of equation [5.12] are interpreted along Keynesian lines then it is clear that the velocity of circulation is not constant so long as the speculative demand for money (i.e. $d - lr$) is non-zero. In particular, the velocity varies positively with the interest rate (the higher the interest rate, the lower the speculative demand and the higher the velocity); it varies widely and may become very small in the liquidity-trap case (where the speculative demand becomes very large); and it is unstable in so far as the speculative demand is unstable, with increases (decreases) in d reducing (increasing) the velocity. In later Keynesian work, velocity is stable and there is no liquidity trap, but it varies with the effect of the interest rate both on transactions demand and on the proportion of money and bonds held in portfolios.

If equation [5.12] is interpreted along modern quantity theory lines, then instability and the liquidity trap are excluded, but velocity still varies positively with the interest rate; however, in so far as l is smaller in this case it varies within a narrower range. The velocity refers to measured income, but the modern quantity theory has the demand for money depending on wealth or permanent income; if, as was argued in Chapter 2, measured income fluctuates more than permanent income over the business cycle, then the (measured income) velocity of circulation varies system-atically with the cycle, being higher in booms when measured income is above permanent income and lower in recessions when measured income is below permanent income. According to modern quantity theory the velocity of circulation also varies with the expected rate of inflation; in hyperinflations, for example, the demand for money is expected to be very low and the velocity correspondingly high.

Finally, according to buffer-stock theory velocity is stable in the long run, varying positively with (permanent) income and negatively with the interest rate, but in the short run it may be quite unstable, with changes to money supply being absorbed in money holdings without any change to the variables on which the demand for money depends.

Thus according to classical quantity theory, velocity is constant. According to Keynesian theory, velocity is unstable: it varies with the interest rate and with fluctuations in confidence and may become very small in the liquidity trap. And according to modern quantity theory, velocity is a stable function of a small number of variables – the interest rate, the business cycle and inflationary expectations: it is not constant but it varies only within a limited range. These differences turn out in Chapter 7 to be of great importance for the questions of what determines aggregate demand and how governments should try to control it.

Empirical evidence

There has been an enormous amount of empirical work on the demand for money, in many countries over many time periods and with a variety of definitions of money, income, 'the' interest rate, and so on; only the key points can be mentioned here.

It seems to be clearly established that the demand for money depends on the interest rate. The actual size of the elasticity varies with the precise definitions of money and the interest rate; however, it appears to be larger than originally expected by Friedman but also smaller than some earlier Keynesian theorists had expected. The demand for money seems to be more closely related to permanent income or wealth than to measured income; but as with consumption in Chapter 2, much of the evidence can also be interpreted in terms of the Keynesian theory with lagged adjustment. The demand for money seems to be proportional to the price level; this was in fact assumed in the theoretical exposition above where the variable on the left-hand side of equation [5.9], for example, was M_d/P rather than M_d, but there is considerable empirical evidence to support this assumption. The demand for money does not appear to be unstable in the way predicted by Keynesian analysis of the speculative demand for money, and there is no evidence of a liquidity trap either during the slump of the 1930s or in other periods. There is considerable evidence of the importance of expected inflation in hyperinflations but less evidence of its importance in more 'normal' periods. There appear to be some economies of scale, particularly in narrow money holdings, and there is some evidence that the wage rate affects the demand for money, which would be consistent with the Baumol–Tobin emphasis on the brokerage fee, broadly defined to include the time and trouble of changing other assets into cash. Finally, the evidence of demand-for-money studies throws little light on the question of how money is best defined: for many countries in many time periods, narrow and broad definitions of money seem to perform equally well as dependent variables in demand-for-money equations.

Conclusions and qualifications

What conclusions can be drawn from the empirical evidence for the various theories of the demand for money discussed earlier in the chapter? Firstly, classical quantity theory, at least in the simple constant-velocity formulations, should be rejected: velocity is not constant; in particular, it varies systematically with the interest rate. Secondly, the specific predictions derived from Keynes's analysis of the speculative demand for money (instability and the liquidity trap) are not borne out by the evidence and this part of Keynesian theory should be rejected. Thus the empirical evidence can be taken to imply rejection of both a constant velocity and an unstable velocity, the two cases which might be characterised as extreme monetarist and extreme Keynesian; instead, the empirical evidence offers support for a 'moderate' (or later) Keynesian *or* monetarist interpretation of equation [5.9].

However, a major qualification which needs to be discussed here relates to the role of institutional change. In the 1970s, and again in the 1980s, empirical work on the demand for money encountered considerable difficulties, First, in the USA economists failed to predict the rise in the velocity of narrow money in the 1972–4 period; conventional demand for money functions suggested that money holdings ought to have been much higher, for equilibrium in the money market, than they actually were, in what has been widely described as the 'Case of the Missing Money' (Goldfeld, 1976). Second, the UK experienced a sharp fall in the velocity of broad money in 1972–3, with a return to the trend level by 1976–7. Third, in the USA and the UK (and in some other countries, particularly Anglo-Saxon ones such as Canada and Australia), there were sustained declines in the velocity of broad money during the 1980s. Fourth, the UK and some other countries saw sustained rises in the velocity of narrow money (the monetary base) in the 1980s.

Given previous disputes it might have been expected that economists would have reacted to these problems by reasserting the instability of the demand for money. But most reaction has taken the form of searching for factors which could explain them, and it is here that the issue of institutional change has been stressed. For example, the 'Case of the Missing Money' is widely seen as the result of institutional changes (such as the introduction of security repurchase agreements and money market mutual funds) which allowed firms and households to economise on their holdings of money. Such innovations, it was argued, were triggered by the high rates of inflation and interest rates in that period, but then proved themselves sufficiently useful to continue in existence after inflation and interest rates had reverted to more normal levels. In a similar way, the declines in the velocity of broad money in the 1980s have been attributed to financial innovations such as the introduction of interest-bearing current accounts at banks which increased the demand for bank deposits, while rises in the velocity of narrow money (the monetary base) have been seen as resulting from rises in the proportion of the workforce holding bank accounts and having their wages or salaries paid directly into those accounts, together with the introduction of automated teller machines which make it easier to obtain cash when required and of non-cash payment mechanisms (e.g. cheque guarantee cards and credit and debit cards).

On the other hand the fall in the velocity of broad money in the UK in the early 1970s is widely regarded as the result of an 'excessive' increase in the supply of money, as in buffer-stock theory. The idea is that prices and income and interest rates were all, for different reasons, unable to adjust rapidly to clear the market, and the exchange rate was floating so that the supply of money could not be adjusted through a balance of payments deficit (see Chapters 11 and 12). Hence the private sector was pushed off its long-run demand for money function, and returned to it only gradually over the next few years.

Thus although there remain some interesting puzzles concerning the demand for money, these have led economists not to overturn the specific conclusions of earlier work or to appeal again to the possibility of instability, but to focus attention on phenomena that had not been considered in as much detail before.

Further reading

This has been a long chapter with a considerable amount of detail. No exercises are suggested, but students should study the chapter carefully to improve their understanding of the material. If further reading is desired, Laidler (1993) is the classic survey of both theoretical and empirical work on the demand for money. Artis and Lewis (1991, Chapter 4) covers the demand for broad money in the UK, while Judd and Scadding (1982) examine the Case of the Missing Money in the US. The *Economic Journal* (1997) contains a useful recent symposium on the demand for money including discussion of the buffer-stock money concept.

Chapter 6

The supply of money

In analytical macroeconomic models of the IS–LM or AD/AS type it is typically assumed that the money supply is fixed exogenously by the monetary authorities, that is $M_s = \overline{M}$. However, there are other areas of analysis such as inflation and open-economy macroeconomics where it is useful to know something of the way in which the money supply is determined, and this is also a prerequisite for any serious empirical analysis of the determinants of monetary growth. It is therefore worth spending a little time on the question of how to analyse the determination of the money supply.

The high-powered money multiplier approach

One of the two main approaches to the question is that of the high-powered money multiplier. This approach essentially assumes that bank deposits and hence the money supply as a whole are determined by the level of the banks' reserves. By definition the money supply M_s is equal to notes and coin held by the non-bank private sector (that is, by 'the public') C *plus* the private sector's bank deposits D; 'high-powered money' H, which is the liabilities of the central bank, consists of notes and coin held by the public C *plus* notes and coin held by the banks *plus* the bank's balances (deposits) at the central bank; and the last two items constitute the banks' reserves R:

$$M_s = C + D \tag{6.1}$$

$$H = C + R \tag{6.2}$$

Dividing equation [6.1] by equation [6.2] produces

$$\frac{M_s}{H} = \frac{C + D}{C + R} \tag{6.3}$$

Dividing the top and bottom of the right-hand side of equation [6.3] by D (which leaves the value of the expression as a whole unchanged) and rearranging gives

$$\frac{M_s}{H} = \frac{C/D + 1}{C/D + R/D}$$

$$M_s = \left[\frac{C/D + 1}{C/D + R/D}\right] \cdot H = hH \qquad\qquad [6.4]$$

$$\text{where } h = \left[\frac{C/D + 1}{C/D + R/D}\right]$$

Equation [6.4] expresses the money supply as equal to the stock of high-powered money times the high-powered money multiplier h, with the latter a function of the two ratios C/D and R/D. So far equation [6.4] has been derived purely by the manipulation of identities and it remains an identity itself. But if the ratios C/D and R/D are constant, or at least stable and predictable, that is they move only within a narrow range and in a way that depends systematically on other variables, then h must also be stable and predictable; and if in addition the stock of high-powered money is fixed exogenously by the monetary authorities, then the money supply must be determined by the stock of high-powered money together with the multiplier. Changes in the money supply, that is monetary growth, can then legitimately be analysed in terms of the changes in the stock of high-powered money and the (relatively small) changes in the multiplier; this is the methodology followed by Cagan (1965), for example, in his study of US monetary growth.

Are these conditions likely to be fulfilled? C/D is the ratio of the private sector's holdings of cash to its deposits. The actual ratio is presumably the outcome of a choice between alternative assets subject to a wealth constraint, comparable to that involved in the demand for money as a whole as analysed in the modern quantity theory section of Chapter 5. If all relative rates of return remain constant, the ratio C/D might be expected to remain constant. But since at least some bank deposits bear interest whereas cash does not, economic agents (that is firms and households) are likely to hold more deposits and less cash at higher interest rates so that the ratio C/D will vary inversely with the interest rate. C/D is therefore unlikely to be constant though it may still be stable and predictable, and that would be enough for present purposes. However, the ratio may also be affected by technological/institutional factors such as changes in the proportion of the labour force which holds bank accounts and has its wages or salaries paid directly into these accounts, or changes in the use of credit cards rather than cash for shopping. And it would be affected by any dramatic loss of confidence in the banking system which led agents to shift out of deposits into cash. Factors such as these could deprive the C/D ratio of the stability and predictability required.

R/D is the ratio of banks' reserves to their deposit liabilities. It is presumably influenced on the one hand by official regulations on minimum reserve ratios and on the other hand by the banks' own awareness of the need for reserves to protect themselves against sudden and large withdrawals of deposits. Subject to official regulations the ratio can be expected to vary inversely with interest rates, for at higher interest rates banks will choose to hold a higher proportion of interest-bearing assets (i.e. loans) and a lower proportion of reserves (which bear less or no interest). This factor is enough to stop the ratio being constant but not to stop it being stable. However, it may also be affected by changes in the technology and management practices of banking, and by fluctuations in public confidence in the banking system, and the effects of these factors could be damaging to the stability and predictability of the ratio.

Finally the stock of high-powered money, although in principle under government control, will be so in practice only if governments behave in certain ways. The stock of high-powered money is the total liabilities of the central bank; hence the change in the stock of high-powered money ΔH is equal to the government's budget deficit DEF *minus* net sales of government debt to the commercial banks and the private sector ΔGD *plus* the government's net payments on external transactions (mainly the central bank's intervention in the foreign exchange market) ET *plus* short-term lending by the central bank to the commercial banks ('money market assistance' in the Bank of England's phrase) MMA:

$$\Delta H = DEF - \Delta GD + ET + MMA \qquad [6.5]$$

Thus the stock of high-powered money is affected *ceteris paribus* by the budget deficit, by the amount of debt the government sells to cover the deficit, by the authorities' intervention in the foreign exchange market (sales of reserves to hold or push up the exchange rate lead to a negative ET and a reduction of H) and by the central banks' day-to-day operations in the money market. Each of these elements can be influenced by government policy, but they are not under the direct or complete control of the government: the budget deficit DEF is affected also by the level of income (Chapter 4), net external transactions ET become endogenous under fixed exchange rates (Chapter 11), government debt sales ΔGD are determined by the behaviour of other economic agents as well as the government, and the central bank's lending MMA is generally influenced by its awareness of the short-term financial pressures on the banks as well as by its medium-term policy objectives. Clearly the government *could* organise its own behaviour in such a way as to make H entirely under its control, but this would constrain its activities in these other areas and it may therefore choose not to do so.

In addition, even if the stock of high-powered money is under the government's control, it will not necessarily be exogenous, in the sense of being determined outside the system. If the government is trying to control H in order to control M_s, then it will want to try to take account in setting H of likely variations in the money multiplier h, and its targets for H and M_s will typically also depend on the state of the economy (e.g. the rates of inflation and economic growth). In such a case it does not make sense to analyse M_s as if it was determined via the multiplier by an exogenously fixed H.

Thus whether the high-powered money multiplier approach is a useful way of analysing how the money supply is determined depends on whether certain conditions are fulfilled. This is essentially an empirical question and one which can be answered only for a specific case; that of the UK is considered below. First, however, it is convenient to examine in general terms the alternative approach to analysing the determination of the money supply, namely the credit counterparts approach.

Flow of funds analysis and the credit counterparts approach

The critique of the high-powered money multiplier approach discussed above led Tobin (1963) and Goodhart (1973), who had been the originators of many of the arguments concerned, to suggest that the stock of money should be approached through analysing the portfolio choices over a wide range of assets and liabilities made by each of the different sectors of the economy. The idea would be to model how the demand and supply of each sector for each sort of financial claim was determined, subject to the wealth constraints of each sector and the obvious requirements that demand for each claim should equal its supply. In the event, the econometric estimation of the behavioural relationships involved proved much more difficult than expected, and in practice many central bank and other economists focused instead on the identities between assets and liabilities which underlie the monetary system.

This 'flow of funds' analysis can be illustrated through Table 6.1, which shows the relationships between the changes in assets and the changes in liabilities held by each sector, for a relatively simple monetary economy. It distinguishes between the government sector (which includes here the central bank), the foreign sector, the private non-financial sector, and the financial sector (where, in recognition of recent changes affecting the financial system, non-bank financial intermediaries (NBFIs) such as building societies are included as well as banks). The first row of the table shows the financial deficit (expenditure *minus* income) of each sector, that is its need for funds: in the government's case this is the budget deficit $G - T$, for the foreign sector it is the current account surplus $X - F$, and for the private non-financial sector it is the excess of investment over saving $I - S$ (the financial sector's financial deficit is assumed to be zero). The other rows of the table show how the change in each financial claim is an increased asset to some sector(s) (positive sign) but an increased liability to other(s) (negative sign). High-powered money, for example, is a liability of the government (central bank) but an asset of the private and financial sectors which hold it.

This simplified table distinguishes only between deposits, non-deposit liabilities (e.g. shares issued by banks), high-powered money, government debt (bonds, Treasury bills and other securities), domestic lending (bank loans) and foreign lending. The latter covers the holding of any sort of claims on or liabilities to the foreign sector, from the government's holding of foreign exchange reserves to the foreign sector's holding of equity or other domestic financial claims and the private sector's corresponding holding of foreign claims. The first row sums to zero because injections must equal withdrawals. Each of the other rows must sum to zero, since it is the same quantity of some financial claim which is a liability of one sector and an asset of one or more other sectors. Each column must also sum to zero, for the columns represent

Table 6.1

	(a) Government	(b) Foreign	(c) Private non-financial sector	(d) Financial sector	(e) Total
1 financial deficit	DEF	$X - F$	$I - S$		0
2 deposits			ΔD	$-\Delta D$	0
3 non-deposit liabilities			ΔNDL	$-\Delta NDL$	0
4 high-powered money	$-\Delta H$		ΔC	ΔR	0
5 government debt	$-\Delta GD$		ΔGD_p	ΔGd_b	0
6 domestic lending			$-\Delta A$	ΔA	0
7 foreign claims	ET	$K - ET$	$-K$		0
8 total	0	0	0	0	0

Key: The columns represent balance sheet constraints for each sector.
The financial deficit is the excess of expenditure over income; $DEF = (G - T)$.
Rows (2–7) represent the identities between assets and liabilities for each kind of
financial claim.
The government sector includes the central bank.
ΔGD_p is the increase in the private non-financial sector's holdings of government
debt.
ΔGD_b is the increase in the financial sector's holdings of government debt.
Δ is the change in the financial sector's lending to the private sector.
ET is the change in the government's stock of foreign exchange reserves.
K is the capital inflow.

the balance sheet constraints of each sector: column (a), for example, shows
that the government must cover its budget deficit and any domestic currency it
needs for the purchase of foreign exchange by issuing government debt or high-
powered money, while the financial sector (d) can acquire additional assets, in
the form of government debt, high-powered money (bank reserves) and loans
to the non-financial sector, only to the extent that it issues additional liabilities
(deposit and non-deposit).

This table can be used to derive what is called the 'credit counterparts
approach' to the supply of money, which examines the changes in assets of
other sectors corresponding to the increase in the money held by the non-
financial private sector. By definition the money supply is equal to the cash
(notes and coin) and the deposits (with banks and NBFIs) held by the private
sector. So the change in money supply must be equal to the change in these
latter:

$$\Delta M_s = \Delta C + \Delta D \qquad [6.6]$$

The identities underlying column (c), row (1) and column (b) in Table 6.1 can
be written as the following equations:

$$I - S + \Delta D + \Delta NDL + \Delta C + \Delta GD_p = \Delta A + K \tag{6.7}$$
$$DEF + (X - F) + (I - S) = 0 \tag{6.8}$$
$$(X - F) + K = ET \tag{6.9}$$

Substituting for $(I - S)$ from [6.8] in to [6.7] and then for $(X - F)$ from [6.9] produces

$$\Delta D + \Delta NDL + \Delta C + \Delta GD_p = \Delta A + K + DEF + (X - F)$$
$$= \Delta A + K + DEF + ET - K$$

Further rearrangement yields the credit counterparts identity:

$$\Delta M_s = \Delta D + \Delta C = DEF + ET - \Delta GD_p + \Delta A - \Delta NDL \tag{6.10}$$

Equation [6.10] allows the growth of (broad) money to be related to the government's fiscal policy (DEF), to its debt management policy (ΔGD_p), to the growth of bank lending to the private sector (ΔA) and to net external transactions (ET). The equation was obtained by the manipulation of identities and it remains an identity itself, but it provides a framework within which monetary growth can be analysed in terms of the growth of the individual credit counterparts together with any interactions between them. If it were the case, for example, that bank lending to the private sector and hence bank deposits were determined via some stable R/D ratio by banks' reserves, then this information could be incorporated in an analysis which uses this framework. However, the framework can encompass any other information on the determinants of bank lending to the private sector, and it also takes more explicit account than the high-powered money multiplier approach of the policy elements which affect the growth of money; if these policy elements $(DEF, ET,$ and $\Delta GD_p)$ fluctuate widely in ways largely independent of each other, then the credit counterparts approach may be particularly valuable.

Empirical applications

Equations [6.4] and [6.10] are both derived from identities. Neither of them can therefore be wrong, but one of them may provide a more illuminating point of departure for an analysis of the determination of the money supply. Is it possible to say which is more appropriate?

Historically, there seems to have been a divide between those countries where the central banks were independent of or at least at arms' length from their governments, and those countries where the relationship was much closer. In the latter, because the central banks tended to be heavily involved either directly or indirectly in financing the government's budget deficit, it seemed natural to apply the credit counterparts approach. At the same time, because the banks were in some cases allowed to include various kinds of short-term government debt (and even, in the UK, some private sector debt) in their reserves, it was difficult to apply the high-powered money multiplier without considerable additional complication. Moreover, in some of these countries (notably the UK), the government has not attempted to control the banks' activities by exerting pressure on their reserves or on the stock of high-powered money, although some economists have maintained that they ought to have been operating in this way. The evolution of H was therefore a by-product of government policies acting on the deficit, the exchange rate and, through different channels, on bank lending. In countries like France and the UK, therefore, both government and outside economists have tended to use the credit counterparts approach as the framework for analysing changes in the money supply. On the other hand in countries with more independent central banks and where monetary policy has typically focused on the control of banks' reserves, such as the US, the high-powered money multiplier framework has been the norm.

It should be emphasised, however, that care needs to be taken in either framework. Those using the high-powered money multiplier approach need to take full account of any important movements in the underlying ratios (associated with changes in interest rates or, for example, financial innovations affecting the demand for cash) and of any extraneous factors affecting the evolution of H. Similarly, users of the credit counterparts approach have to be careful to integrate in the analysis any interactions between the various counterparts: if, for example, the government systematically sells more debt to the private sector when its deficit is larger, DEF and ΔGD_p will move together and DEF on its own may have no ability to predict or explain changes in the money supply.

Conclusion

Two ways of approaching the determination of the money supply have been outlined. Neither can be shown to be either right or wrong in itself, but one or other may be more appropriately applied in a specific country and period. However, that application needs to be undertaken with considerable care.

Exercises

Use official statistics for the last few years in the country in which you are studying to show

(i)   how, if at all, the C/D and R/D ratios have changed in recent years;
(ii) how DEF and ΔGD_p have varied; and
(iii) how ΔA and ΔM_s have varied.

Further reading

A detailed discussion of the evolution of the two approaches to the determination of the money supply can be found in Cobham (1991). The high-powered money multiplier analysis was used effectively in the US context by Friedman and Schwartz (1963) and Cagan (1965), while the original critiques of this framework are Tobin (1963) and Goodhart (1973; see also his 1989, Chapter VI).

Chapter 7

The IS–LM model

In this chapter the various elements of aggregate demand discussed in the five preceding chapters are brought together in a single analytical model, the IS–LM model, so called because its two curves represent respectively points where Investment is equal to Saving (or, in the more general case, injections equal withdrawals) and where Liquidity preference (the demand for money) is equal to the Money supply. The IS–LM model goes beyond the simple Keynesian cross model of national income determination by adding a monetary sector and allowing for the simultaneous interactions between investment, the interest rate and the demand for money, and between saving, income and the demand for money. It is therefore an extremely useful and versatile model, which can be used to discuss the effects of changes in exogenous expenditure, fiscal and monetary policy, and so on; it can also be used to discuss these effects under alternative assumptions about the underlying parameters which correspond to one very important phase of the Keynesian–monetarist controversy. Although the controversy has now moved on and has in any case ceased to be of such importance in macroeconomics, the IS–LM model is still an extremely important piece of analytical apparatus in macroeconomics and it should be thoroughly mastered.

For this reason the following exposition takes care to explain a large part of the material in three separate 'languages': in words, in terms of diagrams, and in terms of algebra. First, each of the curves is derived, together with an analysis of the determinants of its slope and the nature of the shifts caused by a number of exogenous changes. The curves are then brought together to derive the overall equilibrium for the model, and to examine how the equilibrium changes in response to exogenous changes. The latter exercise is then repeated under alternative sets of 'extreme' assumptions about the parameters (slopes) of the curves. The topics of crowding out and the transmission mechanism are then considered as mechanisms which underpin the overall results.

The goods market: IS

The IS curve is drawn on a diagram with real income on the horizontal axis and the interest rate on the vertical axis, and it shows all the combinations of income and the interest rate at which the market for goods and services is in equilibrium, in the sense that expenditure is equal to output. One way of approaching the IS curve is to think of it directly as involving a modification of the Keynesian cross model in which, when the interest rate is lower, investment is higher and therefore, by the usual multiplier process, income is higher. However, it is preferable to approach it in terms of the underlying equilibrium condition, which is the condition that total injections equal total withdrawals, or in the simple case (no government sector and no foreign trade sector) investment equals saving.

Consumption is assumed to be a function of (measured) income; it is not possible to use the permanent income hypothesis of consumption in an IS–LM model without introducing dynamic considerations which are difficult to handle at this level, so it is assumed that consumption is positively related to income and may or may not have a positive autonomous element (it makes little difference here). Saving is equal to income *minus* consumption.

$$C = a + bY, \quad a > 0, 0 < b < 1$$
$$S = Y - C = -a + (1 - b)Y \tag{7.1}$$

Investment is assumed to be partly autonomous and partly related to the interest rate; this is again a relatively simple formulation designed to avoid difficult dynamics, but other influences on investment can be taken account of to some extent by shifts of the function, that is changes in the autonomous element. In symbols,

$$I = j - ir, \quad j > 0, i > 0 \tag{7.2}$$

Here j is the autonomous element of investment and i is the parameter linking investment to the interest rate.

Now consider a position of equilibrium, where investment is equal to saving. How can equilibrium be maintained if the interest rate is increased? At higher levels of the interest rate, investment is lower, therefore to maintain equilibrium, saving must also be lower; and saving will be lower only if income is lower. Alternatively, starting from the original equilibrium position, how can the equilibrium be maintained if income is increased? At higher levels of income, saving is higher, so to maintain equilibrium, investment must be higher; and investment will be higher only if the interest rate is lower. Thus along the IS curve, which shows the equilibrium combinations of income and the interest rate, higher levels of the interest rate are associated with lower levels of income, and higher levels of income are associated with lower levels of the interest rate. The IS curve therefore slopes downwards from left to right as in Figure 7.1.

This verbal derivation is in some ways the most important for an intuitive understanding of the IS curve, but it is also useful to derive the curve

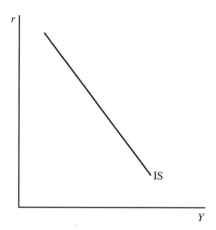

Figure 7.1

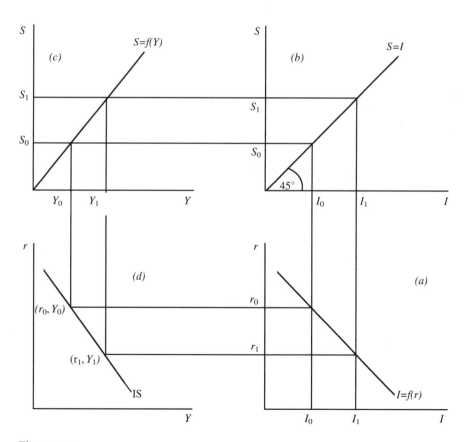

Figure 7.2

geometrically and algebraically. Figure 7.2 shows a method of deriving it geometrically. It is a 'four-quadrant' diagram constructed so that each pair of axes which are parallel and opposite to each other refers to the same variable: in quadrants (a) and (b) for example, the horizontal axis measures investment, while in quadrants (b) and (c) the vertical axis measures saving. This means that it is possible to draw connecting lines between the quadrants to join up in a single model all the parts of the diagram. (Notice that the scale of the horizontal axes for Y in quadrants (c) and (d) is much smaller than that for the S and I axes in quadrants (a), (b) and (c).)

Quadrant (a) shows the inverse relationship between investment and the interest rate. Quadrant (c) shows the positive relationship between saving and income. Quadrant (b) imposes the equilibrium condition that investment should be equal to saving: at all points along a 45° line from the origin the level of the variable measured along the horizontal axis is the same as the level of the variable measured along the vertical axis. And quadrant (d) shows the IS curve derived from these other relationships. The derivation is carried out as follows: starting in quadrant (a), choose some interest rate r_0; from quadrant (a) it can be seen that at r_0, investment is I_0; project this up to quadrant (b), which shows that when investment is I_0 the equilibrium condition will be satisfied only when saving is S_0; project this level of saving across to quadrant (c), which shows that saving is S_0 only when income is Y_0. Thus for the interest rate r_0 a level of income Y_0 has been derived such that investment equals saving. The income Y_0 and the interest rate r_0 can now be projected downwards from quadrant (c) and leftwards from quadrant (a) respectively to mark out the point (r_0, Y_0) in quadrant (d): this is a combination of income and interest rate at which $I = S$ and it is therefore a point on the IS curve. This whole exercise is then repeated for interest rate r_1 to find income Y_1 so that a second point (r_1, Y_1) can be plotted in quadrant (d). If the relationships in quadrants (a), (b) and (c) are linear (straight line) as they are in Figure 7.2, then the IS curve will also be a straight line so that it can be drawn simply by joining up the two points derived and projecting the line at each end. If, however, the relationship between investment and the interest rate, for example, is non-linear, say convex to the origin as in Figure 7.3, then the IS curve is also non-linear, in which case more points need to be plotted to derive the curve; in this case the IS curve will also be convex to the origin.

In principle, the effect on the IS curve of different values of the underlying parameters or of changes in the exogenous variations can be ascertained by a careful consideration of the verbal derivation of the curve or by using the four-quadrant model. However, it is often easier to be precise on these matters by using algebra; algebraically the IS curve is derived as follows:

$$S = -a + (1 - b)Y$$
$$I = j - ir$$
$$I = S$$
$$j - ir = -a + (1 - b)Y \qquad [7.3]$$

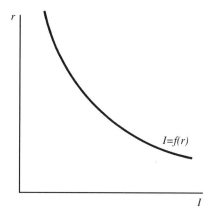

$I=f(r)$

Figure 7.3

Equation [7.3] can be rearranged to obtain r as a function of Y:

$$ir = j + a - (1 - b)Y$$

$$r = \frac{j+a}{i} - \frac{1-b}{i} \cdot Y \qquad [7.4]$$

or to obtain Y as a function of r:

$$(1-b)Y = j + a - ir$$

$$Y = \frac{j+a}{1-b} - \frac{i}{1-b} \cdot r \qquad [7.5]$$

Now from equations [7.4] and [7.5], which each express the relationship of the IS curve, it is possible to derive three values which define the IS curve in geometric terms and make it easy to analyse the effect of changes in exogenous variables and parameters. First, the intercept of the IS curve on the horizontal axis is equal to the value of income when the interest rate is zero: from equation [7.5] when $r = 0$,

$$Y = \frac{j+a}{1-b}$$

therefore $(j + a)/(1 - b)$ is the horizontal intercept. Similarly, the intercept on the vertical axis can be derived from equation [7.4]: when $Y = 0$

$$r = \frac{j+a}{i}$$

so that $(j + a)/i$ is the vertical intercept. Finally, the slope of the IS curve is the coefficient on Y, the variable measured on the horizontal axis, in equation [7.4] which expresses r, the variable measured on the vertical axis, as a function of Y: the slope is therefore $-(1 - b)/i$.

This completes the formal derivation of the IS curve for the simple model with no government sector and no foreign trade sector. However, many of the interesting results which can be derived from the IS–LM model involve government expenditure and/or taxes and foreign trade. How does the simple model need to be modified to accommodate these additional sectors? In terms of the verbal derivation, first, the equilibrium condition now becomes the equality of injections and withdrawals, where injections include government expenditure and exports as well as investment while withdrawals include taxes and savings as well as imports. The additional elements are assumed to be determined as in Chapter 4: exports X and government expenditure G exogenous, imports F and taxes T each partly exogenous and partly income-related. However, the basic principle of the analysis remains, that movements along an IS curve involve changes in the interest rate and income such as to maintain the equality of interest-related injections and income-related withdrawals.

In the geometric derivation the four-quadrant diagram of Figure 7.2 needs to be modified as follows: in quadrant (a) an $I + G + X$ line has to be constructed by adding $G + X$ horizontally to the I line; quadrant (b) now has $I + G + X$ on the horizontal axis and $S + T + F$ on the vertical axis; and quadrant (c) now shows total withdrawals $S + T + F$, as a function of income (the slope of the line will now be larger, reflecting the tax rate t and the marginal propensity to import f as well as the marginal propensity to save $(1 - b)$). In other respects the model and the way these three quadrants are used to derive the IS curve in quadrant (d) are unchanged.

The algebraic derivation of the IS curve in this more complex model is worth doing in full. Investment is as before, but consumption is now a function of disposable income $(Y - T)$, and the functions for government expenditure, taxes, exports and imports are as in Chapter 4:

$$C = a + bY_d$$
$$Y_d = Y - T$$
$$S = Y_d - C = -a + (1 - b)Y_d$$
$$I = j - ir$$
$$G = \overline{G}$$
$$T = \overline{T} + tY$$
$$X = \overline{X}$$
$$F = \overline{F} + fY$$

The equilibrium condition is now that total injections should equal total withdrawals; substituting from the above and rearranging,

$$I + G + X = S + T + F$$
$$j - ir + \overline{G} + \overline{X} = -a + (1 - b)(Y - \overline{T} - tY) + \overline{T} + tY + \overline{F} + fY$$
$$j - ir + \overline{G} + \overline{X} = -a - (1 - b)\overline{T} + \overline{T} + \overline{F} + (1 - b)(Y - tY) + tY + fY$$
$$j + \overline{G} + \overline{X} - ir = -a + b\overline{T} + \overline{F} + Y(1 - b - t + bt + t + f)$$
$$j + \overline{G} + \overline{X} - ir = b\overline{T} - a + \overline{F} + Y(1 - b + bt + f) \qquad [7.6]$$

From equation [7.6] it is possible to find r as a function of Y:

$$ir = j + \overline{G} + \overline{X} - b\overline{T} + a - \overline{F} - Y(1 - b + bt + f)$$

$$r = \frac{j + a + \overline{G} - b\overline{T} + \overline{X} - \overline{F}}{i} - \frac{1 - b + bt + f}{i} \cdot Y \qquad [7.7]$$

or Y as a function of r:

$$Y(1 - b + bt + f) = j + \overline{G} + \overline{X} - b\overline{T} + a - \overline{F} - ir$$

$$Y = \frac{j + a + \overline{G} - b\overline{T} + \overline{X} - \overline{F}}{1 - b + bt + f} - \frac{i}{1 - b + bt + f} \cdot r \qquad [7.8]$$

The intercept of the IS curve on the horizontal axis is the value of Y when $r = 0$, that is

$$\frac{j + a + \overline{G} - b\overline{T} + \overline{X} - \overline{F}}{1 - b + bt + f} \qquad [7.9]$$

The intercept on the vertical axis is the value of r when $Y = 0$, that is

$$\frac{j + a + \overline{G} - b\overline{T} + \overline{X} - \overline{F}}{i} \qquad [7.10]$$

The slope of the IS curve is the coefficient on Y in equation [7.7] (it is also equal to the vertical intercept [7.10] divided by the horizontal intercept [7.9]):

$$-\frac{1 - b + bt + f}{i} < 0 \qquad [7.11]$$

These three values [7.9], [7.10] and [7.11] are more than enough (strictly only two are necessary) to define the IS curve on a diagram. They can now be used to identify the impact on the IS curve of changes in the exogenous variables or of different values for the parameters. The effects of such changes and differences can also be worked out through a careful verbal analysis or through the appropriate modification of the four-quadrant model, and students should make sure for themselves that they can understand the effects in those terms. Here, however, the analysis will be carried out in terms of the algebra, which makes possible greater precision, although the emphasis is on the direction rather than the size of the various effects.

Consider first an increase in j, the autonomous element of investment, reflecting an increase in firms' optimism about future sales. From [7.9] it can be seen that the horizontal intercept of the IS curve increases, since j is a positive element in [7.9]. From [7.10] it can be seen that the vertical intercept also increases. And from [7.11] it can be seen that the slope is unchanged since j does not enter into the value of the slope. Therefore an increase in j causes the IS curve to shift outwards to the right, but remaining parallel to the original IS curve, as in Figure 7.4.

Now consider in turn the effects of an increase in a, autonomous consumption; an increase in $\overline{G}$, exogenous government expenditure; and an increase in $\overline{X}$, exogenous exports: in all of these cases, just as in the case of the

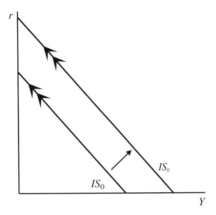

Figure 7.4

increase in j, the horizontal and vertical intercepts are increased and the slope is unchanged, so the IS curve must shift outwards to the right as in Figure 7.4.

Next consider the effect of increases in $\overline{T}$, autonomous taxes, and $\overline{F}$, autonomous imports: both of these enter into the horizontal and vertical intercepts as negative terms, so when they are increased the intercepts are reduced; neither enters into the slope so the slope is unchanged. Therefore increases in autonomous taxes or in autonomous imports shift the IS curve inwards to the left.

The intuitive explanation of the results of the last three paragraphs is that these changes alter the amount of injections or withdrawals at any level of the interest rate and hence alter the level of income associated with each level of the interest rate in equilibrium. Indeed, the horizontal shifts of the IS curve correspond exactly to the changes in income predicted in the Keynesian cross model. Variations in the parameters t, b and f, on the other hand, affect the way in which withdrawals vary with income and hence the slope of the IS curve. Take first t, the tax rate: this does not enter into the vertical intercept [7.10] which is therefore unaffected by t, but it enters positively into the denominator of the horizontal intercept [7.9], which must therefore be reduced when t is increased; and since t enters positively into the numerator of the slope [7.11] the absolute value of the slope is increased when t is increased. The effect of an increase in t is therefore to pivot the IS curve around the vertical intercept to become steeper, as in Figure 7.5.

In the case of b, the marginal propensity to consume, the question of interest is not so much 'what happens if b increases?' as 'how would the IS curve be different if b were larger?', since b is not a policy instrument like t. The analysis of the intercepts is more complicated here because b enters into both the numerator and the denominator of the horizontal intercept [7.9]. However, for present purposes an analysis of the slope is sufficient: b enters negatively into the numerator of the slope (which can be rearranged as $1 - b(1 - t) + f$ where $0 < t < 1$), so that the larger is b, the smaller is the slope (in absolute terms) and the flatter is the IS curve. On the other hand, the effect of an increase in f,

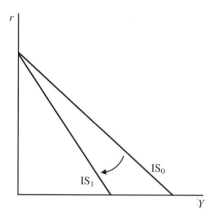

Figure 7.5

the marginal propensity to import, is essentially the same as that of an increase in t because it enters the intercepts and slope in the same way as t.

Finally, consider the effect of different values of the parameter i which relates investment to the interest rate. The investment equation used here, $I = j - ir$, can be represented diagrammatically as in Figure 7.6 where j is the intercept on the horizontal axis and the slope of the line is $1/i$. The question of interest here is 'how would the IS be different if i were larger or smaller?', that is how would the IS differ if the investment function of Figure 7.6 was either very flat (I_1) or very steep (I_2) as in Figure 7.7, reflecting either a high or low interest-elasticity of investment (note that i is not the same as the interest-elasticity but it is closely related to it: the elasticity is $(\Delta I/\Delta r) \cdot (r/I) = i \cdot (r/I)$). The analysis of the intercepts of the IS is complicated here because different interest-elasticities of investment as in Figure 7.7 involve different values of j as well as of i. However, an analysis of the slope of IS alone is sufficient for present purposes: i

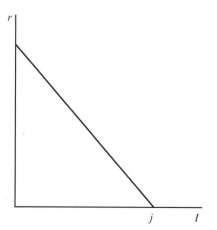

Figure 7.6

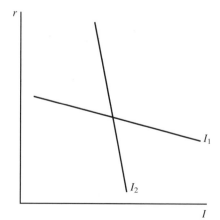

Figure 7.7

Table 7.1

Increase in	Effect on horizontal intercept	Effect on vertical intercept	Effect on slope	Movement of IS curve
$j, a, \overline{G}$ or $\overline{X}$	+	+	0	shifts to right
$\overline{T}$ or $\overline{F}$	–	–	0	shifts to left
t or f	–	0	+	pivots on vertical intercept, becomes steeper
b	(?)	(–)	–	becomes flatter
i^*	(+)	(?)	–	becomes flatter

Note * including implied increase in j.

is the denominator of the slope so that when i is larger (as with I_1 in Figure 7.7) the (absolute) slope of the IS curve is smaller (IS_1 in Figure 7.8), and when i is smaller (I_2 in Figure 7.7) the (absolute) slope of the IS is larger (IS_2 in Figure 7.8). In intuitive terms, the more sensitive investment is to the interest rate, the larger is the variation in investment associated with a given variation in the interest rate, and hence the larger the variation in the equilibrium level of income.

The results of the last six paragraphs are tabulated in Table 7.1, which shows whether the intercepts or slope increase (+), decrease (–) or stay the same (0) in response to an increase in each exogenous variable or parameter, and hence how the IS curve moves. The spaces for the effect on the intercepts of increases in b and i are filled in for the sake of completeness but they do not need to be remembered. The table will be referred to below when the IS and LM curves are put together.

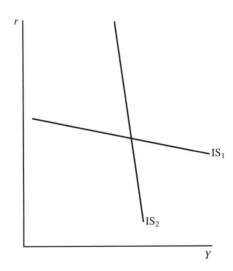

Figure 7.8

The money market: LM

The LM curve is the locus of all the combinations of interest rate and real income at which the money market is in equilibrium, that is demand for money equals supply of money. It is assumed that the supply of money is fixed exogenously by the government, i.e. $M_s = \overline{M}$, and that the demand for (real) money varies positively with real (measured) income and negatively with the interest rate, as in the 'moderate' Keynesian–monetarist demand for money function [5.9], $M_d/P = d + mY - lr$.

Consider first some position of equilibrium where demand for money equals supply. How can equilibrium be maintained if income is increased? An increase in income raises the demand for money, but the money supply is fixed and equilibrium requires demand to equal supply: the only way equilibrium can be maintained is if the interest rate is also increased, so that the increase in the demand for money caused by the increase in income is exactly offset by a decrease in the demand for money caused by the increase in the interest rate. Thus along the LM curve increases in income are associated with increases in the interest rate. In diagrammatic terms the LM curve slopes upwards from left to right as in Figure 7.9.

In geometric terms the LM curve can be derived through a four-quadrant model comparable to that of Figure 7.2 for the IS curve, provided the demand-for-money function can be split into income-related and interest-related components (which fits easily with the Keynesian analysis of transactions *plus* precautionary and speculative demands for money, but less easily with the modern quantity theory). Such a model is given in Figure 7.10. As with Figure 7.2, axes which are parallel and opposite to each other have the same variable measured on them so that it is possible to join the four quadrants in a single model. Quadrant (a) represents the speculative demand for (real) money varying with the interest rate in the simplified linear form of equation [5.8]. Quadrant (c) shows the transactions and precautionary demand for (real) money varying with income. Quadrant (b) imposes the equilibrium condition that demand for real money equals supply of money: it is constructed as an isosceles triangle with 45° angles, such that for all points on the curve the sum of the horizontal and vertical coordinates is the same, equal here to the (exogenously fixed) real money supply (note that the price level as well as the nominal money supply is taken as exogenously fixed here). Thus the line in quadrant (b) shows for a given speculative demand for money what the transactions and precautionary demand needs to be for overall money demand to equal supply. Quadrant (d) shows the LM curve derived from the relationships of the other three quadrants, as follows: choose an interest rate r_0, use it in quadrant (a) to find the speculative demand for money; project this up to quadrant (b) to find the transactions and precautionary demand for money consistent with money market equilibrium; project this across to quadrant (c) to find the level of income Y_0 at which the transactions and precautionary demand for money is at the required level; project

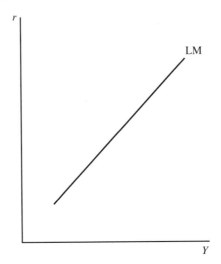

Figure 7.9

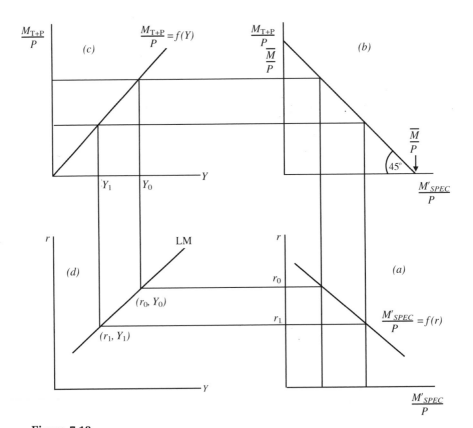

Figure 7.10

income Y_0 downwards from quadrant (c) and interest rate r_0 leftwards from quadrant (a) to mark out the point (r_0, Y_0) in quadrant (d); repeat the exercise for another level of the interest rate r_1; finally, draw a line through the points (r_0, Y_0) and (r_1, Y_1): this is the LM curve.

An alternative derivation, which is less neat but does not require the separation between income-related and interest-related components of the demand for money, starts from the diagram in Figure 7.11. Real money balances are measured along the horizontal axis, and the interest rate on the vertical axis. The money supply line is vertical at the exogenously fixed level (it is invariant with respect to the interest rate). Alternative demand-for-money curves are drawn for different levels of income: they slope downwards from left to right because demand for money is inversely related to the interest rate, and the curve for income level Y_1 is above that for the lower level of income Y_0 because the demand is positively related to income. The LM curve itself is derived by plotting the equilibrium points (r_0, Y_0) and (r_1, Y_1) on a separate graph with income on the horizontal axis.

The algebraic derivation of the LM curve involves the 'moderate' demand-for-money function, the assumption that the money supply is exogenously fixed and the equilibrium condition that the demand for money is equal to the supply:

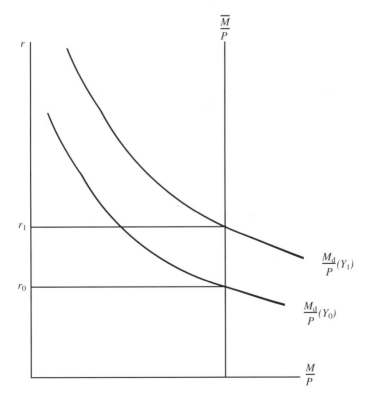

Figure 7.11

$$\frac{M_d}{P} = d + mY - lr$$

$$M_s = \overline{M}$$

$$M_s = M_d$$

Substituting and rearranging

$$\frac{\overline{M}}{P} = d + mY - lr \qquad\qquad [7.12]$$

Equation [7.12] can be used to obtain r as a function of Y:

$$lr = d - \frac{\overline{M}}{P} + mY$$

$$r = \frac{Pd - \overline{M}}{Pl} + \frac{m}{l} \cdot Y \qquad\qquad [7.13]$$

or Y as a function of r:

$$mY = \frac{\overline{M}}{P} - d + lr$$

$$Y = \frac{\overline{M} - Pd}{Pm} + \frac{l}{m} \cdot r \qquad\qquad [7.14]$$

The intercept of the LM curve on the horizontal axis is the value of Y when $r = 0$, that is

$$\frac{\overline{M} - Pd}{Pm} \qquad\qquad [7.15]$$

The intercept on the vertical axis is the value of r when $Y = 0$, that is

$$\frac{Pd - \overline{M}}{Pl} \qquad\qquad [7.16]$$

Comparison of [7.16] and [7.15] shows that if one is negative, the other is positive: the alternatives are illustrated in Figure 7.12. The slope of the LM curve is the coefficient of Y in equation [7.13], that is

$$\frac{m}{l} > 0 \qquad\qquad [7.17]$$

The last three values [7.15], [7.16] and [7.17] can now be used to identify the effects on the LM curve of movements in the exogenous variables and the underlying parameters. Consider first the effect of an increase in $\overline{M}$, the exogenous money supply: this enters positively into the horizontal intercept, negatively into the vertical intercept, and not at all into the slope. The effect of an increase in $\overline{M}$ is therefore to shift the LM curve to the right, parallel to itself, as in the movement from LM_1 to LM_2 in Figure 7.12. Now consider the case of an increase in P, the price level: this enters into the numerators of [7.15] and [7.16] with the opposite sign to $\overline{M}$, and does not feature in [7.17]. Thus an increase in P must shift the LM curve to the left, as in the movement from LM_2 to LM_1 in Figure 7.12. Next consider the constant term d: this can be thought of as the constant in the Keynesian speculative demand for money function,

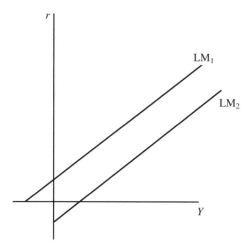

Figure 7.12

and Keynesian theory predicts that d will fluctuate. d enters into [7.15–7.17] in the same way as P; therefore an increase in d (increase in the speculative demand) shifts the LM to the left. The intuitive explanation of these results is that an increase in the supply of money enables equilibrium in the money market to occur at a higher income and/or a lower interest rate; while anything that increases the demand for money (increases in P or d) requires equilibrium to occur at a lower income and/or a higher interest rate.

The significance of the parameters m and l, which measure the sensitivity of the demand for money to income and the interest rate respectively, lies as with parameters b and i in the IS curve, not in the effect of a change but in the contrast between the LM curves implied by different values. It can best be analysed by concentrating on the slope [7.17] which is the ratio of the two. Since m is the numerator of the slope, the larger m is, the larger (steeper) is the slope. However, economists' ideas of the size of m do not vary widely, and it is l which is the key determinant of the slope of the LM curve. Since l is the denominator, the larger l is (the larger the interest-elasticity of the demand for money), the smaller (flatter) is the slope. If l is very small m/l is very large and the LM curve is very steep, as with LM_1 in Figure 7.13. But if l is very large m/l is very small and the LM curve is very flat, as with LM_2 in Figure 7.13.

The results of the last two paragraphs are tabulated in Table 7.2. The effects of variations in m and l (including in the latter case the associated increase in d) on the intercepts are given for completeness, but are not important.

Overall equilibrium

It is now possible to put the IS and LM curves together in order to find the equilibrium values of income and the interest rate, which are jointly endogenous in this model, and to analyse how the overall equilibrium

Table 7.2

Increase in	Effect on horizontal intercept	Effect on vertical intercept	Effect on slope	Movement of IS curve
M	+	−	0	shifts to right
P or d	−	+	0	shifts to left
m	(−)	(0)	+	becomes steeper
l^*	(−)	(?)	−	becomes flatter

Note* including implied increase in d.

changes in response to changes in the exogenous variables. For the moment it will be assumed that the IS curve slopes downwards and the LM curve slopes upwards, with both slopes near the middle of the possible range, as in Figure 7.14. The IS curve shows all the combinations of income and the interest rate at which the market for goods and services is in equilibrium, while the LM curve shows all the combinations at which the money market is in equilibrium. The point (r_e, Y_e) where they intersect is the only point on the diagram where both the goods and services market and the money market are in equilibrium; it is also assumed that this overall equilibrium is stable, in the sense that the economy tends automatically to move towards it. The algebraic equivalent of finding this point by the intersection of the curves is solving the equations [7.7] and [7.13] simultaneously for Y and r. If this is done the solutions can be analysed to find the effects of changes in exogenous variables. However, such an exercise is greatly facilitated by the use of calculus, and since knowledge of calculus is not assumed in this part of the book the present exposition of the effects of these changes is primarily a diagrammatic one.

How does this overall equilibrium change in response to changes in the exogenous variables? Since the effects of such changes on the individual curves have already been established and are summarised in Tables 7.1 and 7.2, the

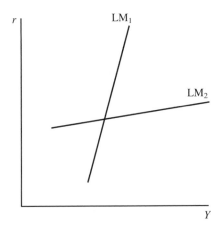

Figure 7.13

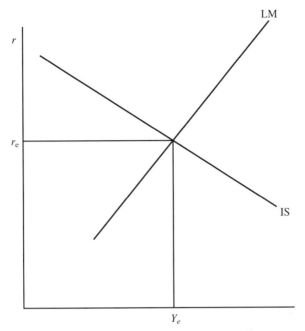

Figure 7.14

effects on the overall equilibrium can be discussed immediately on the basis of those results. Take first an increase in autonomous investment, autonomous consumption, or exports: the effect of each of these (from Table 7.1) is to shift the IS curve to the right from IS_0 to IS_1 in Figure 7.15, and this results in a new overall equilibrium with a higher level Y_1 and a higher interest rate r_1. Next consider an increase in autonomous imports: this shifts the IS curve to the left, for example, from IS_1 to IS_0 in Figure 7.15, and therefore has the opposite effect on the overall equilibrium, reducing both the interest rate and income. Now consider the effect of an increase in the price level: from Table 7.2 this shifts the LM curve to the left, from LM_0 to LM_1 in Figure 7.16, which raises the interest rate and reduces income. An increase in the autonomous element of the speculative demand for money d has the same effect.

The exogenous variables discussed in the last paragraph are all outside at least the *direct* control of the government. But what of the policy instruments which the government can manipulate? Within the present model there are essentially three: government expenditure and taxation (fiscal policy) and the money supply (monetary policy). From Table 7.1 increases in government expenditure shift the IS curve to the right as in Figure 7.15, raising both income and the interest rate, while increases in (autonomous) taxes have the opposite effect. An increase in the tax rate t causes the IS curve to pivot inwards around the vertical intercept, and therefore also causes income and the interest rate to fall. And from Table 7.2 an increase in the money supply shifts the LM curve to the right, for example, from LM_1 to LM_0 in Figure 7.16, reducing the interest rate and increasing income.

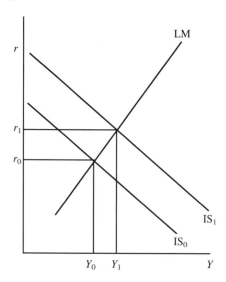

Figure 7.15

These changes have been discussed in terms of the conventional slopes of the IS and LM curves. However, macroeconomists have at times – particularly in the 1960s – differed sharply about these slopes, and these differences turn out to have important policy implications. They can be analysed most conveniently in the simplified form of what will be called 'extreme Keynesian' and 'extreme monetarist' assumptions about the underlying parameters.

The extreme Keynesian position assumes first that investment is completely insensitive to the interest rate (for example, because it is dominated by animal

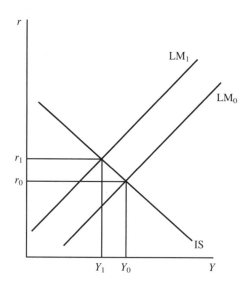

Figure 7.16

spirits): the parameter i and the interest-elasticity of investment are zero. It was established above (Table 7.1) that the smaller i is, the steeper is the IS curve; when i is zero the slope of the IS curve is infinity (from [7.11]), so the IS curve is vertical. Secondly, the extreme Keynesian position assumes the special case of the liquidity trap in the speculative demand for money, in which the demand for money is perfectly interest-elastic and the parameter l is equal to infinity. It was established above (Table 7.2) that the larger l is, the flatter is the LM curve; when l is infinite the slope of the LM curve (from [7.17]) is zero, so the LM curve is horizontal.

Thus the extreme Keynesian version of the IS–LM model is that depicted in Figure 7.17. What effect do changes in the exogenous variables have here? It is important to note that such changes shift the IS and LM curves to the right or left, *not* upwards or downwards. For the IS curve the vertical intercept [7.10] is infinite because $i = 0$, so that changes in exogenous expenditure do not affect it, but the horizontal intercept [7.9] is finite and is affected. For the LM curve the vertical intercept is that (fixed) level of the interest rate at which the liquidity trap occurs; in algebraic terms the value of [7.16] is dominated by d and l, both of which are infinite, so that changes in $\overline{M}$ and P do not affect it, while the horizontal intercept [7.15] is *minus* infinity and is also unaffected by such changes. Now anything which shifts the IS curve to the left or right has a large effect on income but no effect on the interest rate: thus fluctuations in (autonomous) investment or exports produce significant fluctuations in income, but at the same time fiscal policy also has a powerful effect on income. On the other hand, anything which shifts the LM curve to the left or right has no effect at all, because when the (horizontal) LM is shifted to the left or right it still intersects the IS curve at the same point: that means that instability of the demand for money (fluctuations in d) and changes in prices have no effect on income or the interest rate, and similarly monetary policy has no power to influence these variables.

In the extreme Keynesian version of the IS–LM model then, 'expenditure shocks', that is fluctuations in exogenous expenditure, produce instability of income; but 'monetary shocks', that is fluctuations in autonomous money demand or prices, cause no such instability; and fiscal policy is powerful while monetary policy is impotent.

The extreme monetarist version of the IS–LM model involves two contrasting assumptions. Firstly, investment is held to be extremely sensitive to the interest rate: i is infinite. This means that the slope of the IS curve [7.11] is zero so that the IS curve is horizontal. Secondly, the demand for money is taken to be completely insensitive to the interest rate: l is zero, the slope of the LM curve [7.17] is infinity and the curve is vertical, as in Figure 7.18. Again changes in the exogenous variables shift the curves to the left or right, rather than upwards or downwards, with the vertical intercept of the IS curve [7.10] dominated by j and i, both of which are infinite, and the vertical intercept of the LM curve [7.16] equal to infinity because $l = 0$. In this case anything which shifts the IS curve to the left or right has no effect on income or the interest rate: expenditure shocks have no effect and fiscal policy is impotent. On the

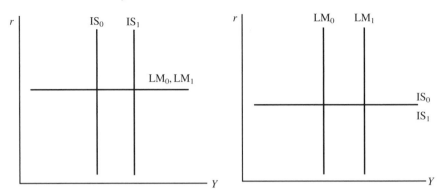

Figure 7.17   Figure 7.18

other hand, anything which shifts the LM curve to the left or right has a large effect on income and no effect on the interest rate: monetary shocks produce instability of income, and monetary policy is powerful.

Crowding out and the transmission mechanism

The last section made use of the findings of previous sections to look at the end results of changes in various exogenous variables under different assumptions about the underlying parameters, but it said nothing of the mechanisms by which these end results are produced and provided little intuitive explanation of the processes involved. It is time to remedy this defect, and to focus on two of the mechanisms underlying the IS–LM model which have featured prominently in macroeconomic debates.

The first of these mechanisms is 'crowding out'. Crowding out takes place when an increase in government expenditure leads to a smaller increase than might otherwise have occurred in overall income and output, not because of any scarcity of resources but because it induces some offsetting reduction in private-sector expenditure; the private-sector expenditure which is now no longer undertaken is said to have been 'crowded out' by the government expenditure. Consider the case depicted in Figure 7.19. From an initial equilibrium of (r_0, Y_0) an increase in government expenditure shifts the IS curve to the right from IS_0 to IS_1; if the interest rate remained unchanged at r_0 then income would increase to Y_2, but on the IS and LM curves given here the interest rate rises to r_1 and income increases only to Y_1, because there is a fall in private-sector investment as a result of the interest rate rise which partly offsets the original rise in government expenditure: this is what is called partial crowding out. Now the degree of crowding out, which can vary in the IS–LM model from 0% to 100%, depends on the slopes of both curves. If the LM curve was horizontal the interest rate would not rise so investment would not be reduced; and if the IS curve was vertical then even if the interest rate rose,

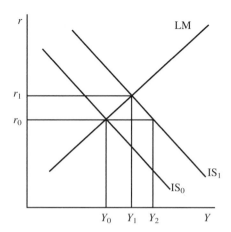

Figure 7.19

investment would not be affected by it. Thus in the extreme Keynesian case of
Figure 7.17 there is no crowding out because both of these conditions are
fulfilled (only one is necessary). On the other hand, if the LM curve was vertical
interest rates would rise sharply in response to any shift in a (non-horizontal)
IS curve; while if the IS curve was horizontal, investment would be extremely
interest-elastic so that an infinitesimal rise in interest rates would produce a
large reduction in investment. Thus in the extreme monetarist case of Figure
7.18 where both of these conditions are fulfilled (again only one is necessary)
there is complete (100%) crowding out: the increase in government expenditure
is exactly offset by a reduction in private investment.

The second of the mechanisms involved in the IS–LM model which needs
comment here is the transmission mechanism, that is the mechanism by which
increases in the money supply are transmitted into increases in income. Within
the IS–LM model as constructed here, there is only one transmission
mechanism (others are considered in later chapters): that by which increases
in the money supply lead to reductions in the interest rate, which lead to
increases in investment and hence (via the multiplier) in income. In Figure 7.20,
for example, an increase in the money supply shifts the LM curve to the right
from LM_0 to LM_1; this reduces the interest rate, which stimulates investment
and hence income rises from Y_0 to Y_1. This particular transmission mechanism
depends on the slopes of the IS and LM curves. In the extreme Keynesian case
of Figure 7.17 where the LM is horizontal and the IS is vertical, there is no
transmission mechanism and increases in the money supply do not lead to
increases in income. In the extreme monetarist case of Figure 7.18 where the
LM is vertical and the IS horizontal, on the other hand, there is a very
powerful transmission mechanism. The conditions required for at least some
transmission from money supply to income are of course the same as those
required for non-zero crowding out: that the LM curve is non-horizontal,
which requires the interest-elasticity of the demand for money to be finite; and
that the IS curve is non-vertical which requires the interest-elasticity of
investment to be non-zero.

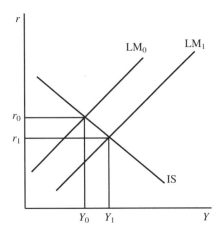

Figure 7.20

Finally, it should be noted that the extreme Keynesian case can be regarded as a representation within the IS–LM model of the simple Keynesian cross model: the latter has no monetary sector and no influence from the interest rate to investment, while in the extreme Keynesian case of the IS–LM model there is a monetary sector but it plays no part at all in the determination of income and there is no influence from the interest rate to investment. It is therefore possible to compare results obtained in, say, the moderate IS–LM and Keynesian cross models by representing the latter as the extreme Keynesian case. It should also be noted that the horizontal LM curve of the extreme Keynesian case could be the result not of a liquidity trap in the demand for money, but of an endogeneity of the supply of money: if the government decides to fix the interest rate rather than the money supply at some particular level, it can do so by supplying whatever quantity of money is demanded at that level of the interest rate. The effect is that the LM curve becomes horizontal at the chosen interest rate, but its slope is the product here of a policy decision by the government rather than of a particular state of the private sector's demand for money.

Qualifications

A number of results have been established in this chapter regarding the effects on overall equilibrium of changes in variables which are exogenous to the IS–LM model, under different assumptions about the underlying parameters. These results were presented in the section on overall equilibrium on the basis of the findings of the earlier sections, and the mechanisms underlying the results were discussed in the last section. There is no need to restate these results here, but several qualifications need to be made.

First, the extreme versions of the IS–LM model deployed here are essentially caricatures of the positions held by Keynesians and monetarists in the 1960s and early 1970s: neither group (with the possible exception of some traditional

Keynesians at Cambridge, England) really thought that the curves were horizontal or vertical, though monetarists thought the LM was steeper and the IS flatter than Keynesians. The caricatures have been used here because they enable certain contrasts to be pointed up more clearly, but it should not be forgotten that they are exaggerations of the views actually held at that time (and are even less close to current views).

There was a stage in the debate when each side claimed the middle ground – a moderate version of the model – for itself but attributed an extreme position to its opponents. Once it was realised that neither side was genuinely at either extreme, the argument became less clear-cut and interest began to move away from arguments about the true empirical values of the underlying parameters towards other theoretical developments of the IS–LM model. One such development involved the incorporation into the model of the hypotheses that consumption and the demand for money depend on permanent income, together with the adaptive expectations hypothesis of permanent income of equation [2.9]. This development led to some interesting results on the relative effectiveness of monetary and fiscal policy and an increased awareness among macroeconomists of the importance of the time lags involved in the process by which the economy adjusts to exogenous changes. More recently, the adoption of rational expectations has reduced the emphasis on time lags but made the issue altogether more complicated. A second and more important development was the incorporation into the model of a government budget constraint (of the kind embodied in column (a) of Table 6.1) linking the budget deficit to government borrowing of a non-monetary kind (the sale of bonds to the private sector) and of a monetary kind (borrowing from the banking system which *ceteris paribus* leads to increases in bank deposits and the money supply). Within the IS–LM framework the government budget constraint introduces certain forms of interdependence between the IS and LM curves, and it requires a more sophisticated distinction between time periods. This literature is discussed in detail in Chapter 14. The results of both these developments have cast some doubt on some of the more traditional IS–LM results, but their main effect has been, not to weaken or strengthen the positions of either Keynesians or monetarists, but to move the whole debate on to other areas and questions.

It should also be noted that the IS–LM model *implicitly* contains a bond market: in the money market which is modelled explicitly, agents are regarded as choosing to hold their wealth in the form of money or bonds, so that for a given stock of wealth a particular demand for money implies also a particular demand for bonds. Thus (although this point is not developed in this book) for any shift in the equilibrium position in the IS–LM model there is some adjustment in the bond market as well as in the money and goods markets.

Finally, the most important shortcoming of the IS–LM model as used here should be emphasised: it assumes a constant price level and a horizontal aggregate supply curve. Much of the rest of this book, and particularly the next three chapters, are taken up with attempts to remedy this defect and to get to grips with the question of inflation.

Exercises

(i)   Show that monetary and expenditure shocks have the same effects on income but not always on the interest rate in a model where only one of the two extreme Keynesian assumptions on the interest-elasticities of investment and the demand for money holds, as where both extreme assumptions hold.

(ii)   Show that monetary and fiscal policies have the same effects on income but not always on the interest rate in a model where only one of the two extreme monetarist assumptions on the interest-elasticities of investment and the demand for money holds, as where both extreme assumptions hold.

(iii)   By comparing expression [7.9] for the horizontal intercept of the IS curve and expression [4.11] for the basic multiplier in the Keynesian cross model, show that horizontal shifts of the IS curve correspond to the multiplier effects of the Keynesian cross model.

(iv)   Use expression [7.15] for the horizontal intercept of the LM curve to show that horizontal shifts of the LM curve correspond to the 'money multiplier' of a crude quantity theory of money in which velocity is constant and prices are fixed but real income varies proportionately with the money supply (that is $M = \bar{k}\bar{P}Y$).

(v)   Explain why the balanced budget multiplier is less than one in a closed economy if the IS is non-vertical and the LM non-horizontal.

(vi)   Find the effect on the government's budget deficit (that is, $G - T$) of a cut in government expenditure in the moderate and the two extreme cases considered in this chapter.

(vii)   Analyse how the interest-sensitivity of the demand for money affects the stability of the economy in the face of: (a) expenditure shocks; and (b) monetary shocks.

(viii)   Analyse the effect on the potency of monetary policy of an increase in the marginal tax rate t.

(ix)   Solve equations [7.4] and [7.13] to find the equilibrium levels of income and interest rate in a simple IS–LM model without government or foreign trade sectors. Consider how the solution for income fits with the analysis of the effect of changes elsewhere in the chapter.

(x)   Repeat exercise (ix) for the fuller IS–LM model using equations [7.7] and [7.13].

Further reading

No further reading is recommended, since the above exercises are both extensive and essential.

Chapter 8

The labour market, Keynes and unemployment

The last six chapters have all been focused primarily on the macroeconomic debates of the 1960s through to the 1970s between Keynesians and monetarists. At this point it is useful to go back to a somewhat earlier debate, that between Keynesian and classical, or rather neoclassical, economists, which was provoked by Keynes's *General Theory*. This involves an explicit consideration of the labour market in addition to the markets for goods and services and for money (and implicitly for bonds) which have been considered so far. It will also be helpful to the discussion of inflation in the next two chapters, since some of the work to be examined there has consciously tried to return to the themes of classical or pre-Keynesian economics.

One of the major claims of the *General Theory* was that equilibrium can occur with employment below the full employment level; classical economics on the other hand regarded the labour market as self-adjusting so that such an equilibrium cannot occur, as is explained in the next section. That provides a basis for discussion of the neoclassical argument that Keynes's unemployment equilibrium depended on the downward rigidity of money wages, and for the explanation of the Keynesian–neoclassical synthesis in which this debate culminated. Finally, some different strands in Keynesian thinking which provide a rationale for the implicit use of a horizontal aggregate supply curve in the Keynesian cross and IS–LM models are considered.

The classical labour market

Classical economics thought in terms of a labour market which is competitive and atomistic, that is where individual workers and employers behave separately as individuals rather than combining in trade unions or employers' associations. The supply of labour is assumed to be positively related to the real wage, which implies that the substitution effect of an increase in the wage (which induces more workers to work and/or induces existing workers to work more hours) outweighs the income effect (which induces workers to choose more leisure and less work). The demand for labour is assumed to depend inversely on the real wage. It can be derived by summing the demands of each firm based on the assumption of profit maximisation which implies that labour is employed up to the point where the marginal input cost, the money wage, is equal to the marginal revenue product, that is the marginal physical product of labour times the marginal revenue from the firm's output. Or it can be derived at the aggregate level from the aggregate production function which relates the total output of goods and services to total labour employed shown in Figure 8.1. This is drawn for a fixed capital stock and given technology (because it is the short-run relationship which is relevant here) and its shape shows the diminishing returns to labour when these other factors are fixed: with competitive labour and goods markets and profit maximisation, the demand for labour depends on its (real) marginal physical product which is the (diminishing) slope of the production function. The downward-sloping demand is graphed in Figure 8.2, together with the upward-sloping supply curve.

The important point to note here is that in the classical model there is no involuntary unemployment. In an atomistic and competitive labour market the real wage adjusts to equilibrate supply and demand: at $(W/P)_e$ in Figure 8.2 the supply of labour is equal to the demand at L_e, and while there are people who would be interested in a job (or would work extra hours) at a higher real wage, all those who wish to work at the real wage of $(W/P)_e$ can find work for the hours they require.

The proposition can also be depicted in an aggregate demand/aggregate supply (AD/AS) diagram, which represents the overall equilibrium for the goods and services and money (and bonds) markets as well as the labour market. In Figure 8.3, AD and AS are plotted on the horizontal axis (in terms of Y, expenditure or income or output) against the price level on the vertical axis. The AD curve slopes downward from left to right, showing that demand

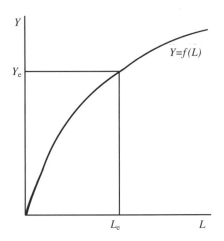

Figure 8.1

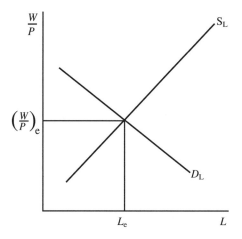

Figure 8.2

is higher when prices are lower (with everything else being held equal); it can be thought of as derived from the classical quantity theory of money, but with the money supply held constant and transactions or income allowed to vary: higher price levels are compatible only with lower levels of transactions or income. In terms of equation [5.4],

$$\overline{M} = \bar{k}PY$$

$$Y = \frac{\overline{M}}{\bar{k}} \cdot \frac{1}{P}$$

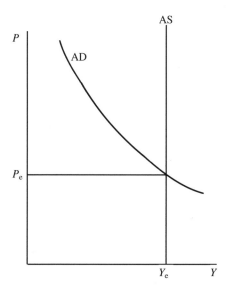

Figure 8.3

Therefore Y varies inversely with P. (Strictly speaking, the AD curve derived on this basis must be a rectangular hyperbola, but this has no particular significance in this case.)

The AS curve is derived from the labour market and the production function of Figure 8.1 and 8.2. The labour market is in equilibrium with employment of L_e and real wage $(W/P)_e$; from Figure 8.1 when employment is L_e, output is Y_e. The flexibility and self-adjusting properties of the classical labour market ensure that whatever the price level, the real wage is always $(W/P)_e$, because money wages adjust appropriately. Thus whatever the price level, employment is L_e and output is Y_e, and the AS curve is vertical. Figure 8.3 depicts overall equilibrium in the classical model, with full employment and a price level determined by the money supply (changes in the latter shift the AD curve and produce equiproportional changes in prices).

The Keynesian–neoclassical debate

The neoclassical critique of Keynes can be thought of as starting from the classical model and arguing that involuntary unemployment could occur in the Keynesian model only because of rigidities in the labour market which prevented the money wage adjusting to maintain the real wage at its equilibrium level. Moreover, if such rigidities existed then the existence of involuntary unemployment could be explained in terms of the classical model of the labour market, without recourse to the ideas of deficient effective demand, the multiplier, liquidity preference, and so on, whose exposition made up the bulk of the *General Theory*. Thus this neoclassical critique implied that

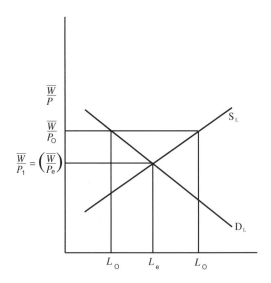

Figure 8.4

Keynes's contribution to economics lay not in any fundamental new insight in economic theory but merely in his recognition of the existence of money-wage rigidity.

In Figure 8.4, for example, if the money wage within this otherwise classical model is fixed at $\overline{W}$, then if prices are P_0 and the real wage is $\overline{W}/P_0$ the supply of labour at L_0 exceeds the demand for it which is L_0'. If the money wage fell in response to this involuntary unemployment so that the real wage fell to $(W/P)_e$, the unemployment would be eliminated. But with the money wage fixed at $\overline{W}$, full employment, that is the position of no involuntary unemployment, occurs only if the price level happens to be P_1.

Keynesian economists were indeed inclined to regard the money wage as inflexible at least in the short run, but they rejected the neoclassical implication that Keynes had contributed little to economic theory. Their reply and the subsequent debate were couched in terms of the IS–LM model, which Keynes himself had not formally developed but whose formulation by John Hicks (1937) Keynes apparently regarded as an acceptable expression of his ideas (see Hicks, 1973). Keynes had considered the question of whether there were any automatic mechanisms by which unemployment would be eliminated. The only such mechanism which he seems to have identified is the following: if wages fall in response to the unemployment, labour costs fall and therefore prices fall; this increases the real money supply (M_s/P) and reduces the interest rate; and the lower interest rate leads to higher investment and hence higher income. In symbols,

$$U \rightarrow W \downarrow \rightarrow P \downarrow \rightarrow M_s/P \uparrow \rightarrow r \downarrow \rightarrow I \uparrow \rightarrow Y \uparrow$$

This can be depicted in the IS–LM model (see Table 7.2) as a shift of the LM curve to the right due to the fall in prices, as in Figure 8.5, with the interest rate falling from r_0 to r_1 and income rising from Y_0 to Y_1. In principle such a mechanism continues to operate until income has reached the full employment

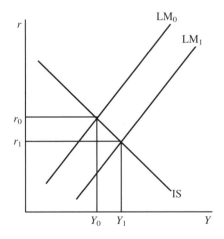

Figure 8.5

level, because at any lower level, money wages and prices fall and the LM curve shifts to the right.

This mechanism has come to be known as the 'Keynes effect', but Keynes himself does not seem to have thought it very important, partly at least because he thought money wages would respond to unemployment only slowly and with considerable social and industrial disruption. Indeed, he suggested that if this was the only automatic mechanism working for the restoration of full employment it would be sensible for governments to intervene themselves by increasing the nominal money supply so that the increase in the real money supply (M_s/P) could be achieved more quickly.

However, there are three cases where the Keynes effect does not restore full employment and these were cited by Keynesian economists in order to refute the neoclassical argument that an unemployment equilibrium can occur only if money wages are rigid. In Figure 8.6 the IS curve is vertical (investment is insensitive to the interest rate) and the reduction in the interest rate caused by the rightwards shift of the LM curve does not result in higher investment or higher income. In Figure 8.7 the LM curve is horizontal (the demand for money is infinitely sensitive to the interest rate) and the interest rate is not reduced by the rightwards shift of the LM curve, so that even if investment is interest-elastic there is no increase in investment or income. And in Figure 8.8 the IS and LM curves have their conventional slopes but the full employment level of income is to the right of the intercept of the IS curve on the horizontal axis, so that full employment would be restored by a rightwards shift of the LM curve only if the interest rate became negative, which is impossible. In these three cases, then, even if money wages are not rigid downwards, it seems that the fall in prices caused by the fall in money wages in response to unemployment does not lead to the restoration of full employment. These special cases therefore appeared to uphold the Keynesian contention that unemployment equilibrium does not depend on money-wage rigidity.

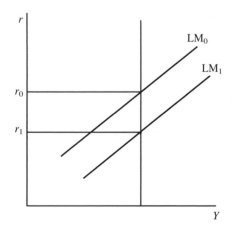

Figure 8.6

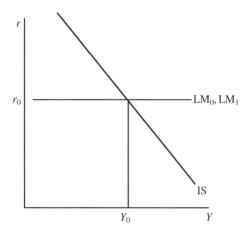

Figure 8.7

However, the neoclassical economists were able to dispose of these special cases by introducing a second automatic mechanism, called the 'Pigou effect' after one of the leading economists of this school. The Pigou effect (anticipated in Chapter 2) involves a wealth effect in the consumption function: consumption is assumed to be positively related to wealth as well as income, and one of the components of wealth is the real money supply (M_s/P). When prices fall, wealth rises and therefore consumption increases. In symbols,

$$U \to W \downarrow \to P \downarrow \to M_s/P \uparrow \to C \uparrow \to Y \uparrow$$

In the IS–LM model this means that the IS curve shifts to the right, and a brief glance at Figures 8.6–8.8 confirms that even in the Keynesian special cases income increases. Indeed, with the Keynes effect shifting the LM curve to the right and the Pigou effect shifting the IS curve to the right, there is no combination of IS and LM slopes for which income does not increase.

Keynesian economists were forced to concede that the Pigou effect exists in principle, but they argued that it is likely to be relatively small in practice because it operates only on 'outside' money and not on 'inside' money which makes up the bulk of the money supply. Money enters into the wealth of the private sector (and hence affects consumption) because of its role as an asset of the private sector, but in general there will be some corresponding liability somewhere in the economy, either for other agents in the private sector or for some other sector. Inside money is defined as *money for which there exists a corresponding private-sector liability*: most bank deposits come into this category since the liability corresponding to bank deposits is the loans owed to the banks by other private-sector agents or (usually in much smaller amounts) by the public sector. In the former case, while private-sector holders of money balances find themselves better off as the result of a price fall, because their money balances have increased in real value, private-sector debtors who have outstanding bank loans find themselves worse off, because their debts are now larger in real terms. There

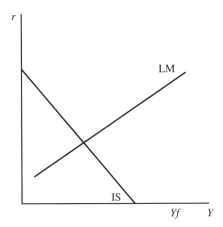

Figure 8.8

is therefore a negative wealth effect for private-sector debtors, which is assumed (in the absence of any explicit statement about distribution) to offset the positive wealth effect for the private-sector holders of money, so that the net effect of a price fall on expenditure is zero for inside money. Outside money on the other hand is *money for which there is no corresponding private-sector liability*: in effect this means money which is 'backed' by the debts of the public sector, whether it is bank deposits for which the corresponding liability is bank lending to the public sector, or notes and coin issued by the central bank for which the corresponding liability is government debt to the central bank. Here it is assumed that the public sector does not feel itself to be worse off and does not therefore reduce its expenditure as the result of the fall in prices, so that there is no negative wealth effect offsetting the positive wealth effect for the private-sector holders of money.

Since most money is inside money and the Pigou effect operates only on outside money, the effect of a given fall in prices is likely to be small; conversely, a given increase in expenditure from the wealth effect requires a large fall in prices. This means that the automatic self-equilibrating mechanisms of the economy operate relatively weakly, but they do operate provided money wages are not completely rigid. This double recognition of the conditional existence of these mechanisms on the one hand and of their weakness on the other, together with the assumption that money wages are in practice relatively rigid downwards, constitutes the basis of the 'truce' between Keynesian and neoclassical economists in which this debate ended in the 1950s. More commonly referred to as the Keynesian–neoclassical synthesis, this truce involved the agreement that if wages are not completely rigid downwards then there exist automatic mechanisms in the economy which would eventually restore full employment if the economy moved away from that position; but that these mechanisms operate only slowly and weakly; while in any case money wages are (it was assumed) largely inflexible. Thus the synthesis awarded the theoretical victory to the neoclassicals (unemployment *does* depend on wage rigidity) but gave Keynesians the justification required for a policy of systematic macroeconomic intervention.

The Keynesian labour market

What does this money-wage rigidity Keynesianism look like in terms of an explicit model of the labour market corresponding to the classical view of Figure 8.2? The demand for labour is the same as in the classical case, that is downward sloping with respect to the real wage because of diminishing returns to one factor when others are fixed. But the supply of labour involves a fixed money wage: the rationale for this is that workers suffer from 'money illusion', in other words they attach importance to and respond to money wages (or other money variables) rather than real wages; and/or that workers are concerned about *relative* wages which are disturbed by changes in money wages (which typically occur separately in individual firms or industries) but not by changes in prices. In Figure 8.9 the supply of labour is perfectly elastic up to the full employment level L_f at the fixed money wage $\overline{W}$, that is there is no labour supplied at less than $\overline{W}$ but any amount up to L_f is supplied at $\overline{W}$, while at L_f there is full employment and no more labour is supplied even if the wage is increased: the supply of labour curve is therefore horizontal up to L_f and vertical at L_f. In Figure 8.9 labour supply is drawn against the money wage, and this is the easiest way to think of it, but for comparison with the classical model (and because the demand for labour depends on the real rather than the money wage) the supply needs to be redrawn against the real wage. This is done in Figure 8.10 where a number of supply curves are drawn corresponding to the real wage produced by the (unchanged) money wage $\overline{W}$ and a number of different price levels. For successively higher price levels, $P_3 > P_2 > P_1 > P_0$, the real wage implied by $\overline{W}$ is successively lower, giving a

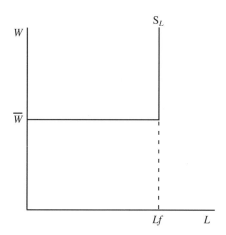

Figure 8.9

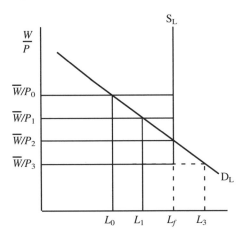

Figure 8.10

series of 'reverse L-shaped' supply curves each vertical at the full employment level L_f. At these lower levels of the real wage the intersection of the supply and demand curves occurs further to the right: at $\overline{W}/P_0$ employment is L_0, at $\overline{W}/P_1$ it is L_1, and at $\overline{W}/P_2$ it is L_f; while if the price level rose to P_3 there would be excess demand for labour $(L_3 - L_f)$ which would push the real wage up to $\overline{W}/P_2$.

This analysis of the labour market can be used to derive an aggregate supply curve. Figure 8.11 shows how on the aggregate production function the successively larger amounts of labour employed, L_0, L_1 and L_f, produce successively larger amounts of output, Y_0, Y_1 and Y_f, up to full employment (where output cannot be increased further because all productive resources are already fully utilised). It is therefore possible to work from Figure 8.10 through Figure 8.11 to construct the AS curve of Figure 8.12: at price level P_0 the real wage $\overline{W}/P_0$ is such that L_0 labour is employed and Y_0 output is produced; at

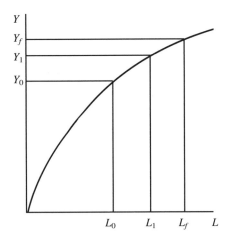

Figure 8.11

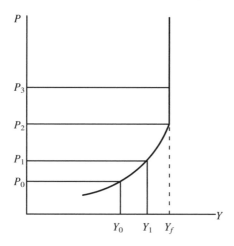

Figure 8.12

price level P_1 the real wage $\overline{W}/P_1$ is lower, labour employed is higher at L_1 and output produced is higher at Y_1; at P_2 and the real wage $\overline{W}/P_2$, full employment is reached with L_f employed and Y_f produced; and at P_3 or any higher level of prices, employment remains L_f and output Y_f because of the physical constraint of the size of the labour force. Thus the AS curve for this money-wage rigidity Keynesianism slopes upwards from left to right up to the full employment level when it becomes vertical.

This AS curve can then be combined with an AD curve to produce a complete model. In the Keynesian case the AD curve is best thought of as derived from the IS–LM model by considering the levels of expenditure associated with different levels of prices, with all the other exogenous variables of the IS–LM model held constant. In Figure 8.13 at higher price levels

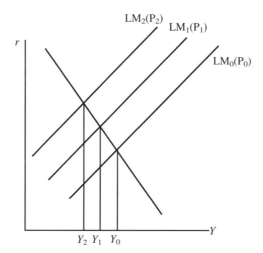

Figure 8.13

$P_2 > P_1 > P_0$ the LM curve is further to the left (see Table 7.2) and aggregate expenditure or demand is lower. The mechanism involved here is essentially that of the latter part of the Keynes effect: higher prices reduce the real money supply, which raises the interest rate and reduces investment and income. In the special cases of vertical IS and horizontal LM this mechanism does not lead to lower aggregate demand at higher price levels; but the introduction of the wealth effect mechanism involved in the Pigou effect ensures that at higher prices the IS curve is also further to the left (real money balances and therefore consumption are lower), and thus aggregate demand must be lower at higher prices. The AD curve is therefore drawn downward sloping in Figure 8.14.

The AD curve can be derived more formally by analysing the algebraic solution to the simultaneous equations of the IS and LM curves. Such an analysis shows clearly that the AD curve is not a rectangular hyperbola if velocity is not constant (that is, if the interest-elasticity of the demand for money is not zero): a rise in the price level is typically associated with a rise in the interest rate, which reduces the demand for money, so that the fall in income is less than proportional to the price rise. It also shows exactly how the AD curve responds to changes in the exogenous variables of the IS–LM model, and how its slope is related to the slopes of the IS and LM curves. However, the algebra involved is necessarily more complicated.

The key result which comes out of both the AD/AS model of Figure 8.14 and the labour market model of Figure 8.10 is that an unemployment equilibrium can exist: if AD is at AD_0, the AD and AS curves intersect at (P_0, Y_0), so the price level is P_0, output is $Y_0 < Y_f$; and from Figures 8.10 and 8.11 labour employed is $L_0 < L_f$. If aggregate demand is increased to AD_1, by means of expansionary fiscal or monetary policy, prices rise to P_1, employment to L_1 and output to Y_1; while aggregate demand of AD_2 produces full employment. Thus while in the classical model of Figures 8.2 and 8.3 an unemployment equilibrium cannot exist, in the Keynesian money-wage rigidity models of Figures 8.10 and 8.14 it can. Moreover, government policy can in

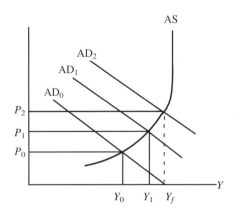

Figure 8.14

principle reduce unemployment by increasing aggregate demand; this increases prices and so lowers the real wage to the level required for full employment.

The rationale for a horizontal AS curve

The Keynesian model of the labour market presented above and the partly upward-sloping, partly vertical AS curve which it generates do not of course provide a justification for the use of fixed-price, aggregate demand only, models like the Keynesian cross or IS–LM models, as in the analysis of the effects of fiscal and monetary policy in Chapter 7, for example. It would probably be fair to say that for many macroeconomists in the 1950s and 1960s this inconsistency was simply ignored, and that macro analysis concentrated overwhelmingly on models of that type, with something on the labour market tacked on at the end. However, it is possible to provide a rationale for the use of fixed-price AD-only models in the form of a rationale for a horizontal AS curve, which can be approached most easily by considering an alternative derivation of that curve from the one given above.

In the preceding parts of this chapter the AS curve was constructed by working from the labour market (in conjunction with a given price level) to the amount of output associated with that price level. An AS curve can also be thought of as the aggregation of the supply curves of each industry in the economy, where the industry supply curve is the aggregation of the supply curves of each firm in the industry. Each firm's supply curve is its marginal cost curve above its average variable cost curve; the competitive firm equates marginal cost to marginal revenue (price) by expanding its output along its marginal cost curve as the price of its output rises. Thus the partly upward-sloping and partly vertical Keynesian AS curve derived above can be regarded as showing how firms expand their output as prices rise (with the money wage and therefore the marginal cost curve fixed) up to the full employment level, at which point even if prices continue to rise, firms are physically unable to produce more output. In the classical case on the other hand, the AS curve is vertical because the assumption of flexibility in the labour market means that the real wage is always at the equilibrium level, so that when prices are higher or lower, money wages and therefore the marginal cost curve are also higher or lower, and the profit-maximising level of output for each firm is always the same.

Now suppose that for each firm the marginal cost curve is horizontal, that is firms can vary their output at least over a certain range without any increase in the average (or marginal) cost of production. Suppose also that industries are oligopolistic and firms do not compete by varying the prices of their outputs. Finally, suppose that prices are determined by costs, primarily wages, so that if the money wage is constant so also is the price level. In this case, for a given level of money wages on the one hand and output prices on the other, the AS curve is horizontal below the full employment level of output and vertical at that level, as in Figure

8.15. Firms are willing to supply different levels of output in response to the demand, but at the same price.

What is happening to the labour market in this case? Since prices are determined by wages, the real wage as well as the money wage is fixed, and there is only one supply-of-labour curve as in Figure 8.16. However, instead of the single fixed demand-for-labour curve as in the classical and Keynesian–neoclassical synthesis cases of Figures 8.2 and 8.10, which is derived from the aggregate production function of Figure 8.1, Figure 8.16 has a number of different demand curves, D_0, D_1, D_2 and D_L. D_L is the same as the demand-for-labour curve in the earlier cases; it is constructed on the assumption that firms can sell as much output as they wish to sell at the current price level, so that the demand for labour depends only on relative prices (that is, on W relative to P). D_0, D_1 and D_2 each have first a downward-sloping portion and then a vertical portion; they are constructed on the assumption that there are limits which firms perceive to the amounts they can sell at the current price. The downward-sloping portions correspond to levels of output *within* those limits, where the demand for labour depends as in the other cases on the relative price of labour, and they constitute sections of the D_L curve. The vertical portions on the other hand correspond to the limits on firms' labour requirements due to the limits on the sales of their output: on these portions, however low the wage fell, firms would still not wish to employ more labour because they do not believe they would be able to sell any more output. Thus fluctuations in aggregate demand, from AD_0 to AD_1 to AD_2 in Figure 8.15, are paralleled by fluctuations in firms' effective demand for labour, from D_0 to D_1 to D_2 in Figure 8.16, and result in fluctuations in labour employed and output produced, with both the money wage and the price level unchanged.

It is therefore possible in this way to provide a rationale for a horizontal AS curve, which means that output is entirely demand-determined and that the Keynesian cross and IS–LM models can be regarded (if the rationale is

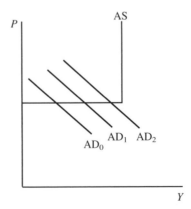

Figure 8.15

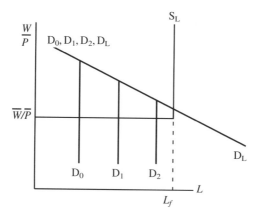

Figure 8.16

accepted) as adequate representations of reality for certain purposes. The elements which are necessary to construct this rationale include imperfect competition, constant marginal costs, and money-wage rigidity, together with some mechanism that links prices directly to wages, such as the 'mark-up' or 'administered' pricing discussed in Chapter 10.

Conclusions and qualifications

Three models of the labour market have been analysed in this chapter, each of them generating a different AS curve which can be used in conjunction with an AD curve to determine prices and output simultaneously. The crucial results of these models concern the possibility of an unemployment equilibrium and (implicitly) the role for macroeconomic stabilisation policy. In the classical model no unemployment equilibrium is possible, the economy is always in a situation of no involuntary unemployment or, in terms of the Keynesian concept, full employment, and there is no need for or gain to be had from a policy designed to stabilise output or employment. In the Keynesian–neoclassical synthesis model the downward rigidity of money wages ensures that an unemployment equilibrium can occur; stabilisation policy can move the economy towards the full employment level but only at the cost of an increase in prices. Finally, in the more orthodox Keynesian model, money-wage rigidity makes an unemployment equilibrium possible while the other assumptions ensure that stabilisation policy can restore full employment without affecting prices.

Two further points should be made. Firstly, the classical model presented here is something of a caricature of the thinking of pre-Keynesian economists: they may have regarded wage flexibility and self-adjustment in the labour market as long-run tendencies, but they did not generally regard full employment as something which held continuously. It is also the case that many of the 'classical' economists Keynes was attacking in his *General Theory* – notably Pigou – advocated programmes of public works in the 1920s and 1930s as a temporary measure to reduce unemployment.

Secondly, it should be stated more explicitly that the works of Keynes, like those of many other great thinkers, have been variously interpreted. For example, it has been argued, both by Cambridge Keynesians who had known Keynes and by some younger economists who have been involved in a 'reappraisal' of Keynes's ideas, that the Keynesian–neoclassical synthesis completely misunderstood the basic thrust of Keynes's analysis. On the other hand, the above discussion of the horizontal AS curve or traditional Keynesian case has skirted over a number of problems and differences relating to the underlying microeconomic assumptions in particular. There is no space to pursue these points here, but students should at least make sharp distinctions in their minds between Keynes himself, the various interpretations of him, and the various brands of Keynesianism.

Exercises

Students should familiarise themselves with the derivation and workings of the AD/AS models presented here by working through the following questions:

(i)   Use the IS–LM model (in diagram form) to derive the effect on the AD curve of increases in: (a) the nominal money supply; (b) autonomous investment; (c) lump sum taxes; and (d) the marginal tax rate.

(ii) Explain how and why real and money wages vary (if at all) along each of the three AS curves constructed in this chapter.

(iii) Analyse the effects on prices and income of increases in autonomous exports and the speculative demand for money in the three versions of the AD/AS model.

(iv) Solve equations [7.4] and [7.13] for income, and interpret the resulting expression for equilibrium income as an AD curve. What is the slope of this AD curve? What changes in exogenous variables would cause the curve to shift, and how?

Further reading

An introduction to the 'Keynes and the classics' debate described in this chapter together with a useful selection of readings is given in section 1 of Surrey (1976). Leijonhufvud (1981, especially Chapters 1, 3 and 4) presents some of the more accessible material from the recent 'reappraisal' of Keynes's economics stimulated by Leijonhufvud and Clower, while Coddington (1983) situates this and the earlier discussion in a broader perspective.

Chapter 9

Inflation: Phillips curves

The previous chapter took a number of steps away from the fixed-price world of the earlier chapters; this chapter and the next confront more directly the question of inflation, defined as a sustained rise in the general level of prices. Much of the analysis of inflation is concerned with a particular piece of analytical apparatus, the Phillips curve, and the present chapter focuses on the evolution and the various forms of the Phillips curve; the next discusses inflation in a broader perspective and examines the main competing approach, that of cost-push theory.

The original Phillips curve

The original Phillips curve was an empirical relationship between the rate of change of money wages ($\dot{W}$) and the rate of unemployment (U) in the UK 'discovered' by Phillips (1958). What he found was an inverse relationship between the two, convex to the origin, as in Figure 9.1, which appeared to be remarkably stable: Phillips estimated the relationship on the data from 1861 to 1913 and found that the combinations of wage change and unemployment recorded in the periods 1913–48 and 1948–57 remained very close to the relationship estimated on the earlier data. Where the wage change/ unemployment combination for a particular year was well away from the estimated curve, Phillips was able to 'explain' this in terms of a rise in import prices initiating a 'wage–price spiral'.

Two years later Lipsey (1960) provided a theoretical rationale for what in Phillips's treatment was essentially an empirical relationship; a brief account of this rationale is given here as a background to the later analysis. Lipsey started from individual labour markets, disaggregated from the overall national labour market by region or by skill, and worked up to the overall macroeconomic relationship. First, he made the simple dynamic assumption that the rate of change of wages varies positively with the proportionate amount of excess demand for labour in the individual labour market. In symbols,

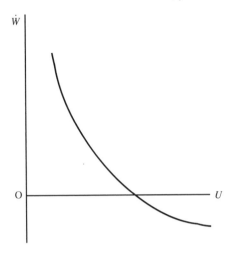

Figure 9.1

$$\dot{W} = \phi ED_L, \quad \phi > 0, \qquad\qquad\qquad\qquad [9.1]$$

where $\dot{W}$ is the proportionate rate of change of wages, that is $\Delta W/W$, and ED_L is the proportionate amount of excess demand for labour, that is the demand *minus* the supply, divided by the supply. Lipsey represented the individual labour market diagrammatically as in Figure 9.2: at W_0 the excess demand for labour is $(L_0 - L_0')$, and Lipsey's assumption means that the larger this amount (and so the further the existing wage W_0 from the equilibrium wage W_e), the more rapidly W would move towards W_e. The dynamic assumption [9.1] is represented diagrammatically in Figure 9.3.

Secondly, Lipsey assumed the sort of relationship between unemployment and the excess demand for labour which is depicted in Figure 9.4 (the latter variable is of course unobservable): here Oa is the amount of frictional

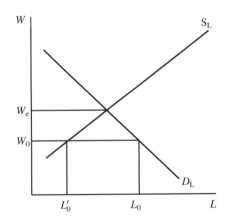

Figure 9.2

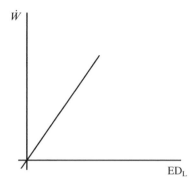

Figure 9.3

unemployment, that is unemployment which exists as the result of the normal process of turnover in the labour market, when the excess demand for labour is zero and the labour market is in balance. As excess demand rises above zero, unemployed workers who are changing jobs find new jobs more quickly and so the rate of unemployment tends asymptotically towards zero, and the line is convex to the origin. But as excess demand for labour falls below zero there is a one-for-one increase in unemployment and the line is straight.

These two assumptions are then combined to construct an 'adjustment function' for the individual labour market by considering the rate of wage change and the rate of unemployment each associated with each particular

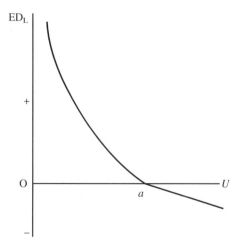

Figure 9.4

level of excess demand. Since the relationship between wage change and excess demand is linear, that between wage change and unemployment has the same shape as that between excess demand and unemployment, as in Figure 9.5.

The final stage in Lipsey's analysis is to construct a 'macro adjustment function' by aggregating the individual labour market adjustment functions, which he assumed to be identical. Lipsey showed that this macro adjustment function (that is, the Phillips curve for the economy as a whole) is non-linear below the horizontal axis if the unemployment rates in individual labour markets differ; that it is further away from the origin, the greater is the difference between the rate of unemployment in the various individual labour markets; and that in principle the government could shift the overall Phillips curve inwards towards the origin if it could reduce the dispersion of unemployment rates between individual labour markets.

The Phillips–Lipsey analysis pre-dated the Keynesian–monetarist debates of the 1960s and was not thought of as belonging to any particular school; perhaps partly for this reason it was taken up rapidly by a wide range of economists in different countries and soon became a basic element of macroeconomic thought. Three important implications were drawn from the analysis. Firstly, it was interpreted as showing that wage change could be explained by market forces rather than trade unions (which could therefore be regarded as impotent): this assumed that the major reason for changes in the excess demand for labour was demand shifts rather than (trade union-induced) supply shifts, although Lipsey had been careful to point out that the analysis was compatible with both and had argued that trade unions might have effects elsewhere in the analysis by influencing the speed of adjustment (ϕ above) or the dispersion of unemployment, both of which could affect the position of the Phillips curve.

Secondly, the analysis was combined with the idea that at least over the long run the rate of change of prices is the same as that of unit labour costs (so that

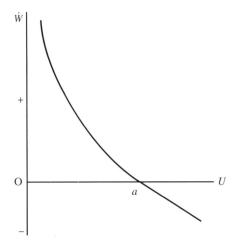

Figure 9.5

profit margins remain unchanged), in order to derive a relationship between the rate of change of prices ($\dot{P}$) and unemployment. The rate of change of unit labour costs is the rate of change of the labour costs per unit of output, that is the rate of change of money wages *minus* the rate of change of output per unit of labour, in other words *minus* productivity growth (g); in symbols,

$$\dot{P} = \dot{W} - g \qquad\qquad [9.2]$$

Thus the original Phillips relationship, which had wage change as a function of unemployment, could be turned into a relationship expressing price change as a function of unemployment, which could then be used to estimate, for example, the rate of unemployment consistent with zero inflation.

Thirdly, the Phillips curve was interpreted as showing that there was a 'trade-off' between inflation and unemployment: less unemployment was possible only with more inflation; less inflation could be obtained only at the cost of higher unemployment. The problem for macro policy was then presented as the problem of choosing and attaining the preferred combination of the two, that is the preferred point on the curve. However, some economists also argued that the trade-off could be favourably modified by the use of an incomes policy (the setting of some kind of norm or limit to the rate of increase in wages and salaries) which would make wages rise more slowly at any given level of unemployment and would therefore shift the Phillips curve inwards towards the origin.

Expectations-augmented Phillips curves

By the mid-1960s Phillips curves had been estimated for a variety of countries and time periods with apparent success. But in the late 1960s and early 1970s many countries began to experience combinations of inflation and unemployment well outside the estimated Phillips curves: the original Phillips curve experienced an 'empirical breakdown'. Even before this, however, the original analysis had been strongly criticised by Friedman (1968) and Phelps (1967).

The easiest way to explain their critique is to refer back to Figure 9.2, which is based on one of the figures in Lipsey (1960): this has an upward-sloping supply-of-labour curve and a downward-sloping demand-for-labour curve, *drawn against the money wage on the vertical axis*. Friedman and Phelps argued that the supply of and demand for labour depend on real wages and not money wages, and hence that the amount of excess demand for labour should determine the rate of change of real wages, not that of money wages. But it is the latter which is relevant for the study of inflation: how does the former connect to and influence the latter? Friedman and Phelps argued (in slightly different ways) that the connecting link is expectations of inflation. Employers are concerned about what is likely to happen to the price of their output since this partly determines what they can afford to pay for labour and so how much labour they want to employ at any particular level of money wages; workers on the other hand are concerned about the real value of any particular level of money wages, and so about the likely change in the prices of the goods and services they buy. Thus both sides of the labour market in effect work out what they think will happen to prices over the period for which they are entering into agreements on wages and employment: they form expectations about inflation, and these expectations feed into the wages on which they agree. Suppose that some level of unemployment U_0 would, if zero inflation was expected, be associated with $\dot{W}_0$ rate of wage change: if 5% inflation was expected, then U_0 would be associated with wage change of $\dot{W}_0 + 5\%$. While Phillips and Lipsey had excess demand determining the growth of money wages, then, Friedman and Phelps had excess demand determining the growth of real wages, and excess demand *plus* expected inflation determining the growth of money wages.

When expected inflation is zero, employers and workers expect the rate of change of money wages to be the same as that of real wages, and in this situation the original Phillips curve (which in Lipsey's rationale did not distinguish between the two) makes sense. But for any other level of expected inflation there must be another Phillips curve above or below that curve by the amount of the inflation expected, and these curves are called 'expectations-augmented' Phillips curves. In Figure 9.6, for example, the lower of the two curves shown is for zero expected inflation ($\dot{P}^e = 0$) and the upper curve is for

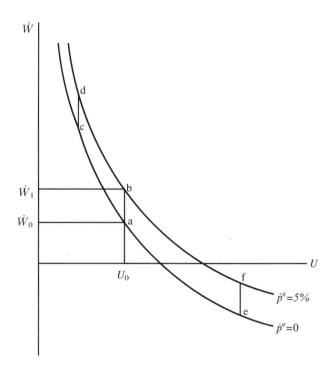

Figure 9.6

expected inflation of 5% ($\dot{P}^e = 5\%$); the vertical distance between the two curves, that is the distance ab=cd=ef, etc., is equal to the difference in expected inflation between the two curves, i.e. 5%. The rate of wage change, given on the vertical axis, can be translated into price change (inflation) by use of assumption [9.2], $\dot{P} = \dot{W} - g$, where productivity growth is conventionally assumed to be constant in the short run. Suppose that g is equal to $\dot{W}_0$ which is associated with U_0 on the $\dot{P}^e = 0$ curve: when unemployment is U_0 and expected inflation is zero, actual inflation is $\dot{W}_0 - g = 0$ so that the expectations of inflation turn out to be correct. At levels of unemployment to the left (right) of U_0 wage change and inflation are above (below) zero, so that expectations are not fulfilled. When expected inflation is 5%, on the other hand, unemployment U_0 is associated with $\dot{W}_1$ wage change but $\dot{W}_1$ is equal to $\dot{W}_0 + 5\%$ because the vertical distance between the curves is 5%, and inflation is $\dot{W}_1 - g = 5\%$, again as expected; while at levels of unemployment above (below) U_0 inflation is below (above) the expected rate of 5%.

It is helpful here to consider the results of two 'notional experiments'. Suppose first that, starting from point V in Figure 9.7 with U_0 and $\dot{W}_0$ and expected inflation of zero, the government decides to stimulate the economy. It could do this by any combination of fiscal and monetary policy, but it is easier to analyse it in terms of an 'extreme monetarist' model of the economy in which nominal aggregate demand is determined solely by the rate of growth of the money supply. In the initial equilibrium the rate of monetary growth must have been the same as the growth rate of (nominal and real) aggregate demand, that is the rate of productivity growth g ($= \dot{W}_0$). Suppose the government now increases the rate of monetary growth $\dot{M}$ to $g + 5\%$. Initially the economy moves upwards and to the left along the $\dot{P}^e = 0$ Phillips curve to a point such as X: the stimulus to aggregate demand increases real output and unemployment falls to, say, U_1 while wage change increases to $\dot{W}_1$. From

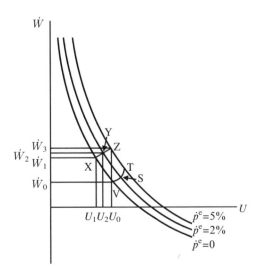

Figure 9.7

assumption [9.2] inflation increases to $\dot{W}_1 - g > 0$. After a while (if not immediately) economic agents – employers and workers – come to realise that prices are rising, and begin to expect that they will continue to rise: the economy therefore moves on to a higher short-run Phillips curve, such as that labelled $\dot{P}^e = 2\%$ in Figure 9.7. Wage change and actual inflation are now higher, because the inflation expectations are contributing to them, and therefore more of the 5% increase in $\dot{M}$ is being absorbed in inflation and there is less 'left over' to stimulate real demand. The economy therefore moves to some point such as Y in Figure 9.7 where unemployment is between U_1 and U_0. However, at Y wage change is now $\dot{W}_2$ and inflation is $\dot{W}_2 - g > 2\%$, and this leads to a further increase in inflation expectations, that is a shift on to a higher short-run Phillips curve at a point between U_2 and U_0. So long as unemployment continues to be less than U_0, actual inflation exceeds expected inflation and the economy continues to shift on to a higher Phillips curve; each time it does so it also moves to the right as more and more of the original increase in $\dot{M}$ is absorbed in inflation and there is a smaller and smaller stimulus to real aggregate demand. The economy follows a trajectory such as VXY, eventually reaching point Z on the $\dot{P}^e = 5\%$ curve, where the whole of the stimulus of the $\dot{M}$ increase is now absorbed in inflation, unemployment is back at its original level U_0, and actual inflation at $\dot{W}_3 - g = 5\%$ is equal to expected inflation so that there is no further shift to a new short-run Phillips curve. Point Z is therefore a point of (long-run) equilibrium, like the starting point V.

Now consider a second experiment. Suppose that, starting again from point V, the government decides to stimulate the economy but this time to ensure that unemployment remains at U_1. In the first instance the economy moves to point X on Figure 9.8 as before. As inflation increases and expected inflation

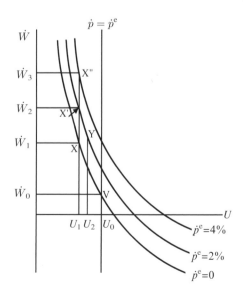

Figure 9.8

rises above zero the economy moves, say, to the $\dot{P}^e = 2\%$ curve, again as before. However, this time the government is determined to keep unemployment at U_1; since otherwise the economy would move to point Y with $U_2 > U_1$, the government finds it has to increase $\dot{M}$ a second time to compensate for that part of the original increase which is now being absorbed by inflation and to maintain the stimulus to real aggregate demand. The economy therefore moves to point X′, with wage change of $\dot{W}_2$ and inflation of $\dot{W}_2 - g > 2\%$: it therefore moves to a higher Phillips curve such as that labelled $\dot{P}^e = 4\%$, the government again has to increase $\dot{M}$ to maintain the stimulus to real demand and keep unemployment at U_1. But at point X″ actual inflation is again greater than expected inflation and the process repeats itself.

What are the key points illustrated by these experiments? Firstly, the only points of long-run equilibrium are points where unemployment is at U_0 and actual inflation is equal to expected inflation: the long-run Phillips curve, that is the line showing the alternative combinations of wage change and unemployment available in long-run equilibrium, is therefore a vertical line through U_0, marked $\dot{P} = \dot{P}^e$ in Figure 9.8. This long-run equilibrium can occur with any (positive or negative) rate of inflation, but it occurs only at U_0 level of unemployment; thus there is no long-run trade-off between inflation and unemployment, although a short-run trade-off still exists (along the individual short-run Phillips curves where $\dot{P}^e$ is given). The level of unemployment which occurs in long-run equilibrium, U_0, has been variously described as the 'natural rate of unemployment' or the 'non-accelerating inflation rate of unemployment' (NAIRU).

Secondly, any attempt to maintain unemployment permanently below U_0 involves a continuous increase in inflation. Conversely, any attempt to maintain unemployment above U_0 involves a continuous decrease in inflation (and after zero inflation has been reached an accelerating fall in prices). For this reason the Friedman–Phelps theory embodied in the analysis of Figures 9.6 to 9.8 is sometimes called the 'accelerationist hypothesis', though it is more often referred to as the 'natural rate hypothesis'. It should also be noted that a reduction in inflation, according to this hypothesis, requires a temporary increase in unemployment as the economy moves downwards to the right along a given short-run curve, in a trajectory such as ZTSV in Figure 9.7.

Adaptive and rational expectations

The existence of a long-run Phillips curve which is vertical at the natural rate of unemployment depends on two things: the absence of money illusion, which ensures that expected inflation is fully incorporated into the determination of actual wage change and inflation (the vertical distance between different short-run curves must be equal to the difference between them in expected inflation); and the existence of some mechanism by which actual inflation is, ultimately if not immediately, fully incorporated into expected inflation. The mechanisms concerned have so far been left rather vague, but must now be considered.

There are two main hypotheses as to how expectations are formed, the adaptive expectations hypothesis and the rational expectations hypothesis. Each can be combined with the natural rate hypothesis to analyse how the economy reacts to certain events and each predicts that actual inflation is in the end fully incorporated into expectations, so that the choice between them does not affect the implications of the natural rate hypothesis regarding the long-run equilibrium. However, the two hypotheses have different implications for the movement of the economy away from and in between positions of long-run equilibrium and hence they have different implications for short-run policy.

The adaptive expectations hypothesis is the one used implicitly by both Friedman and Phelps in their original expositions of the natural rate hypothesis and used explicitly in a large amount of later work on the latter; it was also used implicitly in the discussion in the previous section of the two 'experiments'. The basic idea of the hypothesis is that economic agents adapt or adjust their expectations in the light of the errors they find they have made in the past. More formally, agents are assumed to change their expectations between one period and the next by some fraction of the difference between their expectations and the actual rate of inflation in the first period. In symbols,

$$\dot{P}^e_t - \dot{P}^e_{t-1} = \delta(\dot{P}_{t-1} - \dot{P}^e_{t-1}), \quad 0 < \delta < 1 \tag{9.3}$$

This can be rearranged to give

$$\dot{P}^e_t = \delta(\dot{P}_{t-1} - \dot{P}^e_{t-1}) + \dot{P}^e_{t-1}$$
$$= \delta\dot{P}_{t-1} + (1 - \delta)\dot{P}^e_{t-1} \tag{9.4}$$

Equation [9.4] expresses current expectations of inflation as a weighted average of previous period inflation and previous period expectations of inflation. Its structure is almost exactly the same (there is a minor difference in the time period of the first term on the right-hand side) as that of equation [2.9] above which expresses permanent income as a function of current measured income and previous period permanent income. And just as equation [2.9] can be used to derive equation [2.8] which expresses permanent income as a weighted average of measured income in all previous time periods, so equation [9.4] can be expanded by using the same equation in lagged form to substitute repeatedly for the last term on the right-hand side, to give expectations of inflation as a weighted average of actual inflation in all previous periods:

$$\dot{P}^e_t = \delta\dot{P}_{t-1} + (1 - \delta)[\delta\dot{P}_{t-2} + (1 - \delta)\dot{P}^e_{t-2}]$$
$$= \delta\dot{P}_{t-1} + \delta(1 - \delta)\dot{P}_{t-2} + (1 - \delta)^2[\delta\dot{P}_{t-3} + (1 - \delta)\dot{P}^e_{t-3}]$$
$$= \delta\dot{P}_{t-1} + \delta(1 - \delta)\dot{P}_{t-2} + \delta(1 - \delta)^2\dot{P}_{t-3} + \delta(1 - \delta)^3\dot{P}_{t-4} + \ldots \tag{9.5}$$

Since the weights on past inflation sum to 1, if actual inflation has always been the same then expected inflation must be equal to it (compare equation [2.6] above): in other words, expectations of inflation in the end, though not immediately, fully incorporate or fully adjust to actual inflation.

This hypothesis clearly has some intuitive plausibility: it suggests that people adjust their expectations or forecasts in the light of the mistakes they find they have made, and on one level at least it would be remarkable if people did not do this. It is also relatively 'tractable', that is it can be incorporated in a variety of mathematical models without much difficulty. However, there are two major problems with the hypothesis. The first is that if there is a systematic trend (upwards or downwards) in inflation – that is inflation is always rising, or always falling – people who form their expectations in this way will be systematically wrong, but they apparently just continue being wrong without changing the way they try to forecast the future. For example, if inflation is continuously rising, adaptive expectations always underpredict inflation. Imagine a gradual rise of inflation from an initial level of zero and consider equation [9.3]: people adapt their expectations in each period towards the level of actual inflation in the previous period, but inflation in the current period is always higher than inflation in the previous period and their expectations in the current period are lower than either. If actual inflation sometimes rises and sometimes falls there will not be systematic errors in expectations of this sort, but their existence in situations where there is a systematic trend in inflation is enough to put a question mark against the hypothesis.

The second problem with the adaptive expectations hypothesis is that it assumes that people take no notice of any information about future inflation other than their past errors. Yet there is a considerable amount of such information available, in the form of reports in the media of the forecasts of professional forecasting agencies (including the government's own forecasting department) on the one hand and in the form of information about variables which might reasonably be supposed to affect the inflation rate on the other hand. For an open economy such as the UK, for example, it is straightforward to show that a devaluation or depreciation of the currency is likely to lead to an increase in prices; it is reasonable to suppose that this is widely understood; and there is in fact some evidence to suggest that expectations of inflation increase sharply following large depreciations. However, adaptive expectations formed according to equation [9.3] would involve no increase in such a situation until *after* the effects of the devaluation had begun to feed through, and only a gradual increase even then.

The rational expectations hypothesis, though first outlined by Muth (1961), was not applied either to expectations of inflation or in other areas of macroeconomics until the early 1970s when Robert Lucas and others began to use it in conjunction with the natural rate hypothesis to derive some striking results. At its simplest the rational expectations hypothesis says that economic agents use all the information available to them in trying to forecast the future. At the level of detailed application in the present context the hypothesis involves two main assumptions: (a) economic agents make their forecasts as if on the basis of a correct model of the economy; and (b) this current model includes the systematic element in government policy. In concrete terms the meaning of these assumptions can be clarified by reference to the first of the two experiments considered above, in Figure 9.7. First, assumption (a) means that agents understand the natural rate hypothesis, realise that nominal aggregate demand is determined by the growth of the money supply, know the value of U_0, and so on. On this basis a 'weak' version of the hypothesis would argue that, when the government decides to increase the growth of the money supply from g to $g + 5\%$, people immediately perceive this and realise it will bring about an inflation rate of 5%; they therefore expect inflation of 5% and the economy moves directly from V to Z without passing through X and Y. However, the 'stronger' (and more common) version of the rational expectations hypothesis goes further than this. Assumption (b) means that people understand how the government typically manipulates its monetary policy: they understand, for example, that the government regularly reacts to, say, a rise in unemployment by $j\%$ above U_0 by increasing monetary growth by $k\%$, and therefore whenever unemployment rises above U_0 by $j\%$ people expect the government to increase monetary growth by $k\%$ and immediately revise their expectations of inflation accordingly.

There is a considerable literature on the rational expectations hypothesis, but two main points stand out from the debate. On the one hand, the hypothesis certainly has some basic plausibility; in particular, it would be odd if economic agents continuously made erroneous forecasts, and there are clearly some situations when they have a financial incentive to obtain the best possible forecasts. On the other hand, many expositions of the rational expectations hypothesis pay little attention to the problems and costs of acquiring the information which is necessary to make accurate forecasts. But finding (or choosing) the 'correct model' of the economy, for example, is by no means straightforward, nor is getting to know the typical behaviour of the authorities in manipulating their policy instruments.

For present purposes it is more important to examine the policy implications of the rational expectations hypothesis when combined with the natural rate hypothesis. The basic point here is that according to these two hypotheses systematic stabilisation policy – that is policy which varies in a systematic way in response to fluctuations in unemployment (or any other variable) – has no effect on unemployment or output, because policy is anticipated by private-sector economic agents who revise their expectations of inflation accordingly, and the result is that the entire effect of policy falls on prices and none of it on real demand and output. There is therefore no short-run trade-off between inflation and unemployment which policymakers can make use of, in contrast to the original Phillips curve where there is a long-run trade-off and the adaptive expectations-augmented curve where there remains a short-run (but no long-run) trade-off. Under the natural rate hypothesis with rational expectations, unemployment and output are affected only by 'surprises' or 'shocks' which cannot be predicted, and it is assumed that expectations adjust quickly after a shock has occurred and is therefore known, so that even in these cases the length of time that unemployment can differ from the natural rate is strictly limited.

Conclusions and qualifications

It should be clear from the above account that the original Phillips curve with its implication of a long-run trade-off between inflation and unemployment has been discredited both by experience and by the theoretical critique of Friedman and Phelps. The natural rate hypothesis put forward by these economists is widely, if not universally (see Chapter 10), accepted together with its implication of a possible short-run but no long-run trade-off. There is a considerable amount of empirical evidence which can be cited in support of the hypothesis, but tests of it involve the simultaneous testing of other hypotheses, notably of a hypothesis of expectations formation and of a hypothesis on the constancy or otherwise of the natural rate, and the results are therefore open to some interpretation and dispute; in the face of these empirical uncertainties, analytical argument has played a major role in attracting support for the natural rate hypothesis. Much of the early work in this area involved the adaptive expectations hypothesis; when combined with the natural rate hypothesis adaptive expectations imply that there is a short-run trade-off between inflation and unemployment which policy-makers can use in their attempts to influence unemployment and output, but no long-run trade-off. However, the adaptive expectations hypothesis suffers from being both mechanical and backward-looking, and an alternative hypothesis of expectations formation has been put forward in the shape of the rational expectations hypothesis. When combined with the natural rate hypothesis, rational expectations imply that there is no short-run (or long-run) trade-off, so that there is no role for systematic stabilisation policy. The empirical evidence on the formation of expectations remains unclear, but most economists find the analytical arguments very persuasive, and rational expectations are now the norm in a wide range of models. At the same time, however, economists have become more conscious of the problems of 'learning', particularly in cases of 'regime change' where the way in which government policy is made is altered.

There are two other qualifications worth making here. First, so far little has been said about the microeconomic underpinnings of the Phillips curve. These are discussed in more detail in Chapter 15, but this is arguably one of the key issues which continue to define the 'visions' of the economy held by different groups of macroeconomists, so that it is worth saying something more about it here. On the one hand, the more traditional interpretation, which can be found in Phillips and Lipsey, in some of Friedman's earlier writings and in Phelps, regards the growth of wages (and prices) as the result or effect of excess demand, that is of a disequilibrium in the labour market (and in that for goods and services). On the other hand, the rational expectations theorists such as Lucas, and Friedman in his later writings, present the Phillips curve as an 'inverted supply curve': workers supply more labour when wages are higher than they had expected (and firms supply more output when prices are higher than they had expected), so that the Phillips curve reflects the response of the supply of labour (and output) to movements in wages (and prices), rather than the movement of wages (and prices) in response to changes in demand relative to supply. On this second interpretation then, fluctuations in unemployment and output are the result of the voluntary choices made by economic agents in flexible and self-equilibrating markets. This interpretation therefore involves a conscious return, in its underlying vision as well as in its key result (that there is no role for stabilisation policy), to some of the themes of classical economics. The 'disequilibrium' interpretation, however, is much closer to the mainstream of developments since Keynes and is consistent with the view (see Chapter 15) that there is some scope for stabilisation policy even if expectations are rational.

A second qualification refers to the nature of the natural rate of unemployment or NAIRU at which the long-run Phillips curve is vertical. Those who regard the Phillips curve as an inverted supply curve tend to regard the natural rate essentially as frictional unemployment, and to focus on the factors such as the level of unemployment benefits relative to wages (the 'replacement ratio') which they think determine how long a time (and how often) individuals choose to spend between jobs. On the other hand, those who hold to the 'disequilibrium' interpretation of the Phillips curve tend to put more emphasis on structural factors such as the dispersion of unemployment rates in different labour markets to which Lipsey drew attention. And some of these economists would also stress the role of past levels of aggregate demand and unemployment in determining the 'employability' of the current labour force and/or the availability of the capital stock with which people can be employed. This is sometimes expressed in terms of the concept of *hysteresis*, a concept from physics which refers to the lasting effects that a temporary magnetising force may have on an electromagnetic field. Here the idea is that the NAIRU may be determined by past levels of actual unemployment. The empirical evidence suggests that in European countries (but not in the USA) the natural rate or NAIRU rose substantially from the mid-1970s (though in the UK it may have fallen back slightly in the more recent period). There has been considerable debate over the causes of these movements, with most discussion focusing on the replacement ratio, structural factors and lagged aggregate demand or unemployment.

Exercises

Suppose that in an economy with an initial high rate of inflation the government decides to reduce inflation to zero. Identify the policies required and use Phillips curves to show their impact on the economy,

(i) for the original non-augmented Phillips curve,
(ii) for the expectations-augmented Phillips curve with adaptive expectations of inflation,
(iii) for the expectations-augmented Phillips curve with rational expectations of inflation, and

(iv) for the expectations-augmented Phillips curve with rational expectations of inflation, in an economy in which the NAIRU is determined partly by recent levels of actual unemployment.

Further reading

The earlier theoretical and empirical work on the Phillips curve is well surveyed in Sumner (1984). Attfield *et al.* (1991) review much of the work on rational expectations. Cross (1993) and *Journal of Economic Perspectives* (1997) contain a number of papers on the NAIRU, while Siebert (1997) and Nickell (1997) consider European unemployment in more detail.

Chapter 10

Inflation: cost-push and a wider perspective

This chapter starts with an account of the cost-push theory of inflation. It then gives a broader perspective on theories of inflation in which the various forms of the Phillips curve from Chapter 9 are located in the context of wider macroeconomic controversies and the target real-wage hypothesis is introduced. It should be noted that although import costs are included in the discussion of cost-push theory below, the analysis of this chapter is essentially appropriate to a closed economy; open-economy considerations are introduced in Chapters 11 and 12, and the various strands of analysis are integrated more fully in Chapter 13.

The cost-push theory of inflation

In historical terms, cost-push theory was important in the 1960s and 1970s, when it formed one of the key elements of the Keynesian side of Keynesian–monetarist debates, but it has become less important and prominent since then. However, it is worth discussing for more than mere historical reasons, because some legacy of the ideas persists in mainstream economics in the form of the possibility of certain kinds of supply side shocks and the issue of the accommodation or non-accommodation of those shocks.

The simplest way to approach the theory is by thinking of the price of an individual good produced by a particular firm: the price can be 'decomposed' or broken down into the cost of the materials used (per unit of the good), the cost of the labour used, any indirect tax (a positive component) or subsidy (a negative component) and the profit, where the latter is by definition the difference between average cost (excluding the cost of capital) and average revenue (net of any tax or subsidy). The same procedure can also be undertaken at the macroeconomic level; the only difference is that when all firms are included in the analysis the materials used by one firm which are also the outputs of another firm can be decomposed in their turn into separate components, so that all material costs disappear except for imports. Thus the value of the total output of goods and services available for domestic use can be expressed as the sum of the value of imports, total labour costs involved, total profits and indirect taxes less subsidies. For present purposes it is convenient to concentrate on output at factor cost rather than at market prices; the former excludes indirect taxes and subsidies.

On this basis the value of output PQ can be decomposed into import costs F, labour costs W and profits R:

$$PQ = F + W + R$$

Now cost-push theory assumes that firms set (or 'administer') their prices to give a constant mark-up above costs. This means that the profit margin is constant, and that profits are a constant proportion, say r, of other costs:

$$R = r(F + W)$$

Hence

$$PQ = F + W + r(F + W) = F(1 + r) + W(1 + r) \qquad [10.1]$$

The average price of a unit of output P can be found by dividing the right-hand side of [10.1] by Q, and the rate of change of P can be expressed as a weighted average of the rates of change in import and labour costs, as follows:

$$P = \frac{F(1 + r)}{Q} + \frac{W(1 + r)}{Q} \qquad [10.2]$$

If r and Q are assumed constant,

$$\Delta P = \Delta F \cdot \frac{(1 + r)}{Q} + \Delta W \cdot \frac{(1 + r)}{Q}$$

$$\frac{\Delta P}{P} = \Delta F \cdot \frac{(1 + r)}{PQ} + \Delta W \cdot \frac{(1 + r)}{PQ}$$

$$= \Delta F \cdot \frac{(1 + r)}{PQ} \cdot \frac{F}{F} + \Delta W \cdot \frac{(1 + r)}{PQ} \cdot \frac{W}{W}$$

$$= \frac{\Delta F}{F} \cdot \frac{F(1 + r)}{PQ} + \frac{\Delta W}{W} \cdot \frac{W(1 + r)}{PQ}$$

$$= \alpha \cdot \frac{\Delta F}{F} + \beta \cdot \frac{\Delta W}{W}$$

or, in the notation of Chapter 9,

$$\dot{P} = \alpha \dot{F} + \beta \dot{W} \qquad [10.3]$$

where $\alpha = F(1 + r)/PQ$ and $\beta = W(1 + r)/PQ$ are the weights on the rates of change of import and labour costs respectively (and $\alpha + \beta = 1$). The reader will have noticed that what is involved here is similar to the construction of a retail price index, except that in this case the price index is being related to the inputs of factors rather than the outputs of goods and services, and the algebraic manipulation goes from the price index to the inputs rather than from the output components to the overall price index.

With profit margins constant, the change in prices can be decomposed in this way into the change in import costs and the change in labour costs (and if output at market prices was being considered then the change in indirect taxes and subsidies would figure in expression [10.3] too). Cost-push theory then regards the latter as the proximate determinants of inflation. In particular, changes in labour costs are singled out as the main cause of inflation, and in the 1970s and 1980s a number of studies tried to relate the change in labour costs to some measure or indicator of trade union militancy, such as the level or rate of change of trade union density (union membership as a proportion of the labour force), or the level of strike activity. Thus inflation is seen as caused by increases in costs; variations in demand have no direct effect on prices and indeed no indirect effect either since cost-push theorists generally consider that the rate of change of wages is also independent of demand conditions. The appropriate way to reduce or prevent inflation is therefore the use of an incomes policy to reduce the rate at which wages increase.

Cost-push and real demand

Even if variations in demand do not cause inflation there is an obvious difficulty in the analysis so far regarding the effect of cost-push inflation on real demand. In the IS–LM framework, for example, an increase in prices shifts the LM curve to the left, reducing real aggregate demand and therefore output as in Figure 10.1, from Y_0 to Y_1 for $P_1 > P_0$. If the LM curve were horizontal because of the liquidity trap or if the IS curve were vertical because investment was interest-inelastic, demand and output would not be affected. But if these extreme cases are excluded (or a real balance effect is introduced) cost-push inflation must lead directly to lower output and higher unemployment. However, the inflation which has been experienced in most industrialised countries has not typically taken this form, and cost-push theorists have usually regarded inflation as 'orthogonal to' or independent of the level of economic activity. The apparent inconsistency is reconciled by positing some

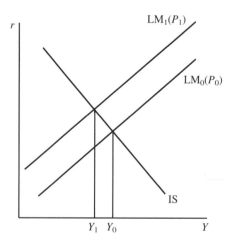

Figure 10.1

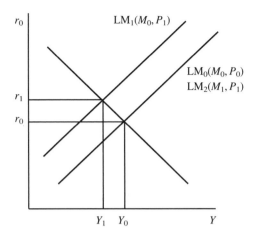

Figure 10.2

process by which the money supply grows in response to inflation in such a way as to maintain the level of real demand unchanged.

Suppose, for example, that the government is committed (for some reason) either to stabilising the rate of interest at r_0 in Figure 10.2 or to maintaining employment at the level corresponding to Y_0. If cost-push pressure increases the price level from P_0 to P_1 and the LM curve shifts to the left from LM_0 to LM_1, the rate of interest will tend to rise to r_1 and the level of aggregate demand and output to fall to Y_1. However, the government could prevent either or both of these things occurring by increasing the nominal money supply from M_0 to M_1 so that the LM curve shifts back to its original position at LM_2, where the real money supply is unchanged from the original position LM_0 because nominal money supply and prices have both increased by the same proportion. Thus the growth of the money supply is caused by and endogenous to inflation here, in such a way as to eliminate the effect inflation would otherwise have had on the level of economic activity. This endogeneity also makes sense of the observed tendency for prices and money to rise together over long time periods.

An alternative possibility is that the money supply responds to inflation, not because of any commitment or specific decisions by the government, but because of some sort of slackness in the system of monetary control. For example, cost-push inflation might have the effect of increasing the budget deficit, if it tends to raise nominal government expenditure by more than it raises nominal tax revenue (which is possible but not necessary, and depends on the ways in which expenditure is controlled and taxes are specified and adjusted); if the monetary authorities do not react by increasing the government's borrowing from the private sector the money supply will increase. A second example is where bank lending to the private sector is determined essentially by the demand for credit; if cost-push inflation leads companies to borrow more to maintain the real value of their working capital, bank lending and the money supply will increase in line with prices.

The precise mechanisms involved in these (and other) cases have not been well developed, and there is relatively little empirical analysis of them, but *some* mechanism that makes the money supply endogenous to inflation is essential to the cost-push theory.

A wider perspective

Classical economics regarded the price level as determined via the quantity theory by the money supply. In the 1940s and 1950s, when the quantity theory had been discredited by the work of Keynes and his followers, there were two theories of inflation current: the cost-push theory as explained above (though with less emphasis on the endogeneity or relevance of the money supply) and the 'demand-pull' theory, according to which excess demand 'pulls up' prices in its wake.

Demand-pull theory can best be thought of in terms of the original unaugmented Phillips curve (which was 'discovered' only towards the end of this period), according to which the excess demand for labour determines the rate of change of wages, while prices are determined either indirectly (via wage costs) by the excess demand for labour or directly by the associated excess demand for goods and services. Excess demand was assumed to be dominated by fiscal policy, so that demand-pull inflation was primarily the result of errors in the government's macro policy causing an overheating of the economy. However, demand-pull and cost-push were regarded in this period not as mutually exclusive but as referring to different sorts of inflation: actual experience might involve an alternation between the two or some combination of them, and different policy responses – lower demand on the one hand and incomes policy on the other – would be appropriate.

As indicated in Chapter 9 the Phillips curve was taken up enthusiastically and rapidly by economists after the publication of Phillips's paper in 1958. Since it was widely interpreted as emphasising market forces rather than trade union power its influence tended, in the first half of the 1960s, to strengthen the support for the demand-pull rather than the cost-push analysis. In the late 1960s, however, the Friedman–Phelps critique of the original Phillips curve was succeeded by the empirical breakdown of the relationship, and this led to a greater polarisation of economists' views on inflation. On the one hand, Keynesian economists interpreted the empirical breakdown as evidence that inflation was after all essentially a cost-push rather than a demand-pull phenomenon, and Keynesian economics became identified with the view that the basic cause of inflation was some kind of social conflict and pressure outside the economic sphere and outside the scope of economic analysis, while excess demand was not even a minor cause of inflation. Moreover, the endogeneity of the money supply in response to inflation, as explained in the preceding section, was given more emphasis as increasing evidence of a stable demand for money accumulated.

On the other hand, the earlier concept of demand-pull inflation was now subsumed in the revised, expectations-augmented, version of the Phillips curve associated with Friedman and Phelps, and the latter was itself situated in a monetarist framework. This monetarist theory of inflation had three main components: firstly, the argument that there was a powerful transmission mechanism from money to aggregate demand, so that excess demand was dominated by monetary factors as in the monetarist version of the IS–LM model; secondly, the assumption that the growth of the money supply was exogenous, that is both able to be controlled and in fact controlled by the monetary authorities; and thirdly, the expectations-augmented Phillips curve analysis with the natural rate hypothesis. Thus exogenous monetary growth determined excess demand which, together with expectations of inflation, determined actual inflation. Finally, where do trade unions fit into this analysis? It was argued that the labour market was not so very different from other markets so that it *did* respond to variations in excess demand, and that trade unions did not necessarily work against the grain of market forces because their bargaining power depended precisely on the degree of excess demand. Moreover, trade unions might even, on occasion, speed up the working of the price mechanism, by hastening the normal tendency for wages in different markets to move roughly in line with each other (abstracting from structural changes in the supply and demand for different sorts of labour).

By the mid-1970s then, there were two well-articulated theories of inflation with sharply differing views on both the causes of inflation and the appropriate policy response. Against the monetarist emphasis on excessive monetary growth resulting from expansionary government policy as the basic cause of inflation stood the Keynesian cost-push emphasis on trade union (and other) 'pushfulness', while against the monetarist prescription of tight monetary control stood the Keynesian advocacy of incomes policy. There are three further developments to be noted here.

The first is the introduction of the rational expectations hypothesis into the monetarist analysis, as discussed in Chapter 9. The effect of this was to introduce a direct connection between monetary policy and inflation expectations, in place of the indirect connection via excess demand and actual inflation which characterised the adaptive expectations analysis, and therefore to make closer and stronger the link between monetary growth and inflation. However, the link now depended on the way in which monetary policy was being used, that is on the extent and nature of the systematic (and therefore predictable) element in policy; expectations of inflation could be affected by the announcement of targets for monetary growth, inflation or other variables, by changes in government or in exchange rate regimes, and so on.

The second development was the introduction of the 'real wage resistance' or 'target real wage' hypothesis on the cost-push side; this hypothesis had been put forward in one form or another well before but it became much more important in the 1980s. On the one hand, real wage resistance can be thought of as a step beyond the money-wage rigidity hypothesis of earlier Keynesianism: real wage resistance means that workers and trade unions resist not merely cuts in their real wage which result from cuts in their money wages but also cuts in their real wages which result from rises in the price level. On the other hand, the target real wage formulation of the hypothesis suggests more aggressive behaviour: here the idea is that workers and trade unions seek to obtain wage settlements which will provide them with a certain target growth in their real wages net of tax. In formal terms the hypothesis can be stated as

$$\dot{W} = \psi \left[\left(\frac{\theta W}{P} \right)^*_t - \left(\frac{\theta W}{P} \right)_{t-1} \right], \quad 0 < \psi \leqslant 1, 0 < \theta < 1 \tag{10.4}$$

where W is the money wage, P is the price level, ψ is a partial adjustment parameter similar to that used in the capital stock adjustment principle (Chapter 4), and θ is the 'retention ratio', that is the proportion $(1 - t)$ of real wages which is retained after (direct) tax has been paid. $(\theta W/P)^*_t$ is the 'aspiration wage', that is the target or desired level of real post-tax wages, and $(\theta W/P)_{t-1}$ is the actual level in the preceding period. Thus the hypothesis says that wages rise by some fraction (which may be unity) of the gap between the aspiration real wage and the lagged actual wage.

The first point to note about this hypothesis is that workers and trade unions are not thought to have money illusion: the gap between aspiration and actual wage levels is equally affected by a cut in money wages W or a rise in prices P and wages respond in the same way in either case. Some treatments of the hypothesis include an expected inflation term on the right-hand side of [10.4], but even without this there is no long-run money illusion. A second point is that any exogenous change in prices will evoke a response from wages, and if prices are determined by a mark-up on wages as in equation [10.3], this will start off an extended process of wage and price inflation. Indeed, the hypothesis provides (in conjunction with [10.3]) a formal rationale for the widespread concept of a 'wage–price spiral'. Thirdly, the hypothesis provides an explicit role in the process of inflation for direct taxation (through the retention ratio), in contrast to all the other theories considered here. And, finally, it should be noted that excess demand can be given a role in the hypothesis, if (as has been done in some analytical and empirical work) either the adjustment parameter ψ or the aspiration wage is allowed to vary (positively) with the level of excess demand.

The third development is the decline of cost-push views in the 1980s and 1990s. One factor in this may have been the widely perceived reduction in the strength of trade unions, notably in the UK. Here, over the 1980s, repeated waves of industrial relations legislation, trade union defeats in some key areas (e.g. coal mining), structural changes in employment patterns and a substantial rise in unemployment had combined to reduce trade union membership and militancy. Despite this, however, there was a significant rise in inflation towards the end of the decade, generally attributed to a boom which was clearly demand-led. Another factor may have been a broader, partly political, trend to emphasise market forces rather than social conflict as explanations of economic phenomena, and to emphasise monetary rather than incomes policy as the cure for inflation. And a third factor may have been the development of the target real wage hypothesis, where excess demand gained a role within cost-push views and workers were no longer perceived as suffering from money illusion. But whatever the causes, among both economists and social commentators the cost-push theory of inflation had almost vanished by the mid-1990s.

Conclusions

With the empirical breakdown of the original unaugmented Phillips curve the analysis of inflation became strongly polarised between cost-push theory on the one hand and monetarist theory on the other. The empirical evidence, which has not been surveyed here, is very mixed. Tests of the full monetarist theory come up against wider problems of the nature of the transmission mechanism and the exogeneity of monetary growth, while tests of the natural rate hypothesis suffer from the particular problem that they also involve a simultaneous test of a theory of how inflation expectations are formed – a problem exacerbated by the emergence of rational expectations as an alternative to adaptive expectations. A further problem relates to the estimation of the natural rate or NAIRU itself: if this is thought to have varied over the period examined, econometric estimation is made considerably more difficult and its results more tentative.

Tests of cost-push theory also come up against wider problems such as the existence of mark-up or administered pricing and the endogeneity of monetary growth. Tests of the target real wage hypothesis, which emerged as the most interesting and best formulated hypothesis on this side of the debate, suffer from the fact that the aspiration real wage cannot be observed but must be either assumed or estimated simultaneously with the rest of the relationship. Moreover, even tests of the hypothesis which exclude a role for excess demand and/or for inflationary expectations are difficult to distinguish from tests of the natural rate hypothesis, since the gap between aspiration and actual wages can always be interpreted as a proxy for excess demand.

By the 1990s, however, opinion had turned decisively away from cost-push theory, and a widespread consensus had developed around the view that in the medium term inflation was a matter of excess demand and expectations, with monetary policy being seen as the key factor in excess demand and expectations being seen as essentially rational (although economic agents might sometimes either fail to understand what the government was trying to do or refuse to be convinced by its protestations, a question considered further in Chapter 16). At the same time the possibility that wages could sometimes be pushed up by trade unions in the short term was also quite widely accepted. However, the recognition that cost-push pressures could not have enduring effects on the price level without monetary accommodation, together with the shift towards greater activism of monetary policy in most industrial countries, implied that wage-push could only be a short-run factor in inflation.

Exercises

Get hold of a recent copy of the Bank of England's *Inflation Report* and read through it, in order to answer the following questions:

(i)   What importance is given to cost-push elements (look mainly at the short-run forecasting of inflation)?
(ii)   What is seen as the driving force behind longer run inflation?
(iii)   How are expectations of inflation brought in, and how far are they adaptive or rational?
(iv)   How would you characterise the Bank of England's overall view of inflation in terms of the different theories discussed in this chapter?

Further reading

Cost-push theories which try to relate inflation to trade union militancy are surveyed in Carline (1985). Artis and Miller (1979) and Artis, Leslie and Smith (1982) discuss the target real wage hypothesis including its relationship to the natural rate hypothesis. Carlin and Soskice (1990) make a brave attempt to combine some of the older cost-push thinking with New Keynesian views, while advanced texts such as Romer (1996) illustrate the disappearance of that thinking in mainstream macroeconomics.

Chapter 11

The open economy under fixed exchange rates

This chapter and the next analyse the implications of the 'openness' of an economy – to trade with other countries and to international capital flows – under fixed and flexible exchange rates respectively. The interest in this analysis lies in the questions of whether and how openness in each case alters any of the central macroeconomic relationships discussed so far, such as the power of fiscal and monetary policy and the causal mechanisms underlying inflation. However, in order to consider these questions it is necessary to examine first the balance of payments and the exchange rate themselves. After an introduction to the foreign exchange market this chapter therefore briefly considers Keynesian thinking on the balance of trade and the monetary approach to the balance of payments under fixed exchange rates, before returning to the basic macroeconomic issues; Chapter 12 deals in a similar way with flexible exchange rates.

The foreign exchange market

The foreign exchange market is the market where currencies (pounds, dollars, etc.) are exchanged; it can be thought of initially in terms of a standard supply and demand model, such as that represented in Figure 11.1. The exchange rate e is usually defined in economics as the value in the domestic currency of a unit of foreign exchange; for historical reasons, the British tend to define exchange rates the other way round, as the number of dollars or marks or yen per pound, but the standard practice of international economics and of the rest of the world will be followed here. The exchange rate can therefore be thought of as the number of pounds per mark; this means that a depreciation of the pound is an *increase* in the exchange rate, that is an upward movement in Figure 11.1 where e is the variable measured on the vertical axis, and an appreciation means a *decrease* in e. The two curves in Figure 11.1 represent the supply and demand for foreign exchange, that is the amount of foreign exchange Q_{FX} (measured on the horizontal axis) which economic agents wish to sell or

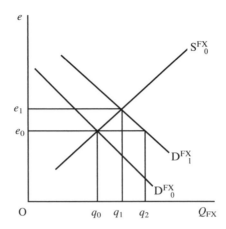

Figure 11.1

buy respectively in return for domestic currency. The supply S^{FX} is the proceeds of exports *plus* the inflow of capital, while the demand D^{FX} is the value of imports *plus* the capital outflow. They are drawn in Figure 11.1 with the conventional slopes of supply and demand schedules; but more is said on this below.

Suppose the initial curves are S^{FX}_0 and D^{FX}_0, with equilibrium at e_0 and q_0, and then consider what happens if demand increases, perhaps because domestic income and therefore the demand for imports has increased, to D^{FX}_1. If the exchange rate is 'floating' or 'flexible' it will move to e_1 where there is equilibrium between the supply and the new demand. But if the exchange rate is fixed at e_0, that is the government has decided to maintain e at e_0, then when D^{FX} shifts outwards to D^{FX}_1 the government (in practice the central bank) will have to maintain equilibrium at e_0 by itself supplying the excess demand for foreign currency at that exchange rate: in this case market demand Oq_2 is equal to the sum of private market supply Oq_0 and government supply q_0q_2. Under fixed exchange rates then, the government or central bank maintains equilibrium in the foreign exchange market at the fixed rate by itself buying or selling foreign exchange to cover any excess supply or demand from private transactions.

This distinction between private and government demands and supplies corresponds roughly to the distinction between *autonomous* balance-of-payments flows, which in this case means not those which are independent of income, but those which are carried out by private economic agents for their own purposes (e.g. for profit) or by government bodies for purposes other than equilibrating the foreign exchange market; and *accommodating* flows which are those carried out by the government to equilibrate the market at a particular exchange rate. A simplified statement of the balance-of-payments accounts can be set out as follows:

exports of goods and services (autonomous)
minus imports of goods and services (autonomous)
plus net payments of interest, profits and dividends (autonomous)
equals current account balance; $B \gtrless 0$
plus net autonomous capital flows/capital account balance $K \gtrless 0$

equals 'overall balance of payments' (current *plus* capital account); $B + K \gtrless 0$
plus official financing (accommodating) $-(B + K) \lesseqgtr 0$

equals zero.   0

The meaning of the first four items here is straightforward. Autonomous capital flows are the flows of capital involved in international purchases of financial and real assets such as bonds and equity, firms and factories. The overall balance of payments $B + K$ is the excess private supply or demand, which is 'made up' by official financing (sales of foreign exchange) of the same magnitude but the opposite sign when the authorities are fixing the exchange rate (if they are not fixing it the exchange rate adjusts until $B + K = 0$). It is necessarily the case that the total of all balance-of-payments flows is zero, but this does not hold for the two aggregates of flows to which most importance is conventionally attached, the current account B and the overall balance of payments $B + K$.

Foreign trade multiplier analysis

Keynesian thinking traditionally emphasised the current account B and paid less attention to the capital account K (where flows were relatively small in the 1940s and 1950s because of the widespread use of exchange controls). One strand in Keynesian thinking is the foreign trade multiplier analysis which involves integrating exports and imports into a Keynesian cross model or an IS–LM model. The results are broadly the same in each case but slightly more difficult to derive in the latter. They are also qualitatively similar if the analysis is modified to incorporate foreign 'repercussion' effects by setting up a two-country model in which one country's imports are the other's exports, so that the incomes of the two countries are linked. The present analysis is therefore in terms of a one-country Keynesian cross model (as in Chapter 4).

Exports are assumed to be autonomous and imports partly autonomous and partly income-related, that is, in symbols

$$X = \overline{X}$$
$$F = \overline{F} + fY$$

Equilibrium income in the full Keynesian cross model was found in Chapter 4 (equation [4.10]) to be:

$$Y = \frac{1}{1 - b + bt + f} \cdot (a - b\overline{T} + \overline{I} + \overline{G} + \overline{X} - \overline{F}) \qquad [11.1]$$

The balance of trade B is equal to exports minus imports:

$$B = X - F = \overline{X} - \overline{F} - fY \tag{11.2}$$

Substituting from [11.1] into [11.2] gives

$$B = \overline{X} - \overline{F} - \frac{f(a - b\overline{T} + \overline{I} + \overline{G} + \overline{X} - \overline{F})}{1 - b + bt + f}$$

which can be simplified as follows:

$$B = \frac{(\overline{X} - \overline{F})(1 - b + bt + f)}{1 - b + bt + f} - \frac{f(a - b\overline{T} + \overline{I} + \overline{G} + \overline{X} - \overline{F})}{1 - b + bt + f}$$

$$= \frac{(\overline{X} - \overline{F})(1 - b + bt)}{1 - b + bt + f} - \frac{f(a - b\overline{T} + \overline{I} + \overline{G})}{1 - b + bt + f} \tag{11.3}$$

Examination of equation [11.2] shows that anything which raises income Y will (*ceteris paribus*) reduce the balance of trade B, while [11.3] shows the quantitative relationships involved between the various exogenous variables and B. Two particular results (which can be derived by means of the technique used in Chapter 4 to derive $\Delta Y / \Delta \overline{G}$) are worth noting:

$$\frac{\Delta B}{\Delta \overline{X}} = \frac{1 - b + bt}{1 - b + bt + f} < 1 \tag{11.4}$$

$$\frac{\Delta B}{\Delta \overline{I}} = \frac{\Delta B}{\Delta \overline{G}} = -\frac{f}{1 - b + bt + f} < 0 \tag{11.5}$$

First, from [11.4], an increase in exports increases B but by a smaller amount; this is because income rises and there is therefore some partially offsetting increase in imports. Secondly, from [11.5], an increase in investment I or government expenditure G reduces B because it raises income and therefore imports.

The conclusion drawn from this sort of analysis by Keynesian economists was that the balance of trade *is* affected by changes in the autonomous variables, in other words the balance of trade is *not* automatically equilibrated. Indeed, for given levels of exports and autonomous imports and a given marginal propensity to import f, it can be seen from [11.2] that there is only one level of income Y at which the balance of trade is equal to zero, and there is no reason why this level should be the full employment level. If there are compelling reasons why governments should avoid deficits or surpluses on the balance of trade (and there are certainly *some* reasons) then macro policy is inevitably constrained. Keynesian economists therefore looked for some other means of influencing the balance of trade, so that policy could aim to achieve both full employment and a zero deficit on the balance of trade; the most important instrument of this kind was the exchange rate, discussion of which is left until the next chapter.

The role of money

Keynesian thinking on the balance of trade or payments traditionally paid little attention to monetary factors, and this has been one of the main criticisms directed against it. In terms of Figure 11.1, for example, when at e_0 there is a deficit on the balance of payments of q_0q_2 this amount of foreign exhange is supplied to the foreign exchange market by the central bank. The central bank receives in return an equivalent amount of domestic currency which means that the domestic money supply is reduced by q_0q_2. But in this case the behaviour of economic agents in the subsequent period is likely to be different, so that the situation depicted in Figure 11.1 is strictly a temporary equilibrium situation. Indeed, it is possible to go further than this and argue that the reduction in the money supply associated with the balance-of-payments deficit will generate a process of adjustment by which the deficit will in time be eliminated (for example, if income falls and therefore imports fall).

This reduction in the money supply can be integrated into an IS–LM model analysis of the foreign trade multiplier as in Figure 11.2: here the vertical line BP shows the unique level of income at which imports are equal to exports and the overall balance-of-payments surplus (there are assumed to be no capital flows here) is zero. From equation [11.2], when B equals zero,

$$B = \overline{X} - \overline{F} - fY = 0$$
$$fY = \overline{X} - \overline{F}$$
$$Y = \frac{\overline{X} - \overline{F}}{f} \qquad\qquad [11.6]$$

Equation [11.6] is the equation of the curve in Figure 11.2; since $\overline{X}$, $\overline{F}$ and f are all constant there is a unique level of income Y_b at which the balance-of-trade (and payments) surplus is zero. From the initial position at Y_b an increase in the money supply shifts the LM curve right to LM_1, but at Y_1 the balance of

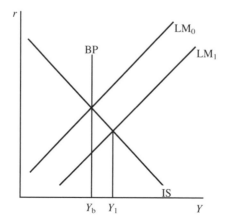

Figure 11.2

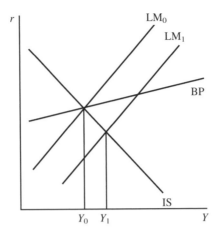

Figure 11.3

payments is in deficit, therefore the money supply falls and the LM curve shifts gradually back to the left until at LM_0 it again intersects the IS curve on the BP line.

Moreover, this framework can be adapted to allow for international capital flows in response to interest rate differentials, by letting the BP curve slope upwards from left to right as in Figure 11.3. Here the capital account inflow K is a positive function of the difference between the domestic and foreign or 'world' interest rate (the latter, r^*, is assumed to be exogenous):

$$K = \mu(r - r^*), \qquad 0 < \mu \leqslant \infty \qquad\qquad [11.7]$$

When the overall balance-of-payments surplus is zero,

$$B + K = \overline{X} - \overline{F} - fY + \mu(r - r^*) = 0$$
$$fY = \overline{X} - \overline{F} + \mu r - \mu r^*$$
$$Y = \frac{\overline{X} - \overline{F} - \mu r^*}{f} + \frac{\mu r}{f} \qquad\qquad [11.8]$$

Equation [11.8] defines the BP curve in Figure 11.3; since μ and f are both positive, the level of income varies positively with the domestic interest rate. In more intuitive terms, along the BP curve the current account surplus is smaller (or the deficit larger) at higher levels of income but with the interest rate higher the capital account deficit is also smaller (or the surplus larger) and the overall balance-of-payments surplus is always zero; to the 'south-east' of the BP curve the balance of payments is in deficit (income is higher and/or the interest rate lower than is required for equilibrium), while to the 'north-west' the balance of payments is in surplus. With high capital mobility, positions such as Y_1 in Figure 11.3 involve substantial capital outflows and therefore larger balance-of-payments deficits; this means that the money supply falls more sharply and the LM curve returns to the long-run equilibrium position LM_0 more quickly. In the limiting case of perfect capital mobility ($\mu = \infty$) the domestic interest

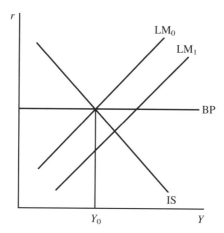

Figure 11.4

rate is unable to diverge from the world interest rate and the BP curve becomes horizontal at this rate as in Figure 11.4. Here when LM shifts to LM_1 the money supply returns *immediately* to its original level and Y remains at Y_0.

In this way it is possible to incorporate a strong monetary element into Keynesian balance-of-trade theory. The key point is that under fixed exchange rates the LM curve always shifts until it intersects the IS curve at the point where the latter intersects the BP curve; and this occurs in response to initial shifts of the IS curve which alter the IS/BP intersection as well as in response to initial LM shifts away from that intersection. Thus it is the intersection of the IS curve and the BP curve that determines the long-run equilibrium here; while the degree of capital mobility determines how quickly the long-run equilibrium is reached after a disturbance.

The monetary approach to the balance of payments

To develop a full monetary model of the balance of payments it is convenient to start elsewhere, with the identity between the liabilities and the assets of the consolidated banking system, that is the commercial banks *plus* the central bank (note that this is a different classification from that used in Table 6.1. The liabilities consist of notes and coin in circulation C and (commercial) bank deposits D, that is the money supply; and the assets consist of the two categories of foreign assets FA (foreign exchange and gold reserves of the central bank) and domestic assets or domestic credit DC (that is, lending to the private and public sectors A and GD_b):

$$C + D = M_s = FA + A + GD_b = FA + DC$$

Taking first differences and rearranging gives

$$\Delta FA = \Delta M_s - DCE \qquad [11.9]$$

which says that the change in foreign exchange reserves, which is the surplus on the overall balance of payments, is equal to the change in the money supply *minus* the 'domestic credit expansion' DCE ($= \Delta DC$). This relationship can also be thought of as derived from a rearrangement of equation [6.10] from Chapter 6,

$$\Delta M_s = DEF + ET - GD_p + A - NDL,$$

where ET corresponds to ΔFA and DEF $-\Delta GD_p + \Delta A - \Delta NDL$ to DCE.

The monetary approach to the balance of payments (MAB) proceeds from equation [11.9], which is only an identity, by introducing a number of behavioural assumptions. Firstly, the money market is assumed to clear, that is $M_s = M_d$ and $\Delta M_s = \Delta M_d$. This means that [11.9] becomes

$$\Delta FA = \Delta M_d - DCE \qquad [11.10]$$

which is no longer an identity. Dividing through by $M_s = M_d$ gives

$$\frac{\Delta FA}{M_s} = \frac{\Delta M_d}{M_d} - \frac{DCE}{M_s} \qquad [11.11]$$

which says that the overall balance of payments as a proportion of the money supply is equal to the proportional growth of the demand for money *minus* DCE as a proportion of the money supply. Secondly, DCE is assumed to be exogenously controlled by the domestic monetary authorities while ΔFA is assumed to be the dependent variable and ΔM_d is determined by changes in the variables on which the demand for money depends. This transforms [11.11] into a theory of how the balance of payments is determined.

The MAB in a very small, very open economy

At this point it is convenient to consider the workings of the MAB under some extreme assumptions which are (it can be argued) relevant for a very small, very open classical economy, one which is highly integrated into the world economy through free trade and capital flows and which is strongly self-equilibrating. The standard demand-for-money function considered in Chapter 5 has the (nominal) demand for money as a function of prices, real income and the interest rate. Suppose that the small open economy's interest rate is determined by the world level of interest rates through capital mobility and the integration of national capital markets; that its price level is determined by the world price level (multiplied by the exchange rate) because of the integration of national goods and services markets under free trade – a hypothesis sometimes referred to as 'purchasing power parity' or the 'law of one price'; and that in this classical or New Classical economy with a vertical aggregate supply curve, real income is always fixed at the (steadily growing) natural rate of output. In symbols,

$$r = r^*,$$

$$P = eP^*, \qquad\qquad\qquad [11.12]$$

$$\frac{\Delta Y}{Y} = \bar{g}, \qquad\qquad\qquad [11.13]$$

where asterisks denote the foreign or world levels of the interest rate or prices and $\bar{g}$ is the (exogenous and constant) rate of productivity growth. The effect of these assumptions is that the demand for money and the growth of the demand for money becomes exogenous to the model; in particular, the interest rate, price level and income growth do not vary in response to variations in domestic monetary policy (DCE). With the interest rate fixed in this manner it is convenient to use the Cambridge quantity theory formulation of the demand for money,

$$M_d = kPY,$$

where k is a constant. Taking first differences and manipulating gives

$$\Delta M_d = kP\Delta Y + kY\Delta P + k\Delta P\Delta Y$$

$$\frac{\Delta M_d}{M_d} = \frac{kP\Delta Y}{kPY} + \frac{kY\Delta P}{kPY} + \frac{k\Delta P\Delta Y}{kPY} \qquad\qquad [11.14]$$

The third term on the right-hand side of [11.14] is relatively very small (it is equal to the product of two proportional growth rates) and can be ignored. From [11.12] the domestic inflation rate $\Delta P/P$ must be equal to the world inflation rate $\Delta P^*/P^*$ if the exchange rate e is fixed. Hence, simplifying and substituting from [11.12] and [11.13],

$$\frac{\Delta M_d}{M_d} = \frac{\Delta Y}{Y} + \frac{\Delta P}{P} \qquad\qquad [11.15]$$

$$\frac{\Delta M_d}{M_d} = \bar{g} + \frac{\Delta P^*}{P^*} \qquad\qquad [11.16]$$

Equation [11.16] can now be substituted into [11.11] to give

$$\frac{\Delta FA}{M_s} = \bar{g} + \frac{\Delta P^*}{P^*} - \frac{DCE}{M_s} \qquad\qquad [11.17]$$

With DCE assumed exogenous and ΔFA the dependent variable, equation [11.17] says the overall balance-of-payments surplus (as a proportion of the money supply) is determined by the sum of the productivity growth rate and world inflation, *minus* DCE as a proportion of the money supply. DCE can best be thought of here as the potential increase in the money supply from domestic sources. What happens according to this theory is that the balance of payments acts as a mechanism by which the demand for money and the supply of money are brought into equilibrium: if the potential increase in the supply of money from domestic sources (DCE) is higher than the economy can absorb (ΔM_d), the excess is removed through a balance-of-payments deficit ($\Delta FA < 0$), while if DCE is less than the growth of the demand for money the economy obtains some more money via a balance-of-payments surplus ($\Delta FA > 0$). The balance of payments is therefore determined by the interaction of domestic monetary policy (DCE) and the arguments of the domestic demand for money.

It should be obvious that the causal mechanisms at work in this MAB model are very different from those in say the IS–LM model as discussed in Chapter 7. There an increase in the money supply leads to some combination of a fall in the interest rate and a rise in real income until the demand for money has risen by as much as the supply. Here a higher growth (the model is a dynamic one) of the potential increase in the supply of money from domestic sources (DCE) causes no change in any of the domestic arguments of the demand-for-money function, which are all completely 'tied down' by the assumptions made above; instead it leads to an outflow through the foreign exchange market, that is a balance-of-payments deficit, which eliminates the excess supply of money.

The MAB in a medium-sized open economy

It is now appropriate to relax the extreme assumptions made in the previous section in order to deal, more informally, with the case of a medium-sized economy such as that of the UK. Here the integration of the domestic markets into world markets is likely to be incomplete and the economy's self-equilibrating tendencies are assumed to be less powerful. Thus the domestic interest rate and prices can diverge to a limited extent from world levels and domestic real income is likely to be affected, again within limits, by domestic monetary policy. The effect of relaxing the assumptions in this way is that the growth of the demand for money is now no longer exogenous: it varies positively with DCE but to a limited extent only, so that some of the effect of an increase in DCE falls on the arguments of the demand for money but the bulk of the effect still falls on the balance of payments. The major *qualitative* results that can be derived from the simple version of the MAB therefore still apply here, although in quantitative terms the results are less neat and clear-cut. Monetary expansion (an increase in DCE) causes a balance-of-payments deficit, but in the short run at least it may provide some limited stimulus to domestic economic activity (and inflation). Similarly, monetary contraction causes a balance-of-payments surplus but it also reduces real income and inflation in the short run.

Macroeconomic implications

There are a number of points that can be drawn out of the above analysis for the basic macroeconomic relationships on which this book is focused. Firstly, in a Keynesian cross or IS–LM model the presence of a marginal propensity to import transfers some of the effects of both expenditure and monetary changes on to the balance of trade: as seen in Chapter 4 it reduces the size of the basic multiplier, so that the effect on aggregate demand of a change in either government expenditure or the money supply is smaller. Secondly, in an open economy under fixed exchange rates macro policy may be constrained by the need to avoid deficits on the balance of trade or payments. This is clearly so for the Keynesian models, where the income level required for balance-of-trade equilibrium may be below (or above) that required for full employment. However, it does not apply in the MAB models where there are strong automatic tendencies to full employment (or rather to the natural rate of unemployment) and appropriate monetary policy (DCE) can deliver balance-of-payments equilibrium at that level of income.

Thirdly, the above analysis has implications for the relative power of fiscal and monetary policy. This was discussed in Chapter 7 in terms of the slopes of the IS and LM curves, but that discussion now needs to be modified by the recognition that under fixed exchange rates, particularly with capital mobility, the effect of monetary policy falls largely on the balance of payments and that of fiscal policy largely on domestic economic activity. In the monetary adaptation of the Keynesian analysis (the IS/LM/BP model), for example, changes in the money supply cause temporary changes in income and in the balance of payments but in the long run (which may come very quickly if capital is highly mobile) the money supply returns to its original level, while in the MAB models the money supply is explicitly endogenous and demand-determined and the effect of changes in DCE is concentrated on the balance of payments.

Finally, the above analysis has implications for the causes of inflation. The Keynesian models assume a fixed price level, at least in the above presentations, but the MAB models imply that under fixed exchange rates open economies have their rates of inflation determined largely by world inflation rather than domestic monetary policy or domestic cost-push factors; this means that neither incomes policy nor monetary contraction can be expected to reduce the inflation.

Conclusions and qualifications

The discussion of the balance of payments given here has been severely restricted, and there are many points at which it would be supplemented or qualified in a textbook on international economics. In particular, the assumptions of perfect goods and capital market integration in the MAB can be relaxed in more formal and rigorous ways than has been done here; and the assumption in the MAB that DCE is exogenous deserves detailed consideration. More importantly, the theory of capital flows which underlies the upward-sloping BP curve can be questioned. It depicts capital mobility in terms of *continuous flows* responding to a *given* interest rate differential, whereas the weight of theoretical argument and empirical evidence favours a stock-adjustment theory of capital mobility in which a given *change* in the interest rate differential causes an international readjustment of capital portfolios with only a temporary and *finite* flow of capital. One way of seeing this point is to consider Tobin's liquidity preference analysis as explained in Chapter 5: in that case a change in the interest rate on the risky asset leads the investor to reallocate her portfolio and move to a new equilibrium, but once she has reached that new equilibrium there is no ongoing change in the distribution of her portfolio. If the flow theory of capital mobility incorporated in the IS/LM/BP model is replaced by the stock adjustment theory, the results for *partial* capital mobility $(0 < \mu < \infty)$ become more complex and less clear-cut, but those for perfect capital mobility are essentially unchanged.

Enough has been said, however, to show that in an open economy under fixed exchange rates some of the basic macroeconomic relationships, notably those concerning money and prices, are different from the relationships analysed earlier for a closed economy. Chapter 12 examines how far such differences exist in an open economy with a flexible exchange rate.

Exercises

(i)   Use the IS/LM/BP model to examine the effect of fiscal expansion under fixed exchange rates (a) when capital is completely immobile (vertical BP curve) and (b) when capital is perfectly mobile (horizontal BP).

(ii) Contrast the results of (i) with those in the text for monetary expansion in these two cases.

(iii) Derive equation [11.9] from Table 6.1, using column (a), rows (4) and (5), and column (d).

(iv) In the MAB explain carefully what happens if, from some initial equilibrium in the balance of payments, the government tightens monetary policy (a) in a very small, very open economy and (b) in a medium-sized open economy.

Further reading

A useful textbook exposition of most of the balance of trade and payments theory is given in Williamson and Milner (1991, Chapters 11–13). On the monetary approach Johnson (1972) is still worth reading.

Chapter 12

The open economy under flexible exchange rates

The aim of this chapter is to consider the implications of openness with flexible exchange rates for the basic macroeconomic relationships. In order to do this it is necessary to examine briefly the various theories as to how (flexible) exchange rates are determined, but it is convenient to start by analysing the effect of a change in a fixed exchange rate. Conventionally, the latter is discussed in terms of the possibility that exchange rate changes may modify the constraint imposed on macroeconomic policy by the openness of an economy in a Keynesian framework, but here it is of interest also for its implications for the workings of fully flexible exchange rates. The chapter starts therefore with Keynesian and monetary approach (MAB) analyses of devaluation, and proceeds via a brief survey of exchange rate determination to an examination of the implications of openness with flexible exchange rates for the basic macro relationships.

The elasticities approach to devaluation

The first strand in Keynesian thinking about devaluation is the elasticities approach. The institutional context which is relevant here is the international monetary system set up at the Bretton Woods conference of 1944; this involved fixed exchange rates which could in principle be changed in certain circumstances, that is the government could decide to fix the rate at e_1 instead of e_0 in Figure 12.1, which reproduces Figure 11.1. Now in that figure it is clear that a depreciation (increase in e) or devaluation (increase in the fixed parity for e) from e_0 to e_1 reduces the balance-of-payments deficit (increases $B + K$): with demand at D_1^{FX} the overall balance-of-payments deficit falls from $q_0 q_2$ to zero. However, this does not occur in every possible case. Figure 12.2 reproduces the S^{FX} curve of Figure 12.1 as S_a^{FX} but also includes another curve S_b^{FX} which slopes downwards from left to right and is flatter than D^{FX}. At e_0 for either supply curve the deficit is $q_0 q_1$. However, at e_1, while on the S_a^{FX} curve the deficit is zero, that on curve S_b^{FX} is $q_2 q_3 > q_0 q_1$: in other words devaluation in the S_b^{FX} case *increases* the deficit (reduces $B + K$). Moreover, the

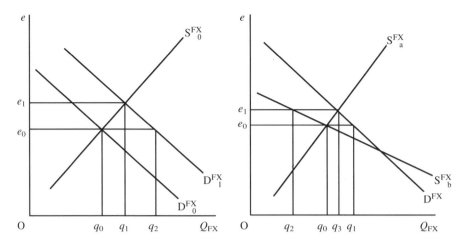

Figure 12.1   **Figure 12.2**

S_b^{FX} case cannot be excluded on logical or *a priori* grounds: the curve shows the capital inflow plus the proceeds of exports (total revenue or price times quantity) at each exchange rate and from elementary supply and demand analysis it is clear that a fall in the price of exports in foreign currency (due to a devaluation of the exchange rate) could increase or reduce the proceeds, depending on whether the demand for them is elastic or inelastic.

The elasticities approach to devaluation is essentially a way of identifying which case is relevant, that is whether a devaluation will or will not increase B in a particular situation (the capital account is assumed to be unchanged). The most important result from this approach, derived on the simplifying assumptions that the domestic and foreign elasticities of supply are infinite and that the initial balance of trade is zero, is the Marshall–Lerner condition:

$$\frac{\Delta B}{\Delta e} > 0 \text{ iff } | \eta_H + \eta_F | > 1, \tag{12.1}$$

that is the balance of trade increases following a devaluation ($\Delta e > 0$) if and only if ('iff') the sum of the domestic elasticity of demand for imports η_H and the foreign elasticity of demand for imports (that is for the devaluing country's exports) η_F is greater than one.

The derivation of this result (and the more complex Robinson–Metzler condition which allows for non-infinite supply elasticities) led to a series of empirical studies designed to obtain estimates of the relevant demand elasticities in order to ascertain whether the condition was likely to be fulfilled or not. By now the results of such studies indicate that except over very short periods (when economic agents do not have time to adjust their behaviour) such conditions are likely to be fulfilled, but in the 1950s the evidence was much less clear-cut and its ambiguity was one of the factors that led to the development of the absorption approach.

The absorption approach to devaluation

The elasticities approach is thought of as one of the strands of Keynesian thinking on the balance of payments, but it fits rather uneasily in this category. It makes no allowance for changes in national income caused by devaluation and the associated changes in demand, but concentrates entirely on the effects on demand of the devaluation-induced change in relative prices. It therefore has no macroeconomic dimension and is a *partial* equilibrium analysis. The absorption approach on the other hand is much closer to Keynesian macroeconomics and was originally presented as avoiding the need for specific estimates of the relevant elasticities (though this claim has since been shown to be incorrect). It begins by rearranging the equilibrium condition for national income,

$$Y = C + I + G + X - F,$$

and defining absorption A as $C + I + G$, so that

$$B = X - F = Y - A, \qquad\qquad [12.2]$$

that is the balance of trade is equal to (and is assumed to be determined by) the amount of goods and services produced domestically Y *minus* the amount consumed domestically A. The change in the balance of trade from a devaluation B can then be obtained as the change in output ΔY *minus* the change in absorption ΔA:

$$\Delta B = \Delta Y - \Delta A \qquad\qquad [12.3]$$

The absorption approach then involves analysing a number of direct effects from devaluation on output and absorption, together with the associated indirect (induced) effects on absorption and output respectively. The two most important of these effects are: (i) the 'idle resources effect' which is the increase in output that results from the switching of (domestic and foreign) demand from foreign output to domestic output in response to the improvement in the competitiveness of domestic output caused by the devaluation; and (ii) the 'cash balances effect' which is the reduction in absorption that results from the efforts of economic agents to restore the real value of their money balances (which has been reduced by the increase in the price level brought about by the devaluation) – this can take the form of a direct real balance effect as firms and households reduce their investment and consumption in order to restore their real balances, or it can involve an indirect effect if they try to restore them by selling financial assets such as bonds, thereby reducing the price of bonds and raising the interest rate, which in turn brings about a reduction in investment.

The absorption approach provides a framework for analysing the effects of devaluation. Its most important implications are that devaluation is more likely to increase the balance of trade if there is a large idle resources effect (the size of the effect depends on the amount of unemployed resources but also on the relevant elasticities of demand); and that the increase in the balance of trade can be assisted by direct policy measures to reduce absorption (reinforcing the cash balances effect by contractionary fiscal or monetary policy), this being particularly important if devaluation occurs at a time of full employment when output cannot increase.

The wage response to devaluation

Both of these approaches were put forward within the fixed price level framework of early Keynesian economics, but as Chapter 10 indicated the money-wage rigidity of that period was superseded by the real wage resistance or target real wage hypothesis. In that case since devaluation raises import prices it sets off an increase in money wages to compensate, which entails further rises in the general price level.

Suppose that money wages rise so as to compensate fully for price increases, and that prices are determined by a proportional mark-up on costs as in equation [10.2] so that the rate of increase in prices is a weighted average of the rates of increase of import and labour costs (equation [10.3]):

$$\dot{P} = \alpha \dot{F} + \beta \dot{W}, \quad \alpha + \beta = 1 \tag{12.4}$$

Suppose for simplicity that import prices rise by the proportion of the devaluation $\dot{e} = \Delta e/e = x$, that is $\dot{F} = x$. The first-round impact on the general price level (before wages react) is therefore

$$\dot{P}_1 = \alpha x$$

Money wages then rise at this rate (αx) to compensate for the price increase, so that there is a second-round impact on the price level from the wage increase (obtained by substituting $\dot{W} = \alpha x$ and $\dot{F} = 0$ in [12.4] as follows:

$$\dot{P}_2 = \beta(\alpha x)$$

However, this leads to a further rise in money wages of $\beta \alpha x$, and a further rise in prices:

$$\dot{P}_3 = \beta(\beta \alpha x)$$

This process is repeated with price and wage increases in each round becoming smaller and smaller (since $\beta < 1$). In the long run the total cumulative impact on the price level is

$$
\begin{aligned}
\dot{P} &= \dot{P}_1 + \dot{P}_2 + \dot{P}_3 + \dot{P}_4 + \ldots \\
&= \alpha x + \beta \alpha x + \beta^2 \alpha x + \beta^3 \alpha x + \ldots \\
&= \alpha x \{1 + \beta + \beta^2 + \beta^3 + \ldots\}
\end{aligned}
\tag{12.5}
$$

The expression in the curly brackets on the right-hand side of [12.5] is a geometric progression whose value is $1/(1 - \beta)$. Substituting this into [12.5] gives

$$\dot{P} = \alpha x \cdot \frac{1}{1-\beta} = \alpha x \cdot \frac{1}{\alpha} = x \qquad [12.6]$$

What this means is that when the wage response is incorporated into the analysis the long-term effect on the price level is to raise it by the full amount of the devaluation, in which case the long-term change in competitiveness is zero. In terms of the elasticities approach the long-term effect on the balance of trade is therefore zero. In the absorption approach there is no long-term idle resources effect while the cash balance effect is strengthened by the (now larger) rise in the price level; however, the effect is (still) likely to be temporary since the increase in the price level is a once-off rather than a continuing process.

The incorporation of a wage response in line with the real wage resistance hypothesis therefore has major results for the Keynesian analysis. It means that exchange rate changes cannot be regarded as a useful policy instrument for altering the balance of trade, for in the long term devaluation does not affect the balance of trade and only promotes inflation. Thus the elasticities and absorption approaches and the long and lively controversy between them have become largely irrelevant.

The MAB approach to devaluation

To analyse devaluation in the MAB case it is necessary to modify equations [11.15] and [11.17] by allowing the exchange rate to vary. From [11.12],

$$\Delta P = e\Delta P^* + P^*\Delta e + \Delta e\Delta P^* \qquad [12.7]$$

Dividing through by $P = eP^*$ and ignoring the third term on the right-hand side on the grounds that it is relatively very small, it is possible to obtain

$$\frac{\Delta P}{P} = \frac{e\Delta P^*}{eP^*} + \frac{P^*\Delta e}{eP^*} = \frac{\Delta P^*}{P^*} + \frac{\Delta e}{e} \qquad [12.8]$$

Substituting [12.8] and [11.13] into [11.15] and then into [11.11] gives

$$\frac{\Delta M_d}{M_d} = \bar{g} + \frac{\Delta P^*}{P^*} + \frac{\Delta e}{e}$$

$$\frac{\Delta FA}{M_s} = \bar{g} + \frac{\Delta P^*}{P^*} + \frac{\Delta e}{e} - \frac{DCE}{M_s} \qquad [12.9]$$

Strictly speaking equation [12.9] refers to continuous growth rates of the variables concerned, while devaluation is a discrete jump in the exchange rate, but it suggests that a devaluation $(\Delta e/e > 0)$ increases the balance-of-payments surplus. However, examination of the derivation of [12.9] makes clear that the devaluation (rise in e) works only by causing an equivalent rise in domestic prices so as to restore the purchasing power parity relationship between domestic and world prices, that is $P = eP^*$. In turn this implies that the effect of devaluation on the balance of payments is merely temporary; the balance increases because devaluation raises domestic prices and therefore the demand for money, but once prices have made the upward adjustment and the supply of money has increased proportionally through a temporary balance-of-payments surplus, there is no further or lasting effect on the balance of payments. This MAB result, that devaluation produces a balance-of-payments surplus but only temporarily, and that its main effect is to raise the domestic price level, is comparable to (and historically preceded) the Keynesian wage-response result discussed above, though different mechanisms are involved in the two cases: prices rise in the MAB case because of competitiveness or market integration effects; in the Keynesian case because of the response of wages to the import price rise. Finally, in a medium-sized open economy where the extreme assumptions are not appropriate, devaluation again causes a rise in domestic prices and a temporary improvement in the balance of payments, but the price rise and the improvement may be spread over a longer period.

The determination of flexible exchange rates

A convenient starting point for the the Keynesian analysis of exchange rate determination is the model of Figure 12.1: as explained in Chapter 11, while the shift of the D^{FX} curve from D_0^{FX} to D_1^{FX} causes a balance-of-payments deficit under fixed exchange rates, it causes an increase in the exchange rate as defined here (that is, a depreciation) from e_0 to e_1 under flexible rates. Indeed, anything that causes a shift in either of the curves can be regarded as causing a change in the exchange rate, though the direction of the change will depend on whether the appropriate elasticity conditions are met. Here it will be assumed that these conditions are met, that is, a balance-of-payments deficit occurs when the exchange rate as defined is less than, rather than greater than, the equilibrium rate. In this case, an expansionary fiscal or monetary policy, for example, would increase imports, shift D^{FX} to the right and depreciate the exchange rate.

This can be analysed more rigorously in the IS/LM/BP model introduced in the previous chapter. For present purposes a full analysis is not necessary but some simple conclusions can be drawn. Firstly, when there is zero capital mobility the BP line is vertical as in Figure 12.3: it should now be thought of as indicating the combinations of income and the interest rate at which the exchange rate is constant. From an initial position of Y_0, a shift of the IS curve or the LM curve to the right increases income and imports and this brings about a depreciation. The depreciation shifts the IS curve further to the right as demand switches towards domestic output and (provided the elasticities conditions are met) shifts BP to the right also, and the new equilibrium occurs where IS and BP intersect on the LM curve. The depreciation-induced shifts of BP and IS to the right ensure that income rises more here than in the fixed exchange rate case; in effect the import leakage has been eliminated.

Secondly, when capital is mobile the BP curve becomes upward sloping; points to the 'south-east' of the curve involve depreciation, points to the 'north-west' appreciation. The same sort of analysis can be used to show that monetary policy is more powerful than under fixed exchange rates, but this is no longer necessarily true for fiscal policy (it depends on the relative slopes of LM and BP). When capital is perfectly mobile, however, the BP curve is horizontal as in Figure 12.4. Here a rightwards shift of the IS curve pushes up the interest rate and causes a capital inflow and appreciation, such that the IS curve is pushed back to its original position. A rightwards shift of LM on the other hand pushes the interest rate down and causes a capital outflow and depreciation so that the IS curve moves to the right as well. Thus the equilibrium is determined here by the intersection of the LM and BP curves, with the exchange rate adjusting so that the IS curve shifts to the left or right as required. With flexible rates then, the dominant element in the IS/LM/BP model is the LM curve (the money supply is exogenous), while the IS curve and the BP curve (unless capital is perfectly mobile) depend on the exchange rate.

In a similar way the MAB can be transformed into a theory of exchange rate determination. Flexible rates mean that there is no intervention in the foreign exchange market so that $\Delta FA = 0$. Thus from equation [12.9],

$$\frac{\Delta FA}{M_s} = \bar{g} + \frac{\Delta P^*}{P^*} + \frac{\Delta e}{e} - \frac{DCE}{M_s}$$

$$0 = \bar{g} + \frac{\Delta P^*}{P^*} + \frac{\Delta e}{e} - \frac{DCE}{M_s}$$

$$\frac{\Delta e}{e} = \frac{DCE}{M_s} - \bar{g} - \frac{\Delta P^*}{P^*} \qquad\qquad [12.10]$$

Equation [12.10] says that the rate of depreciation varies positively with DCE and negatively with productivity growth and world inflation. The underlying mechanism here is that domestic monetary policy determines the domestic rate of inflation (as in the quantity theory) and then the exchange rate adjusts to keep domestic and world prices in line: from equation [12.8],

$$\frac{\Delta e}{e} = \frac{\Delta P}{P} - \frac{\Delta P^*}{P^*}$$

However, neither of these approaches can be regarded as adequate. The IS/

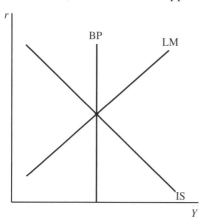

Figure 12.3

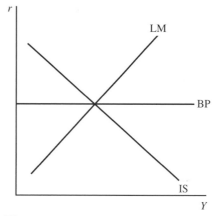

Figure 12.4

LM/BP model can incorporate capital movements, but it includes no impact from the exchange rate on the domestic price level. The MAB approach, on the other hand, depends heavily on purchasing power parity, for it is on that basis that the exchange rate adjusts. However, the evidence of recent years is that the exchange rate has a considerable impact on the price level but significant short-term deviations from purchasing power parity may occur.

Moreover, neither of these models deals properly with capital mobility under flexible exchange rates. In the fixed exchange rate models of Chapter 11 and the flexible rates models discussed so far in this chapter, the capital inflow is assumed to be related to the differential between domestic and world interest rates (equation [11.7]):

$$K = \mu(r - r^*), \quad 0 < \mu \leqslant \infty \qquad [12.11]$$

In the IS/LM/BP model an upward-sloping BP curve reflects a positive but non-infinite value of μ, whereas with perfect capital mobility μ is infinite and capital moves so quickly that no interest rate differential can ever exist and $r = r^*$: this is the horizontal BP line case, and it is also the assumption made in the MAB. However, if exchange rates are not completely fixed, equation [12.11] is inappropriate: investors are interested in the rates of return on financial assets denominated in different currencies *including any change in the value of the currency*. The choice between holding US and UK government bonds, for example, depends not only on the relevant yields but also on the expected depreciation of sterling. This suggests that capital flows should respond to the difference between the interest rate differential and the expected depreciation of the domestic currency:

$$K = \mu'(r - r^* - \dot{e}^e) \qquad [12.12]$$

where $\dot{e}^e$ is the expected depreciation ($\dot{e} = \Delta e / e$). With perfect capital mobility there is continuous equilibrium in the capital markets; this means that the contents of the brackets in [12.12] are always equal to zero, that is

$$r = r^* + \dot{e}^e \qquad [12.13]$$

Equation [12.12] represents what is often called 'uncovered interest parity' (where 'uncovered' refers to the fact that investors are not covering themselves against possible exchange rate change through the forward or futures market for foreign exchange). It is the starting point for the models of the 'asset market approach' to exchange rate determination on which recent work has concentrated. This approach involves modelling the exchange rate as the price of a financial asset (foreign currency) determined in ways comparable to those in which the prices of other financial assets such as bonds are determined, rather than as determined by balance-of-payments flows. Typically models of this sort specify the sensitivity of capital flows μ' and the (rational) determination of exchange rate expectations $\dot{e}^e$, they assume purchasing power parity in the long run but not the short run, and they incorporate at least some elements of a wider model of aggregate demand and supply. There is no space to discuss individual models here but two key points are worth making.

The first is that changes in exchange rate expectations, caused perhaps by changes in expectations about future monetary policy, can be independent causes of change in the exchange rate: the latter therefore reacts sensitively to all sorts of 'news' which affects expectations. The second is that where capital mobility is high (μ' is infinite or near-infinite) but the goods and services markets are sluggish, these models typically predict an *overshooting* of the exchange rate in response to a change in monetary policy: with financial markets flexible and financial prices adjusting rapidly but goods and services (especially labour) markets relatively inflexible and prices and wages adjusting slowly, the burden of a change in the money supply falls heavily in the short run on interest rates and hence on the exchange rate, which moves in the short run *beyond* its new long-term equilibrium value and then returns gradually to that value. If, for example, an increase in domestic monetary growth causes the domestic interest rate r to fall below the world interest rate r^*, equation [12.13] can hold only if expected depreciation $\dot{e}^e$ is negative, that is only if the exchange rate is expected to appreciate; but that can occur only if the exchange rate immediately depreciates by more than it is expected to depreciate in the long run. An overshooting model of this kind, and some further discussion of the determination of the exchange rate, can be found in Chapter 18.

Macroeconomic implications

The first point to be made here is that once a wage response is included in the Keynesian analysis of devaluation, exchange rate changes do not get rid of the constraint imposed on macro policy by the openness of an economy under fixed exchange rates; instead exchange rate changes in the long run affect domestic prices rather than economic activity or the balance of payments, in this Keynesian analysis as well as in the MAB. Moreover, flexible rates (as opposed to changes in fixed parities) do not eliminate the constraints either, though they may change the way in which the constraints make themselves felt. In broad terms any policy measures which would create a balance-of-payments deficit under fixed rates will bring about the depreciation of a flexible rate and increase the rate of inflation. Thus what are balance-of-payments problems under fixed rates become inflation problems under flexible rates; and in some sense it is the fixed exchange rate situation which is the odd one out: policies which cause inflation in a closed economy may cause balance-of-payments deficits in open economies under fixed rates but they cause inflation in open economies under flexible rates. Thus fixing the exchange rate can be regarded as a way of fixing the domestic price level to the world price level and 'anchoring it' in a way that is not otherwise possible. Such a policy will not work, however, if it is accompanied by inappropriately expansionary macroeconomic policies (or strong, independent, domestic wage-push pressures).

A second point is that the relative power of fiscal and monetary policy under flexible exchange rates to influence domestic economic activity is nearer to the closed-economy situation. Since increases in the money supply cannot be 'exported' via balance-of-payments deficits under flexible rates, they impact more strongly on domestic economic activity, and the exogeneity of the money supply under flexible rates acts as a stronger dampener to the effects of fiscal policy: crowding out, in other words, is likely to be greater under flexible than under fixed rates. Moreover, the exchange rate turns out to operate as a strong transmission mechanism for the effect of money on nominal income: more or less all models of exchange rate determination predict that an increase in the money supply will result in a depreciation of the exchange rate and depreciation leads to an increase in the price level, so that an increase in the money supply causes a strong rise in prices and therefore nominal income (there may also be some temporary rise in real income from the temporary improvement in international competitiveness).

Conclusions and qualifications

It should be clear that in some respects an open economy with a flexible exchange rate operates like a closed economy; in particular, the money supply exerts a more powerful influence on the price level than under fixed exchange rates. However, the parallel should not be pushed too far. Flexible exchange rates do not eliminate the links between countries; they make them more complicated, particularly when capital is mobile. Moreover, exchange rates can move in 'exaggerated' ways which increase the shocks and disturbances to which economies are subject, as is shown both in the theoretical analyses of overshooting and in the experience of exchange rate volatility since 1973.

Exercises

(i)   What, if anything, do the mechanisms brought into operation by devaluation in the elasticities, absorption and MAB analyses have in common?
(ii) Use the IS/LM/BP model to examine the effect of a fiscal expansion under flexible exchange rates (a) when capital is completely immobile (vertical BP curve) and (b) when capital is perfectly mobile (horizontal BP).
(iii) Contrast the results of (ii) with those for monetary expansion in these two cases.

Further reading

The effects of devaluation and theories of exchange rate determination are discussed in Williamson and Milner (1991, Chapters 12 and 14). A more recent but more difficult survey of models of exchange rate determination is MacDonald and Taylor (1992).

Chapter 13

The current state of macroeconomics

At this stage of the book it should be useful to draw together the threads of the various analytical developments covered, and to return explicitly to the different schools of thought which were identified in Chapter 1 but have featured less prominently in most of the other chapters. This chapter therefore starts by outlining the development of macroeconomics in terms of schools of thought from the Keynesian–monetarist debates of the late 1960s and early 1970s up to the early 1980s. It summarises the position of the three main schools of thought at that time in terms of their versions of the aggregate demand/aggregate supply model. It then examines the development of macroeconomics since the mid-1980s, and locates the main current schools of thought in relation to the previous versions of the AD/AS model. The chapter concludes with some broader comments on the state of and prospects for macroeconomics.

Macroeconomics from the mid-1970s to the early 1980s

As was indicated in Chapter 1 most of the debates in macroeconomics in the 1960s and early 1970s were in some sense debates between Keynesianism and monetarism. The first strand of those debates related to the determinants of aggregate demand, where there were four main points at issue: the stability and interest-elasticity of the demand for money; the exogeneity of the supply of money; the existence and strength of the transmission mechanism from money to money income; and the existence and degree of the crowding out of private-sector expenditure by government expenditure. The second strand of the debates related to the causes of inflation – cost-push or expectations-augmented monetary demand –and to the appropriate policie – incomes policy or monetary discipline. A third element in the debates concerned the exchange rate regime preferred by each school: most (but not all) monetarists argued for flexible exchange rates and most (but not all) Keynesians for fixed exchange rates.

On each of these various issues the following decade saw a process of convergence between the views of some of the former members of the monetarist school and some of the former members of the Keynesian school, so that neither 'Keynesianism' nor 'monetarism' any longer represented a distinct school of thought in the way that it had done before. On the demand for money, the accumulation of empirical evidence ruled out the extreme cases of zero and infinite interest-elasticity, while the variations in velocity which seemed to have occurred in the early 1970s and again in the early 1980s were widely interpreted as specific shifts of, or short-run movements away from, otherwise stable demand functions rather than as instances of continuing instability. On the money supply the experience of a period of monetary targeting and explicit official attempts to control the money supply convinced many economists both that the money supply was not just endogenously determined by economic activity and/or inflation (or the balance of payments) and that monetary control was not an easy or straightforward undertaking.

While evidence of a significant interest-elasticity of investment continued to be elusive, other possible transmission mechanisms were identified: the (flexible) exchange rate as discussed in Chapter 12, expectations of inflation particularly in so far as they are directly ('rationally') affected by perceptions of government policy, and the real balance effect. The latter had been treated as a mere theoretical curiosum in the earlier period but empirical evidence and some analytical developments (notably that of 'buffer-stock money' gave it greater credibility. The debate on crowding out developed in a number of directions, the most important of which was that of the government budget constraint literature (discussed in Chapter 14), whose conclusions lent support to the original positions of neither Keynesians nor monetarists.

On the causation of inflation, the introduction of the target real-wage hypothesis eliminated the existence of money illusion as a point of contention between Keynesians and monetarists, and in some cases the predictions of this hypothesis were similar to those of the expectations-augmented Phillips curve. At the same time the insistence of monetarists that union push was non-existent and/or irrelevant and the insistence of Keynesians that excess demand was similarly non-existent and/or irrelevant were both weakened, while experience raised question-marks against both incomes policies and policies of pure monetary contraction. Finally, the experience of exchange rate flexibility since 1973 blunted the enthusiasm of some former advocates of flexible rates while Keynesians had to concede the improbability of a return to a Bretton Woods-type system of fixed rates in the foreseeable future.

In this way some Keynesians and some monetarists came together at least to some extent on all of the key issues which had divided them in the earlier period; they also converged in a number of other areas related to both theory and policy. Other Keynesians, however, reinforced their attachment to (some interpretation of) 'pure' Keynesianism: they remained deeply sceptical about price and wage flexibility and about the responsiveness of economic agents to the signals of the price mechanism; they conceded nothing to monetarism, and nothing to the Keynesian–neoclassical synthesis of the 1950s which they regarded as part of a process of 'corruption' of Keynes's original ideas.

On the other hand, other monetarists moved sharply in a different direction. The New Classical macroeconomics started from the use of a different (rational expectations) hypothesis about the formation of expectations and a different ('inverted supply curve') interpretation of the Phillips curve, and developed into a school which aimed to reconstruct the whole of macroeconomics on the basis of more explicit microeconomic foundations and complete price and wage flexibility. By means of new analytical and mathematical techniques and of what some economists would regard as audacious simplifications, it derived results which challenged not merely the traditional Keynesian predictions and policy recommendations but also the monetarism out of which New Classical macroeconomics itself developed.

The thinking of traditional Keynesians, the Keynesian–monetarist convergence and the New Classical school can be usefully illustrated through use of the AD/AS model.

Traditional Keynesianism

For traditional Keynesians the aggregate supply curve is horizontal up to the full employment level of national income Y_f and then vertical, as in Figure 13.1. The rationale for this relationship, as discussed in Chapter 8, involves a fixed money wage, constant marginal costs and a constant mark-up of prices over costs; thus the price level is fixed, at P_0 in Figure 13.1. There is imperfect competition between firms, and firms are not willing to lower their own price in

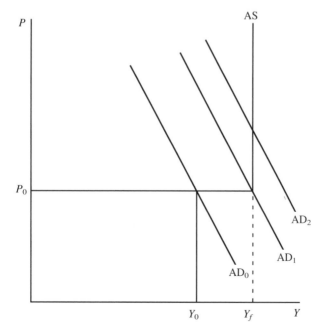

Figure 13.1

order to increase their own sales; instead of maximising profits by producing that output at which marginal cost equals marginal revenue, firms simply produce the output which they can sell at the existing fixed price level. There is therefore an effective demand constraint on individual firms' sales and output, which corresponds to the effective demand constraint on total output and which generates an effective demand constraint on firms' demand for labour: firms demand only that labour required to produce the output they expect to sell. At Y_f a physical constraint on productive resources is reached, no more output can be produced whatever the price, and the AS curve becomes vertical.

The traditional Keynesian aggregate demand curve, on the other hand, is relatively steep as in Figure 13.1. It can be thought of as derived from a Keynesian version of the IS–LM model with a relatively flat LM curve and a relatively steep IS curve, so that variations in the price level (shifts of the LM curve) cause little change in equilibrium income (aggregate demand). For the same reasons the *position* of the AD curve is dominated by expenditure factors and fiscal policy: the transmission mechanism is weak, and the degree of crowding out is low. The downward slope may also reflect changes in international competitiveness, with lower domestic prices improving competitiveness and therefore increasing net exports (exports *minus* imports).

The workings of the traditional Keynesian AD/AS model can be explored by considering first the effect of a shift of the AD curve from say AD_0 to AD_1 in Figure 13.1: this increases output from Y_1 to Y_f, thus restoring full employment, without raising prices, but any further shift of the AD curve to the right, say to AD_2, would raise prices instead of income because of the capacity constraint. Secondly, the effect of cost-push inflation can be analysed as an upwards shift in the AS curve from AS to AS_1 in Figure 13.2, caused by an increase in the money wage (with a constant mark-up): given a non-vertical AD curve this tends to reduce output to Y_1 but if the government is committed to maintaining full employment it boosts aggregate demand to AD_1 so that income remains at the full employment level.

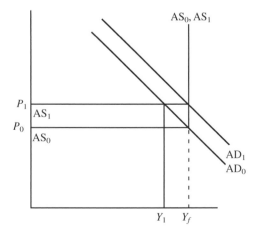

Figure 13.2

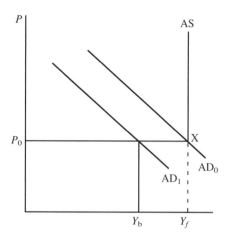

Figure 13.3

Traditional Keynesianism was developed mainly for the case of an open economy on a fixed exchange rate; indeed it can be argued that it did not properly confront the implications of flexible exchange rates. However, it takes very seriously what it perceives as the implication of fixed rates that there may be a conflict between the objectives of internal balance (which occurs at point X in Figure 13.3) and external balance, that is balance of trade or payments equilibrium. At the fixed price level P_0 and the existing (fixed) exchange rate, the income level where this equilibrium occurs may be Y_b in Figure 13.3: in this case the government can maintain demand at AD_0 and run a balance-of-payments deficit, or contract demand to AD_1 so that external balance is achieved. Alternatively, it can use some other instrument such as the exchange rate (providing the appropriate elasticity conditions are met and a wage response can be prevented) or import controls (tariffs or quotas) to shift Y_b so that it coincides with Y_f; then with an increase in aggregate demand to AD_0 (partly from the devaluation or import controls and partly from the use of fiscal policy) both objectives can be fulfilled at the same time.

Thus the typical policy recommendations of this school were as follows: the government should use fiscal policy to maintain full employment, together with an incomes policy to prevent inflation and an exchange rate change or import controls as required to prevent balance-of-payments deficits.

The Keynesian–monetarist convergence

For economists of the Keynesian–monetarist convergence there was a vertical long-run AS curve comparable to the classical AS curve of Chapter 8 and an upward-sloping short-run AS curve as in Figure 13.4; the latter is drawn for a fixed level of expected prices or of the money wage while the former is drawn on the assumption that both of these are fully adjusted to actual prices.

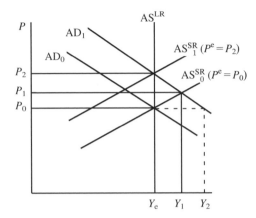

Figure 13.4

One way to understand this analysis is to relate the AD/AS model of Figure 13.4 to the expectations-augmented Phillips curve model of Chapter 8 and Figure 13.5: this needs to be done carefully since the latter refers to rates of change of wages and prices and the former to levels of wages and prices, but if care is taken it can be a useful exercise. The long-run Phillips curve is the combination of points at which actual inflation is equal to expected inflation; it is vertical at the natural rate of unemployment U_0. The long-run AS curve is the combination of points at which actual prices are equal to expected prices; it is vertical at the natural rate of output Y_e which corresponds to the classical labour market equilibrium L_e of Figure 8.2. Clearly Y_e and U_0 describe the same situation in terms of goods and labour markets. In the short run an expansion of demand (from a position of zero inflation) which reduces unemployment from U_0 to U_1 is associated with an increase in the growth of money wages from $\dot{W}_0 = g$ to $\dot{W}_1$; but at the point $(\dot{W}_1, U_1)$ actual inflation

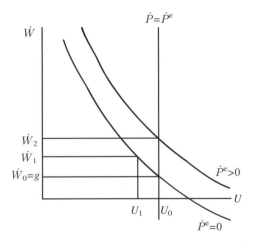

Figure 13.5

$(= \dot{W}_1 - g)$ is above expected inflation $(= 0)$ and expected inflation will rise, so that this is only a short-run, temporary, equilibrium. In the same way an expansion of aggregate demand from AD_0 to AD_1 in Figure 13.4 is associated with increases in output to Y_1 and in prices to P_1, but at (P_1, Y_1) the actual price level P_1 is greater than the expected price level P_0 (the level at which short-run aggregate supply coincides with long-run aggregate supply and AS^{SR} intersects AS^{LR}) so that expected prices will rise. The long-run equilibrium involves an upward shift of both the short-run constant-$\dot{P}^e$ Phillips curve and the short-run constant-P^e AS curve and the return of unemployment and output to their natural rates at points such as $(\dot{W}_2, u_0)$ and (P_2, Y_e).

A second way to understand the long-run/short-run aggregate supply analysis is in terms of the target real-wage hypothesis. Here the long-run AS curve shows the points at which the actual real wage is equal to the target real wage, while points to the right (left) of it are points where prices have risen (fallen) without the money wage adjusting to compensate, so that the actual real wage is below (above) the target level. Thus when aggregate demand increases, output expands in the short run along the AS^{SR} curve, but after a while the money wage rises to compensate for the price increase, the AS^{SR} curve shifts upwards and in the long run equilibrium is re-established at (P_2, Y_e) with the real wage at its original level.

It is important to note that in general, causation goes from aggregate demand to output and employment and thence to prices and wages in this analysis: in terms of Figure 13.4 the shift of aggregate demand from AD_0 to AD_1 causes an excess demand of $(Y_2 - Y_e)$ at the initial price level P_0; this leads to a rise in the price level in the short run to P_1; but at P_1 prices are above their expected level and/or the real wage is below its target level so that further adjustments take place which involve prices rising to P_2, where the original demand stimulus is totally absorbed in higher prices and no real stimulus remains. It should also be noted that while the general analysis is most obviously compatible with an adaptive mechanism of expectations formation it does not preclude changes in expectations of a more rational kind in response to perceptions of specific policy measures or other events; it does, however, deny that such effects are sufficiently continuous or strong to keep output for most of the time at Y_e.

For the convergence economists the AD curve is definitely non-vertical, as drawn in Figure 13.4; it is also not a rectangular hyperbola. It can best be thought of as derived from a moderate version of the IS–LM model supplemented by a real balance effect. Its position is affected by both fiscal and monetary policy and by both expenditure and monetary factors more generally.

The implicit context of the convergence model of AD/AS as discussed so far is that of a closed economy or an open economy with a flexible exchange rate (in the latter case exchange rate volatility, including the overshooting of the exchange rate in response to changes in monetary policy, may cause significant short-run fluctuations in net exports and hence aggregate demand). However, it is relatively straightforward to adapt it to the fixed exchange rate, open economy case. The main point here is that under fixed exchange rates the price level is determined primarily by world prices: this can be thought of in terms of a division of output into those goods and services that can be traded on international markets ('tradables'), whose price is set on those markets, and those goods and services that cannot be so traded ('non-tradables' such as restaurant and hairdressing services), whose price is determined by domestic demand and supply. The effect of this in the model is that the short-run AS curve does not shift: it always intersects the long-run AS curve at the overall price level where the price of non-tradables is in some sense in line with that of tradables. Both full employment (that is the natural rate of unemployment) and balance-of-payments equilibrium occur at Y_e so that there is no long-run conflict between internal and external balance, but in the short run variations in aggregate demand cause balance-of-payments deficits (to the right of AS^{LR}) or surpluses (to the left of AS^{LR}). These deficits or surpluses then cause reductions or increases in the money supply which shift the AD curve so that output returns to Y_e.

The workings of the model have already been explored to some extent, but there are two further points worth making. Firstly, although stimulating demand when the economy is at Y_e affects output only in the short run and affects only prices in the long run, when output is below the natural rate there *is* some scope for reflationary policies. In Figure 13.6 for example, at the initial position of (P_0, Y_0) expected prices and the money wage must be falling and the short-run AS curve must be shifting downwards: if the government wishes to see output restored to Y_e it could wait for this process to take its full course and

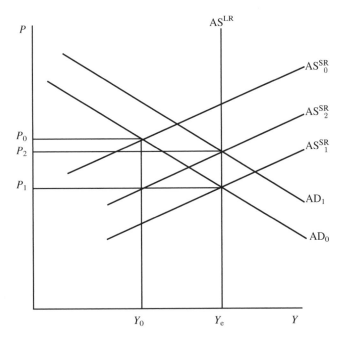

Figure 13.6

for the economy to return to (P_1, Y_e), but it could also speed it up by giving a limited stimulus to demand so that the economy moves to a position such as (P_2, Y_e). Secondly, it should be noted that for this school cost-push factors may exert short-run effects on money wages and prices which cause upward shifts of the short-run AS curve; the latter is expected, however, to adjust over time in the usual way unless the 'push' is renewed or accommodated by an increase in aggregate demand, so that the effect on prices (or inflation) is short-lived. In the long term prices and inflation are dominated by demand factors.

Finally, the policy recommendations of the Keynesian–monetarist convergence can be summarised as follows: monetary and fiscal policy should be used to keep output and employment near their natural rates without causing inflation by creating excess demand, while any initial inflation should be eliminated by a gradual tightening of aggregate demand which gives time for price expectations and money wages to adjust and avoids large fluctuations in employment. Gradualist policies of this sort, if pursued in each country, should also minimise the volatility of flexible exchange rates, while the avoidance of domestic excess demand should prevent balance-of-payments deficits under fixed rates. There is no place for import controls as an instrument of macro policy and no place for incomes policies of the usual kind, though it is conceivable that a new and permanent kind of incomes policy could contribute to the stabilisation of the economy, for example, by reducing the equilibrium real wage and raising the equilibrium levels of income and employment.

New Classical macroeconomics

For New Classical macroeconomists the primary AS curve is vertical. As with the vertical long-run AS curve of the convergence model or the classical AS curve, it can be derived from a model of the labour market in which supply and demand depend on the real wage and the real wage adjusts to clear the market.

However, in this case it is sometimes more convenient to derive it from a diagram of the labour market with money wages on the vertical axis as in Figure 13.7. Here the supply and demand curves are drawn for specific levels of prices; they slope upwards and downwards respectively in the normal way since for a given price level the real wage varies with the money wage; and they each shift up or down by the same amount for a change in prices. For example, when the price level is P_0 the relevant curves are S_0 and D_0, and equilibrium occurs at the money wage W_0 and the real wage W_0/P_0. If prices were P_1 any given amount of labour would be supplied only at an appropriately higher money wage, while the marginal revenue product of labour would be higher so that firms would be prepared to pay correspondingly more for the same amount of labour: S_1 and D_1 are therefore the same vertical distance above S_0 and D_0 and they intersect at W_1, where $W_1/P_1 = W_0/P_0$. Equilibrium in the labour market therefore occurs at L_e and the level of output Y_e at which the AS curve is vertical in Figure 13.8 is the output produced when L_e labour is employed.

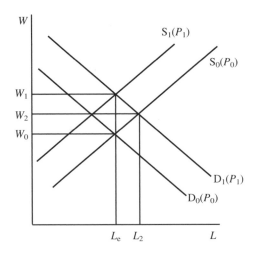

Figure 13.7

This analysis can be related to the expectations-augmented Phillips curve with rational expectations. Y_e in Figure 13.8 is the natural rate of output corresponding to U_0, the natural rate of unemployment in the Phillips curve analysis reproduced in Figure 13.9. And movements up and down the long-run vertical Phillips curve, on which expected inflation is always equal to actual inflation, correspond to movements up and down the AS curve of Figure 13.8, on which prices are always equal to their expected level: the economy moves up and down these curves because economic agents rationally (and correctly) anticipate government policy and therefore prices.

The AD curve in the New Classical model is flatter than that in the convergence model, as in Figure 13.8. It can best be thought of as derived from

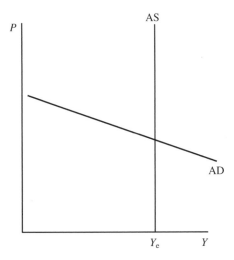

Figure 13.8

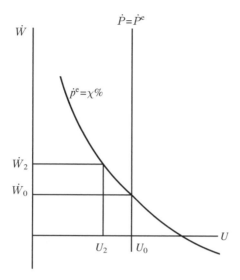

Figure 13.9

a monetarist version of the IS–LM model where the IS curve is relatively flat
and the LM curve is relatively steep, supplemented by a real balance effect and
other wealth effects (notably the effect of prices on the real value of non-money
financial assets and hence on expenditure), and modified by the use of rational
expectations for expected (or permanent) income in the consumption and
money demand functions. The position of the AD curve is not much affected
by fiscal policy because there is a high degree of crowding out, both the indirect
crowding out via the interest rate which was discussed in Chapter 7 above and
direct crowding out through what is called 'ultra-rationality', which involves
rational private-sector agents anticipating the future tax liabilities which result
from current budget deficits financed by the issue of bonds. Instead, the
position of the AD curve is dominated by monetary policy; there is a strong
transmission mechanism from money to money income involving interest rate,
real balance and other wealth effects.

This vertical AS curve was characterised above as the *primary* New Classical
AS curve, and it is the only AS curve which is relevant in the New Classical
model to the use of stabilisation policy: rational expectations involves
economic agents anticipating (correctly) the policy measures undertaken by
the government and their implications for prices (or inflation), so that actual
and expected prices (inflation) are equal. However, in the presence of other
'surprises' and 'shocks', rational expectations may not always be correct, and
in that case unemployment and output may depart temporarily from their
natural rates. In Figure 13.7, for example, if a demand shock of some kind
causes prices to rise from P_0 to P_1 and employers anticipate this but workers
do not, then the relevant curves are S_0 and D_1 and equilibrium occurs
(temporarily) at W_2 and L_2. Workers supply more labour because they do not

realise that prices have risen and therefore think that the real wage is higher when the money wage is W_2. Employers employ more labour because the money wage has risen by less than prices so that the real wage has fallen. Thus L_2 labour is employed and Y_2 output is produced in Figure 13.10: output expands along a secondary AS curve, the upwards-sloping AS ^{surprise} function. This movement corresponds to the movement along a short-run Phillips curve drawn for a fixed rate of expected inflation, as in Figure 13.9.

It should be noted that the Phillips curve is being interpreted here as an 'inverted supply curve', that is, as showing how labour supply responds to wages, while the AS ^{surprise} curve shows how output responds to prices. This is very different from the alternative 'disequilibrium' interpretation of the Phillips curve discussed above for the convergence model, where wages and prices are regarded as responding to (excess) demand (see Chapter 15 for further discussion).

It should also be noted that the labour market model of Figure 13.7 can be used to discuss the determinants of the natural rate of unemployment. For example, the level of unemployment benefits which workers can obtain when out of work can be considered as setting a floor to the supply curve, on the grounds that workers are willing to work only for a wage which is significantly above the benefit level. In Figure 13.11 the supply curve S_0 shows the supply of labour when benefits are B_0; but if benefits are raised to B_1, supply shifts to S_1 and the equilibrium amount of labour employed falls from L_0 to L_1. It is factors like this together with some aspects of the alleged behaviour of trade unions which are typically stressed by New Classical macroeconomists when analysing variations in the actual rate of unemployment, which they interpret mainly as movements in the natural rate of unemployment.

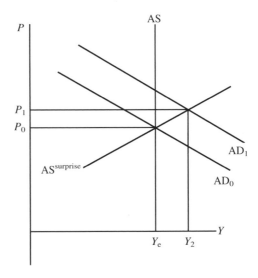

Figure 13.10

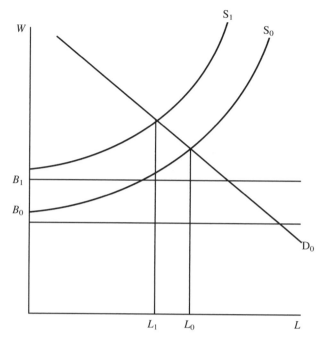

Figure 13.11

New Classical macroeconomics is generally expounded in the context of a closed economy or an open economy with a flexible exchange rate, and this is the policy regime strongly preferred by its exponents. For an open economy on a fixed exchange rate the analysis would have to be adapted: with a fixed exchange rate the prices of internationally tradable goods and services are exogenously determined (on world markets) so that a strong element of price inflexibility has to be incorporated into the model. The effect is to bring the New Classical model much closer to that of the convergence model discussed in the previous section.

Enough has already been said about the workings of the New Classical AD/AS model: essentially, stabilisation policy which shifts the AD curve causes movements in prices, not output, since it is the vertical AS curve which is relevant here; and inflation is strictly a monetary demand phenomenon rather than a cost-push one. Finally, the typical policy recommendations of the New Classical school can be summarised as follows: the government should use monetary policy to prevent inflation, while any initial inflation should be reduced rapidly by an immediate and non-gradualist reduction in monetary growth, since expectations can be expected to adjust rapidly and there should therefore be no significant cost in terms of unemployment or lost output; benefit levels and trade union legislation should be manipulated to influence the supply of (and the demand for) labour so as to promote employment; and the exchange rate should be allowed to float freely.

Macroeconomics since the mid-1980s

In the period since the mid-1980s the traditional Keynesian school has all but vanished, in Europe (where it was always stronger) as well as in the US. Its place has been taken to some extent by a younger generation of 'Post-Keynesian' economists who have devoted much of their effort to 'rediscovering' Keynes's own ideas and have laid great emphasis on unavoidable uncertainty and other obstacles to the smooth functioning of the price mechanism. However, a larger and more influential grouping, also from a younger generation, is that of the 'New Keynesian' economists who have set out to construct microfoundations, particularly models which incorporate conventional assumptions of utility and profit maximisation but predict some inflexibility of prices and/or wages, in order to provide an underlying justification for longstanding Keynesian notions of how the macroeconomy works (New Keynesian ideas are discussed in more detail in Chapter 19).

The New Classical macroeconomists remain important, but they have not come to dominate macroeconomics in the way that some observers and participants of earlier debates had expected. One reason is that they have found it difficult to explain why economies in which markets clear perfectly exhibit more or less regular fluctuations in economic activity (see Chapter 19). At the same time some of their ideas have been challenged with at least partial success by the New Keynesian school, while other ideas that were originally New Classical – notably rational expectations – have been absorbed (with some qualifications) by an eclectic mainstream group of macroeconomists which developed out of the Keynesian–monetarist convergence (another phenomenon which was always stronger in Europe) and more generally from non-traditional Keynesians and non-New Classical monetarists. This Mainstream group is differentiated from the New Classical school by its insistence that some markets often clear only imperfectly, and from the New Keynesians (on whose models it sometimes draws) by its focus on the conventional and policy concerns of macroeconomics.

Most contemporary debate between schools of thought is therefore between the New Classical view that divergences from the natural rates of output and unemployment are relatively few, random and short-lived, and a Mainstream (and to some extent New Keynesian) view that such deviations can, despite the underlying rationality of expectations and the long-term self-equilibrating properties of market economies, be more common, regular and lasting. In terms of the AD/AS model the New Classical view has already been expounded; in this later period supply side shocks to the AS curve should perhaps be given more importance. The Mainstream view, on the other hand, can be represented by a modified convergence-type AD/AS model in which expectations are sufficiently rational and elastic to move the short-run AS curve up and down rather more quickly, but in which expectations are often not sufficiently accurate for deviations from the natural rate to be merely ephemeral aberrations. At the same time, as in the convergence view, the underlying vision is of prices and wages being set by fallible economic agents in response to movements in demand and other variables, rather than of agents responding with their supply decisions to prices and wages automatically set at some equilibrium, market-clearing level by some pure market mechanism.

Comments and qualifications

This chapter itself provides a conclusion to Part One of the book, and therefore needs no conclusion of its own. However, a few brief comments and qualifications should be made on the above account of the main schools of thought in current macroeconomics.

First, the differences between these schools have been identified entirely in terms of their (positive) perceptions of how the economy works, without reference to any differences in their (normative) views of what are the appropriate objectives of macro policy. In conventional expositions the objectives of policy are listed as full employment, price stability, external equilibrium (meaning equilibrium on the balance of payments under fixed exchange rates and stability of the real exchange rate under flexible rates) and economic growth (though the latter is increasingly regarded as a question of micro rather than macro policy). At this stage it is more important to understand the differences in the constraints on achieving these objectives which the various schools see in the workings of the economy and this book has therefore concentrated on these differences, but it should be noted that there may also be important differences between the schools in the weights they attach to each of the objectives of macro policy.

Second, it should be emphasised that the exercise of identifying schools of thought in the way that has been done here inevitably involves some simplification: there are some important differences *within* the schools, particularly perhaps within the Mainstream school, and the division into schools is not of course immutable. Students who pursue their studies of macroeconomics further will become more aware of these differences and will come to see the extent of the simplification made here. But if that simplification has provided a framework and a structure which help students to understand the controversies on which this book has focused, it will have served a useful purpose.

Third, what can be said about the current relative strengths of the various schools of thought? The Post-Keynesians remain a small and perhaps misunderstood (though hardly persecuted) sect, whose lack of influence may owe as much to their somewhat introverted outlook as to the strength or weakness of their intrinsic arguments. The New Keynesians have had some notable successes in creating partial equilibrium models of markets which do not clear perfectly, quickly or even efficiently, but they have had rather less to say on the conventional concerns of macroeconomics. The New Classical macroeconomists have probably failed to fulfil their original promise and intention of revolutionising (or counter revolutionising) macroeconomics, but they remain highly influential, especially in North America. Lastly, what might be called the 'centre ground' of macroeconomics has undergone a remarkable revival in the form of what has been referred to here as the Mainstream school, which has been able to absorb key elements from other schools while retaining its basic attachment to imperfect market-clearing.

At the same time, macroeconomics is perhaps becoming less factionalised in the 1990s than it was in earlier decades. One sign of this is that many of the main policy debates, e.g. over European monetary union, are largely debates within the Mainstream rather than between schools. Such a development, if it is genuine, must surely be welcome after the unproductive heat generated by some of the earlier debates. It may also be a sign of the (overdue) maturing of macroeconomics (it should be noted that microeconomists have not shown the same tendency to polarise in schools in recent decades). On the other hand, there are still many controversies to be resolved, and ones which concern fundamental issues such as the determination of the NAIRU and the macroeconomic implications of financial structures.

Exercises

Students should check their understanding of the AD/AS model by working through the following questions:

(i)   Explain how different sloped AD curves are derived from different views on the magnitude of the parameters in the IS–LM model and on the strength of real balance effects.
(ii)   Analyse the effect of a deflationary fiscal and monetary policy in the three versions of the AD/AS model given in this chapter.
(iii)   Suppose the government wishes to reduce prices (the static analogue of reducing inflation): for the Mainstream and New Classical schools, examine on what factors the unemployment cost involved in reducing prices depends.

Further reading

The nature and extent of the Keynesian–monetarist convergence are explored in more detail in Cobham (1984). Klamer (1984) contains some fascinating, though now rather dated, interviews on the state of macroeconomics with a variety of US economists. Vercelli and Dimitri (1992) contains a range of interesting papers, of which the more accessible and relevant are by Leijonhufvud, Stiglitz, Phelps, McCallum and Laidler. Chick (1995) contains a defence of, and further references to, Post-Keynesian economics. See also the references in Chapter 19.

Part 2

Chapter 14

The IS–LM model with a government budget constraint

The last section of Chapter 7 referred to further developments in the IS–LM model including the subject of the 'government budget constraint'. This literature originated at least in part in the Keynesian–monetarist debate with the monetarist claim that fiscal policy was largely impotent because any rise in government expenditure would crowd out private sector expenditure, except insofar as fiscal expansion brought about an accompanying monetary expansion. However, the discussion soon went beyond the simple confines of that debate, becoming dominated by more technical arguments rather than Keynesian–monetarist attitudes, and it pushed both sides of that debate to shift their ground. The present analysis is confined to the context of a closed economy and concentrates on the key issue of the contrast between 'money-financed' and 'bond-financed' increases in government expenditure. Conventional or moderate slopes of IS and LM are assumed because the emphasis is on other matters.

Definitions and starting points

The results which follow are derived from particular assumptions within a clearly specified framework, which it is important to set out in advance. First, the 'government budget constraint' is simply the constraint that government expenditure has to be paid for either out of tax revenue or out of government borrowing of some kind. More precisely, the difference between expenditure and revenue (i.e. the budget deficit) must be financed by some combination of borrowing from the private sector, via issues of bonds, and borrowing from the banking sector (central bank plus commercial banks), which implies increases in the supply of money. Formally this can be written as

$$P(G - T) = \Delta M + \frac{\Delta B}{r}$$

where P is the price level, G and T are government expenditure and tax revenue, ΔM is the increase in the supply of money, r is the market interest rate and $\Delta B/r$ is the increase in the stock of bonds. Bonds are assumed to be non-redeemable, for simplicity, and to be issued in units such that each bond pays a coupon of 1 per annum. Thus B is both the number of bonds and the total amount of interest payments payable each year, $1/r$ is the price of a single bond (see equation [5.7] above), and B/r is the total value of the stock of bonds outstanding. Given the IS–LM context, the price level is assumed to be fixed and units for the price index are chosen so that $P = 1$. Government expenditure is assumed to be fixed, while tax revenue is assumed to be partly autonomous $(\overline{T})$ and partly dependent on income (tY). Thus the constraint can be written as

$$G - T = \Delta M + \frac{\Delta B}{r}, \quad \text{where} \quad T = \overline{T} + tY. \tag{14.1}$$

The key implication of this constraint is that, whenever and so long as the government's budget is not balanced, there must be a change in one direction or the other in the money supply and/or the stock of bonds.

Secondly, two wealth effects are considered here. The wealth of the private sector (W) can be seen as the sum of the capital stock (K), the stock of bonds and the supply of money:

$$W = K + B/r + M \tag{14.2}$$

Both consumption (as in the Pigou effect) and money demand are assumed to vary positively with wealth:

$$C = C(Y_d, W), \quad \frac{\partial C}{\partial W} > 0$$

$$M_d = M_d(Y, r, W), \quad \frac{\partial M_d}{\partial W} > 0 \tag{14.3}$$

such that an increase in wealth raises consumption at each level of income and therefore shifts the IS curve to the right; an increase in wealth also raises money demand and therefore shifts the LM curve to the left. There is no *a priori* theoretical reason for supposing that either one of these effects is greater than the other, but as will become obvious shortly different results hold in each case. The capital stock K is assumed to be constant, and all wealth effects are due to rises in money or bonds.

Thirdly, it is convenient here to distinguish between three different time periods: the very short run (VSR) which includes the immediate effects of, say, an increase in government expenditure and any associated change in money or bonds, the short run (SR) which also includes the wealth effects from any change in money or bonds, and the long run (LR) which is the eventual position where the government's budget is once again balanced so that there is no further ongoing change in money or bonds taking place. It should be obvious that the SR/VSR distinction is a notional rather than a chronological one.

Fourthly, the discussion is concerned with the effect of an increase in government spending where the resulting deficit is covered either by an increase in money or an issue of bonds, and where the government decides in advance how to finance its deficits and then sticks to that decision.

Model 1: The government budget constraint without wealth effects

Consider first the case of a 'bond-financed' increase in government expenditure, that is an increase in G where any resulting budget deficit will be financed by an issue of bonds (and any surplus would be used to redeem bonds). In the top part of Figure 14.1 the increase in G causes a shift from IS_0 to IS_1, while the issue of bonds in this case (where there are no wealth effects) does not shift the IS or LM curves (although interest rates rise as the economy moves up the LM curve, because nominal bond prices have to fall as the private sector has to be offered better yields to persuade it to hold more bonds). The lower part of Figure 14.1 shows government expenditure (which is autonomous) and tax revenue (which is partly income-related) and hence the deficit/surplus as the vertical distance between the two. While initially the budget was balanced at Y_0, G has now risen from G_0 to G_1, total tax revenue has risen to some extent with income, but overall there is now a deficit since G exceeds T by the amount ab. Thus in the short run or very short run (there is no difference here) income rises to Y_1 and there is a budget deficit. This means that in the next 'round' the government must issue more bonds to cover its deficit. However, the issue of bonds again has no effect on IS or LM and the economy stays at Y_1 (although this is not strictly a long-run equilibrium in the sense defined above).

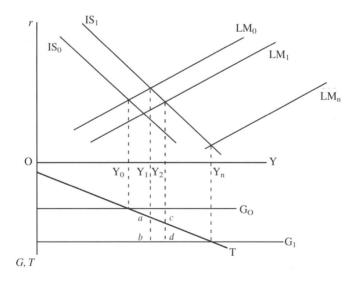

Figure 14.1

Now consider the case of a 'money-financed' increase in government expenditure, that is an increase in G with any deficit covered by an increase in money (or any surplus used to withdraw money from circulation). The increase in G shifts the IS curve as before, but now the increase in money shifts the LM curve from LM_0 to LM_1, so that in the short run/very short-run income rises to Y_2. Note that Y_2 must be greater than (to the right of) Y_1 because LM has shifted as well as IS: in other words a money financed increase in G must have a more powerful effect on income in the short run than a bond-financed increase, because of the greater crowding out of private-sector investment through the induced rise in the interest rate in the bond-financed case. However, the budget will still be in deficit to the extent cd, and this means that in the next 'round' the government must borrow from the banking sector and increase the money supply again, so that LM shifts further to the right. Indeed, this will happen in every round up to the point where income and therefore taxes have risen sufficiently for the budget to be balanced once more, at LM_n and Y_n. In the long run, therefore, a money-financed increase in G is much more powerful than a bond-financed increase.

The long-run multipliers in these models can easily be calculated from the government budget constraint [14.1] rather than from the equations describing the IS and LM curves. If changes from the initial equilibrium to the new long-run equilibrium are denoted dG, dY, etc., then since in the new equilibrium income must have risen enough for taxes to have risen by as much as government expenditure so that that the budget is again balanced, the following equation must hold:

$$dG = dT = tdY$$

Dividing through by t and by dG and rearranging gives

$$\frac{dY}{dG} = \frac{1}{t} \qquad [14.4]$$

as the long-run multiplier for a money-financed increase in G.

Model 2: The government budget constraint with wealth effects

When wealth effects are incorporated into the analysis, different results are obtained. Here it is convenient to start with the case of a money-financed increase in G. In the very short run there are the same shifts from IS_0 to IS_1 and from LM_0 to LM_1 and income rises to Y_1 in Figure 14.2. In the short run, because wealth has risen (from the increase in money supply), the IS shifts to the right and the LM to the left. Overall the IS shifts twice to the right, but the LM shifts first to the right and then to the left. However, it is possible to establish that the net shift of the LM curve must be to the right. The initial shift to the right is from the increase in money supply (to finance the budget deficit) and the subsequent shift to the left is from the increase in money demand due

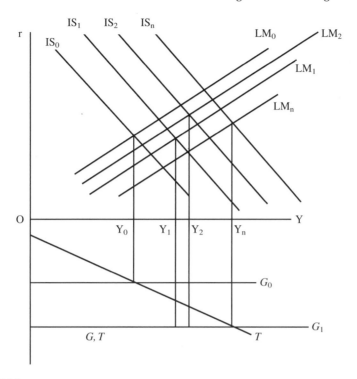

Figure 14.2

to the wealth effect. But since physical capital (K), money and bonds are all 'normal' assets (in the sense that when wealth increases, the demand for each of them will increase), the induced increase in money demand must be less than the increase in total wealth and therefore also less than the increase in money supply. Thus the initial rightward shift of LM must be greater than the subsequent leftward shift. With a net shift of the LM curve to the right and two rightwards shifts of IS, income must rise, to Y_2 in Figure 14.2. Y_2 is drawn to the right of Y_1; in principle (depending on the size of the two wealth effects) Y_2 could be to the left of Y_1, but it must be to the right of Y_0. At this point the budget is still in deficit, so in the next round the government will further increase the money supply, which causes a net rightward shift of LM and a rightward shift of IS: income therefore rises, and the same pattern will repeat itself in subsequent rounds until the budget deficit is again balanced at Y_n with IS_n and LM_n. In this case, then, although the path by which the economy approaches Y_n is different from that in Model 1, the long-run multiplier depends on the government budget constraint in the same way and must therefore be the same as in [14.4], i.e.

$$\frac{dY}{dG} = \frac{1}{t}.$$

There are larger differences in the results for a bond-financed increase in G. Here the initial shift in IS takes the economy to Y_1 in the very short run, in

Figure 14.3. For the short run the wealth effects from the bond issue need to be added; these involve a rightward shift of IS to IS_2 and a leftward shift of LM to LM_1. Since it is possible for the former to outweigh the latter or for the latter to outweigh the former, both cases must now be considered. First, if the rightward shift of IS outweighs the leftward shift of LM, that is to say the net wealth effects are expansionary, income rises in the short run to Y_2. Taxes rise but there is still a budget deficit, so in the next round the government issues more bonds, and – given that the net wealth effects are expansionary – income rises again. Clearly income will go on rising in successive rounds until taxes have risen enough for the budget to be balanced again and the government ceases to issue more bonds, at Y_n. But at that point income must have risen exactly as much as with the money-financed increase in G, and the long-run multiplier must be the same as in [14.4], i.e.

$$\frac{dY}{dG} = \frac{1}{t}.$$

This is a surprising result, given the view taken in earlier debates that fiscal expansion supported by monetary expansion was bound to be more effective than fiscal expansion on its own, but the long-run equilibrium level of income (if it is reached) must be the same in both cases because it is determined by the

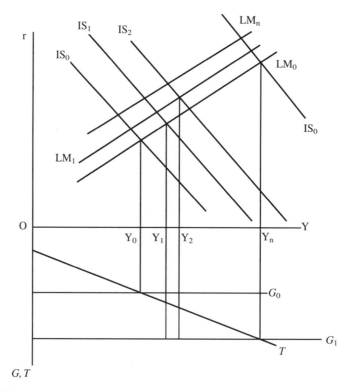

Figure 14.3

same mechanism. (Note, however, that the interest rate will be higher in this case, and private-sector investment therefore lower.)

On the other hand, in the case where the net wealth effects are contractionary so that the leftward shift of LM dominates the rightward shift of IS as in Figure 14.4, income in the short run at Y_2 must be lower than in the very short run at Y_1, though it may be higher or lower than the initial level Y_0. Since the budget is in deficit (income has risen less, if at all, and therefore taxes have risen less, if at all), the government issues more bonds in the next round. The bond issue again causes IS to shift right and LM to shift left, income falls, taxes fall and the budget deficit in the next round will be even larger. Thus, as the government keeps issuing bonds to cover a widening budget deficit, and successive bond issues lead to successive (and larger) falls in income, income goes to zero.

This case, where income does not end up at a point where the budget is balanced, is referred to as the 'instability' case, though it should be noted that this is not the normal meaning of instability (which is the idea that if the economy is pushed away from some equilibrium position it fails to return to that position). The 'stability condition' which ensures that income rises rather than falls is simply that net wealth effects are expansionary, i.e. that when bonds are issued income rises, which can be written

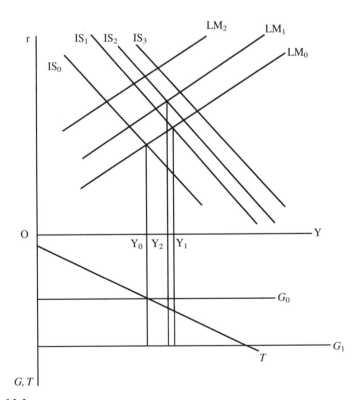

Figure 14.4

$$\frac{\partial Y}{\partial B} > 0 \qquad\qquad\qquad\qquad\qquad\qquad\qquad\qquad [14.5]$$

where ∂ is used to indicate the change in each round. Instability never occurs with money-financing, but may occur with bond-financing. A nice twist implied here is that the operation of a monetary rule, that is of a rule by which the money supply is increased each year at a fixed rate equal to the underlying productivity growth rate (as advocated by Friedman, 1960), is equivalent to bond-financing: whatever happens to the government's budget is not allowed to affect the rate of monetary growth. Instability is therefore more likely with a monetary rule than with a more Keynesian type of monetary policy, where the money supply is allowed to rise to accommodate increases in nominal income.

Model 3: The government budget constraint with wealth effects and an explicit treatment of interest payments

So far, a once for all increase in total government expenditure G has been considered. But a more complete analysis would take into account the effect of variations in the stock of bonds on the interest payments which the government has to make: clearly when the government issues bonds it commits itself to spending more in succeeding periods on coupon payments. The previous treatment can be rationalised only on the rather awkward assumption that as coupon payments increase, the government cuts some other element of its spending to keep the total unchanged. If instead coupon payments are treated explicitly as an item of government expenditure separate from spending on goods and services G, and for consistency tax revenue is assumed to be levied on coupon receipts as well as factor incomes, then the government budget constraint needs to be redefined as follows:

$$G + B - T = \Delta M + \frac{\Delta B}{r}, \text{ where } T = \overline{T} + tY + tB. \qquad\qquad [14.6]$$

In this model the case of a money-financed increase in G is the same as in Model 2, because the stock of bonds does not change and therefore total coupon payments remain the same. However, for a bond-financed increase in G it is necessary to take account of the change in B. In fact there are now three cases to be considered. The first is when the net wealth effects are contractionary (i.e. the rightward shift of IS is outweighed by the leftward shift of LM): in this case income falls each time new bonds are issued. This result is essentially the same as that for Model 2, but the fact that the government's total expenditure $G + B$ is rising further (because of the increase in coupon payments) means that the budget deficit widens more quickly and income falls more quickly towards zero. In the second case, the net wealth effects are expansionary, and income rises and goes on rising until tax revenues have risen by enough to balance the budget. Here, because during this process the government has been issuing bonds, its total expenditure $G + B$ rises by more than the original increase in G, and therefore income and tax revenues have to rise by more for the budget to be balanced again. This means that the long-run multiplier is actually greater for a bond-financed increase in G than for a money-financed increase, essentially because in this case there is a further induced rise in government spending on coupon payments. However, there is also a third case, for even though net wealth effects are expansionary it is possible that in successive rounds the increase in tax revenues (due to the rise in income and the rise in coupon payments) may be smaller than the rise in the coupon payments themselves, in which case the budget deficit becomes larger rather than smaller and a long-run equilibrium with a balanced budget is never reached. This is a new case of instability, for which there is no parallel in Model 2.

The long-run multiplier for the second case of Model 3 can be derived in the same way as that for Models 1 and 2 from the relevant government budget constraint [14.6]: since in the new equilibrium income must have risen enough for taxes to have risen by as much as total government expenditure so that the budget is again balanced, the following equation must hold:

$$dG + dB = dT = tdY + tdB.$$

Rearranging gives

$$tdY = dG + (1 - t)dB.$$

Dividing through by t and by dG gives

$$\frac{dY}{dG} = \frac{1 + (1 - t)dB/dG}{t}. \qquad [14.7]$$

If bonds are issued when G is increased (i.e. if dB/dG is positive), then this multiplier must be greater than that for Models 1 and 2 given by equation [14.4] above. On the other hand if no bonds are issued (i.e. the money-financing case) the multiplier collapses to that in [14.4].

Finally, the stability condition for Model 3 can be derived by considering what is required in each round for the budget deficit to get smaller rather than larger: the rise in total tax revenue must be greater than the rise in coupon payments, i.e.

$$\partial T = t\partial Y + t\partial B > \partial B.$$

Rearranging and dividing through by t and ∂B gives

$$\frac{\partial Y}{\partial B} > \frac{1 - t}{t}, \qquad [14.8]$$

which is a stricter condition than that for Model 2 given in [14.5].

The question of stability

The literature on the government budget constraint was initiated by Ott and Ott (1965) and Christ (1968), while Model 3 was produced by Blinder and Solow (1973). The latter in particular sparked a considerable debate focused mainly on the question of stability. Blinder and Solow themselves had tried to argue that the economy was unlikely to be unstable, in the sense used in this literature, which implied that a bond-financed increase in government spending was more powerful than a money-financed increase. Their arguments hinged on a number of issues such as the nature of the investment function assumed. There is obviously something unsatisfactory in talking about a long run where the capital stock has not changed, or if it has, this has had no effect on anything else, but Blinder and Solow's attempt to allow for changes in the capital stock – which suggested that instability was less likely – was soon countered by Tobin and Buiter's (1976) model in which an accelerator mechanism for investment makes instability more likely. Other arguments by Blinder and Solow for stability were also shown to be open to question, while their definition of a fiscal expansion as a permanent rise in G plus continuing induced rises in B is clearly a somewhat special definition. Thus within this framework the question of whether the economy is stable or not remains an open one.

Ricardian equivalence

The most important counter-argument to the main government budget constraint literature, which steps outside the above framework, is that of ultra-rationality or Ricardian Equivalence (Barro, 1974). The basic idea here is that the 'ultra-rational' private sector perceives that bond financing implies higher taxation in the future to pay for the interest on and redemption of the bonds, and once this effect is taken into account the private sector's wealth is not increased by bond issues. In other words, for the private sector the financing of government expenditure by bond issues is equivalent to its financing by current taxation, and bonds are 'not net wealth'. In this case there are no wealth effects associated with bond issues and Models 2 and 3 above can be dismissed as irrelevant (except insofar as the wealth effects associated with increases in money alter the path – but not the destination – of the economy). A money-financed increase in government spending is therefore unequivocally more powerful than a bond-financed increase.

Consider for simplicity a switch in the way government expenditure is financed in the form of a cut in taxes financed by an issue of bonds, to be redeemed (with interest) in the following year. This raises current disposable income but reduces expected future disposable income (because of the expected tax increases). The private sector therefore invests the proceeds of the tax cut now in order to be able to pay the higher taxes next year, and does not increase its consumption. A more formal way of seeing this is to consider private-sector wealth, redefined to include as a negative item the present value of expected future tax liabilities. Suppose that $D_t, D_{t+1} \ldots D_{t+\infty}$ is the stream of increased payments by the government on debt interest (coupons) and redemptions, while $T_t, T_{t+1} \ldots T_{t+\infty}$ is the stream of additional tax revenues which will have to be levied to pay for the coupons and redemptions. The present value of the bonds is obtained by discounting to the present the D_{t+i} stream, while the present value of the increased tax liabilities associated with the bond issue is obtained by discounting to the present the T_{t+i} stream. If the private sector uses the same interest rate to discount both the present benefits of the tax reduction and the future increases in taxation, the change in wealth can be written as

$$\Delta W = \sum_{i=1}^{i=\infty} \frac{D_{t+i}}{(1+\rho)^i} - \sum_{i=1}^{i=\infty} \frac{T_{t+i}}{(1+\rho)^i} \qquad [14.9]$$

where ρ is the private sector's discount rate. But in each period the D and T elements are the same, that is $D_{t+i} = T_{t+i} \forall i$, and therefore $\Delta W = 0$.

In parenthesis, it should be noted that the expression given here for the value of the bonds is consistent with the formula for the price of a non-redeemable bond with a coupon of B per annum given above in [5.7] and used in [14.1]: the former gives the present value of such a bond as

$$\frac{B}{(1+r)^1} + \frac{B}{(1+r)^2} + \frac{B}{(1+r)^3} \cdots = B \left\{ \frac{1}{(1+r)} + \frac{1}{(1+r)^2} + \frac{1}{(1+r)^3} \cdots \right\}. \qquad [14.10]$$

In a geometric progression where $0 < \alpha < 1$ then

$$1 + \alpha + \alpha^2 + \alpha^3 + \cdots = \frac{1}{1-\alpha}.$$

Since $0 < 1/1 + r < 1$, the expression on the right-hand side of [14.10] can be written as

$$B \left\{ \frac{1}{1 - \frac{1}{1+r}} - 1 \right\} = B \left\{ \frac{1+r}{r} - 1 \right\} = \frac{B}{r}. \qquad [14.11]$$

The idea that bonds are not net wealth, so that Models 2 and 3 can be dismissed and the size of the government deficit is important only for its impact on the money supply, is a controversial element of New Classical Macroeconomics. Critics have argued that people are not sufficiently well-informed and/or far-sighted to act in this way. They have also suggested that, although intragenerational transfers may cancel each other out along the above lines, intergenerational transfers may not, for the current generation may choose to consume at the expense of future generations, especially if there is long run economic growth which will compensate the later generations. The assumption that private sector agents use the same discount rate for the stream of payments associated with bonds and the stream of tax liabilities can be shown to require perfect capital markets and no risk aversion; in particular agents must be able to borrow and lend at the same rate and to borrow at the same rate as that at which the government borrows. Otherwise agents might welcome a tax cut financed by a bond issue as an indirect way of borrowing at a lower rate of interest than they would normally be able to obtain. Ricardian Equivalence also requires that all future interest and redemption payments come out of higher taxes levied on the same level of income; but if a tax cut or increase in government spending financed by a bond issue leads to an expansion of income then that will generate higher tax revenue without any increase in the rate at which taxes are levied and without a fall in disposable income; in that case the private sector must benefit in net terms from a bond-financed tax cut, and it would not be rational for the private sector to keep its consumption unchanged (more formally it would be rational for the private sector *not* to discount the two income streams at the same rate). Finally, it should be noted that to eliminate the surprising results of models 2 and 3 *full*, 100%, ultrarationality is necessary: if there is any wealth effect from bond issues at all the long-run results must eventually be reached.

Conclusions and qualifications

The government budget constraint literature has produced an array of results corresponding to different models and cases, between which theoretical considerations are insufficient to adjudicate. The obvious way to decide between them is to bring empirical evidence to bear on the issues, but, as so often in economics, this has turned out to be both more difficult to do and less decisive in its implications than might have been hoped. Direct evidence indicates that wealth effects exist on private-sector expenditure, and also (though perhaps less strongly) on money demand, but the extent of ultra-rationality is unclear. Indirect evidence from simulations of large macro models seems to suggest that increases in government spending involve higher crowding out when monetary policy is more tightly controlled and/or when exchange rates are flexible. However, such evidence is not strong enough to determine which model and which cases are relevant.

In any case there are a number of important qualifications that should be made. First, the literature as a whole proceeds by examining the consequences of government actions under the assumption that deficits/surpluses are financed 100% by either money or bonds, but it is open to governments to use some combination of the two. If this is done then the possibility of instability can be excluded (e.g. if some combination is used which ensures that the wealth effect on the LM curve is exactly offset by the effect of the increase in money supply so that the LM curve does not shift). Thus it must always be possible to devise some method of financing which guarantees that an increase in government spending will lead to a long run increase in income: instability and crowding out can then be seen as the results of inappropriate financing (or of real resource constraints which have been excluded here). Similarly, the literature typically assumes that the method of financing is fixed at the beginning of the experiment and not subsequently changed. But the long run here is not a matter of lagged effects which, once they are started off, must gradually work their way through the system. On the contrary, there is nothing to prevent governments changing their minds on the mix of financing somewhere along the way (and that is presumably one reason why no instances of a country's income imploding to zero as the result of contractionary net wealth effects have ever been recorded).

Secondly, the literature pays little attention to the intrinsic value of government expenditure: if, for example, it is assumed that infrastructural or educational spending can affect productivity and/or the capacity of the economy the longer-run effects may be quite different. Thirdly, while the focus of the literature is on modes of financing of government spending, the same essential budget constraint and wealth effect mechanisms will operate for changes in (autonomous) private spending: if, for example, there is a rise in autonomous investment (from a starting position of budget balance) income and taxes will rise and there will now be a budget surplus; the government must therefore decide whether to use that surplus to retire bonds or money, and that decision and the associated wealth effects will shift the IS and LM curves, and so on.

The principal contribution of the government budget constraint literature should be sought, therefore, not in the precise results arrived at but in the way it has pushed economists to integrate the financing of budget imbalances into the determination of income and to think about stocks and flows, and the way in which it has exposed shortcomings in the original views of both Keynesians and monetarists. The literature remains, however, rooted in the earlier debates: despite attempts to introduce price flexibility in one form or another the model is essentially a model of aggregate demand which needs to be combined with a theory of aggregate supply. But when it is combined with some form of expectations-augmented Phillips curve, many of the questions discussed in the government budget constraint literature can be short-circuited: if the economy tends towards some natural rate of unemployment or NAIRU then the long-run multiplier for an increase in government expenditure, whatever the method of financing, must be zero.

Exercises

(i)   Show that when an increase in G takes place from an initial position of budget balance the government's budget must now be in deficit. (Hint: it is easiest to analyse the issue first within the simple income–expenditure model, and then consider how the result would differ within the complete IS–LM model.)

(ii) Work through the check list of results given in Box 14.1 for government expenditure multipliers in each model and each case, to make sure you can derive and understand each one.

(iii)   Work through the corresponding check list of results given in Box 14.2 for the multiplier effects of a rise in autonomous private sector investment in each model and each case. (Hints: (a) when investment rises income and taxes rise, and there is now a budget surplus: the government must either retire money or retire debt; (b) the retiring of either money or debt reduces wealth, which leads to a leftwards shift of IS and a rightwards shift of LM; (c) the long-run equilibrium is determined as before by the income level at which the budget is balanced – this may be the same as the original level or, if the stock of bonds and therefore the government's spending on coupon payments has changed, different from it.)

Box 14.1   Checklist of results for increase in G

Model 1:

$$\frac{dY}{dG}(LR, M) = \frac{1}{t} > \frac{dY}{dG}(SR, M) > \frac{dY}{dG}(SR, B) = \frac{dY}{dG}(LR, B)$$

Model 2:

$$\frac{dY}{dG}(LR, M) = \frac{1}{t} > \frac{dY}{dG}(SR, M) > 0$$

$$\frac{dY}{dG}(SR, M) \gtrless \frac{dY}{dG}(VSR, M) > 0$$

$$\frac{dY}{dG}(SR, B) \gtrless \frac{dY}{dG}(VSR, B) \quad \text{as} \quad \frac{\partial Y}{\partial B} \gtrless 0$$

$$\text{if} \quad \frac{\partial Y}{\partial B} > 0, \quad \frac{dY}{dG}(LR, B) = \frac{1}{t} = \frac{dY}{dG}(LR, M)$$

$$\text{if} \quad \frac{\partial Y}{\partial B} < 0, \quad \frac{dY}{dG}(LR, B) < 0 \quad (Y \to 0)$$

Model 3:

$$\frac{dY}{dG}(LR, M) = \frac{1}{t} > \frac{dY}{dG}(SR, M) > 0$$

$$\frac{dY}{dG}(SR, M) \gtrless \frac{dY}{dG}(VSR, M) > 0$$

$$\frac{dY}{dG}(SR, B) \gtrless \frac{dY}{dG}(VSR, B) \quad \text{as} \quad \frac{\partial Y}{\partial B} \gtrless 0$$

$$\text{if} \quad \frac{\partial Y}{\partial B} > \frac{1-t}{t} > 0, \quad \frac{dY}{dG}(LR, B) = \frac{1 + (1-t)dB/dG}{t} > \frac{1}{t} = \frac{dY}{dG}(LR, M)$$

$$\text{if} \quad \frac{1-t}{t} > \frac{\partial Y}{\partial B} > 0, \quad \frac{dY}{dG}(LR, B) >> 0 \quad (Y \to \infty)$$

$$\text{if} \quad \frac{\partial Y}{\partial B} < 0, \quad \frac{dY}{dG}(LR, B) < 0 \quad (Y \to 0)$$

Key: the brackets attached to each multiplier indicate the time period (long run LR/short run SR/very short run VSR) and the method of financing (100% money-financing M, 100% bond-financing B).

Box 14.2 Check list of results for increase in autonomous investment j

Model 1:

$$\frac{dY}{dj}(LR, B) = \frac{dY}{dj}(SR, B) > \frac{dY}{dj}(SR, M) > \frac{dY}{dj}(LR, M) = 0$$

Model 2:

$$\frac{dY}{dj}(SR, M) \gtrless \frac{dY}{dj}(VSR, M) > 0$$

$$\frac{dY}{dj}(SR, M) > 0 = \frac{dY}{dj}(LR, M)$$

$$\frac{dY}{dj}(SR, B) \gtrless \frac{dY}{dj}(VSR, B) \quad \text{as} \quad \frac{\partial Y}{\partial B} \gtrless 0$$

$$\text{if} \quad \frac{\partial Y}{\partial B} > 0, \quad \frac{dY}{dj}(LR, B) = 0 = \frac{dY}{dj}(LR, M)$$

$$\text{if} \quad \frac{\partial Y}{\partial B} < 0, \quad \frac{dY}{dj}(LR, B) > 0 \quad (Y \to \infty)$$

Model 3:

$$\frac{dY}{dj}(SR, M) \gtrless \frac{dY}{dj}(VSR, M) > 0$$

$$\frac{dY}{dj}(SR, M) > 0 = \frac{dY}{dj}(LR, M)$$

$$\frac{dY}{dj}(SR, B) \gtrless \frac{dY}{dj}(VSR, B) \quad \text{as} \quad \frac{\partial Y}{\partial B} \gtrless 0$$

$$\text{if} \quad \frac{\partial Y}{\partial B} > \frac{1-t}{t} > 0, \quad \frac{dY}{dj}(LR, B) < 0 = \frac{dY}{dj}(LR, M)$$

$$\text{if} \quad \frac{1-t}{t} > \frac{\partial Y}{\partial B} > 0, \quad \frac{dY}{dj}(LR, B) << 0 \quad (Y \to 0)$$

$$\text{if} \quad \frac{\partial Y}{\partial B} < 0, \quad \frac{dY}{dj}(LR, B) >> 0 \quad (Y \to \infty)$$

Further reading

Excellent surveys of the theoretical government budget constraint literature (with some references to the empirical evidence) can be found in Currie (1976, 1981). Artis (1979) provides an encompassing formal model. Blinder and Solow (1973) is perhaps the most important paper in the main debate, while Barro (1974) is the key paper on Ricardian Equivalence. Cook and Jackson (1979) is a good collection of papers in the area.

Chapter 15

Policy ineffectiveness and rational expectations

The basic concept of rational expectations, and the idea that this makes macroeconomic stabilisation policy ineffective, have already been discussed in various chapters in Part One. This chapter presents a formal model of the policy ineffectiveness proposition based on Sargent and Wallace (1976), and uses this to discuss some of the criticisms made of such models. It starts, however, with a simpler model of an expectations-augmented Phillips curve with rational expectations (based on Gordon, 1976).

The Phillips curve with rational expectations

The basic idea underlying the expectations-augmented Phillips curve is that inflation (and here the emphasis will be on price rather than wage inflation) is a function of excess demand, thought of as the current rate of unemployment relative to some natural rate or NAIRU, plus expected inflation. Formally, this can be written as

$$\dot{p}_t = \beta(u_N - u_t) + \dot{p}_t^e, \quad \beta > 0 \tag{15.1}$$

where $\dot{p}_t$ is the (proportional) rate of inflation, u_N is the natural rate or NAIRU, u_t is the actual current rate of unemployment, and the superscript e denotes expectations. Rearrange this equation to put actual unemployment on the left-hand side and add a term for supply side shocks:

$$u_t = u_N - \frac{1}{\beta}(\dot{p}_t - \dot{p}_t^e) + \gamma_t^s \tag{15.2}$$

where γ_t^s is a random variable, with expected value of zero, for supply side shocks which may affect unemployment such as unanticipated changes in hours of work or productivity. According to [15.2] unemployment can deviate from the natural rate only if there is a shock or if inflation is different from what was expected. Since by their nature the government cannot create or predict shocks, the only way it can influence unemployment is by boosting inflation relative to the rate that was expected.

Now consider what drives inflation in the economy. Suppose for simplicity that this is an economy where the crude quantity theory reigns, so that inflation is proximately caused by monetary growth, as follows:

$$\dot{p}_t = \dot{m}_t + \gamma_t^d \tag{15.3}$$

where $\dot{m}_t$ is the proportional rate of monetary growth and γ_t^d is a random variable, with expected value of zero, for demand shocks which may affect inflation. If expectations are rational, the private sector knows how the economy works, so that it knows inflation is caused according to [15.3]. It therefore uses [15.3] in forming its expectations about inflation:

$$\dot{p}_t^e = \dot{m}_t^e \tag{15.4}$$

since the expected value of the demand shock is zero.

Next consider the setting of monetary policy in this economy. Suppose that the monetary authority sets the rate of monetary growth equal to some constant (perhaps similar to the underlying productivity growth rate as in Friedman's monetary rule) plus some term in the difference between actual and natural unemployment (in the previous period, which is assumed to be the latest which it can observe), because the authority has a Keynesian view that it should be trying to prevent fluctuations in unemployment:

$$\dot{m}_t = \psi_0 + \psi_1(u_{t-1} - u_N) + \gamma_t^m, \ \psi_1 > 0 \tag{15.5}$$

where γ_t^m is a random variable, with expected value of zero, for shocks which may affect the rate of monetary growth. Because of rational expectations, the private sector knows that this is how monetary growth is set, so it uses [15.5] in trying to forecast the rate of monetary growth:

$$\dot{m}_t^e = \psi_0 + \psi_1(u_{t-1} - u_N) \tag{15.6}$$

Equations [15.3–15.6] can be used to work out the difference between actual and expected inflation:

$$\dot{p}_t - \dot{p}_t^e = \dot{m}_t - \dot{m}_t^e + \gamma_t^d = \gamma_t^m + \gamma_t^d \tag{15.7}$$

[15.7] can then be substituted in [15.2] to give

$$u_t = u_N - \frac{1}{\beta}(\gamma_t^m + \gamma_t^d) + \gamma_t^s \tag{15.8}$$

Equation [15.8] says that unemployment is determined by the three shocks, supply side, demand and monetary, that are included in the model. Moreover, the policy parameters ψ_0 and ψ_1 do not appear in [15.8], which means that policy decisions – that is, decisions about the appropriate magnitudes for ψ_0 and ψ_1 – do not affect unemployment. The reason for this can be found in the way this result was derived above: because of rational expectations the private sector knows how the monetary authority sets monetary growth and uses that knowledge to forecast inflation; if the monetary authority chose to set monetary growth in a different way the private sector would know that and again use it to forecast inflation. Thus any variations in the way the monetary authority behaves affect expected, as well as actual, inflation, and do not affect the difference between them; from [15.8] above the authority cannot therefore affect unemployment.

This simple introductory model demonstrates the policy ineffectiveness proposition within an expectations-augmented Phillips curve framework with perfect market clearing (this point is discussed later in this chapter). However, it is also useful to demonstrate policy ineffectiveness within an explicit aggregate demand framework.

Monetary growth and aggregate demand

One focus of earlier Keynesian–monetarist debates was the choice between 'rules' and 'discretion', that is, the choice between monetary policy (and macroeconomic stabilisation policy more widely) being determined according to rules set in advance and monetary policy being wielded with discretion by the monetary authority in each period. In particular, Friedman (1960) had argued that monetary growth should be set at a fixed rate, year in and year out, corresponding to the underlying productivity growth rate of the economy: this would allow a minor element of countercyclical policy, insofar as monetary growth would be higher than nominal income growth in a recession and lower in a boom, but at the same time it would guarantee price stability and prevent policymakers using monetary policy for political reasons (stimulating expansion before an election and then cutting it back afterwards) or making the cycle worse as a result of mistakes in their forecasting. Keynesian economists, on the other hand, had argued that it would always be better to allow policymakers to use all the information available to them in making their decisions, so that a *feedback rule*, in which the current state of the economy 'feeds back' into current policy decisions, was preferable: such a rule can be thought of as systematic discretion. In what follows the superiority of the feedback rule in a non-rational expectations economy will be demonstrated; then it will be shown that if expectations were in fact rational a no-feedback rule would be better.

Suppose income or output y is equal to some constant (which could include autonomous expenditures of various kinds), a term in lagged output (for consumption and other income-related expenditure), a term in the rate of monetary growth (to incorporate the idea that higher monetary growth reduces the interest rate and, in this and other ways, stimulates expenditure) and a random disturbance term, as follows:

$$y_t = \alpha + \lambda y_{t-1} + \beta \dot{m}_t + u_t, \quad \lambda > 0, \beta > 0 \tag{15.9}$$

where u_t is a random variable with mean of zero and variance σ_u^2. The monetary authority tries to control output by manipulating monetary growth. It sets the latter by choosing appropriate values for the parameters in the monetary growth function:

$$\dot{m}_t = g_0 + g_1 y_{t-1} \qquad \qquad [15.10]$$

according to which it can set monetary growth as some combination of a constant g_0 and a term in lagged output $g_1 y_{t-1}$ (note that this exhausts the possibilities within this particular simple framework). In order to see how policy affects output, substitute [15.10] into [15.9]:

$$y_t = \alpha + \lambda y_{t-1} + \beta(g_0 + g_1 y_{t-1}) + u_t$$
$$= (\alpha + \beta g_0) + (\lambda + \beta g_1) y_{t-1} + u_t. \qquad [15.11]$$

A 'Keynesian' policymaker wishes to minimise the variability of output and to ensure that on average output (and employment) is at some target (full employment) level y^*. To see what this means, first take the steady state mean of y by taking the expected values of both sides of [15.11] (the steady state mean is the expected value of y in the steady state, i.e. when no change is occurring such that $y_t = y_{t-1}$):

$$E(y) = (\alpha + \beta g_0) + (\lambda + \beta g_1)E(y)$$
$$= \frac{\alpha + \beta g_0}{1 - (\lambda + \beta g_1)}. \qquad [15.12]$$

Next, take the variance of y by taking the variance of both sides of [15.11] (note that the variance of a constant is zero and that if the variance of y is var y then the variance of cy is c^2 var y):

$$\text{var } y = (\lambda + \beta g_1)^2 \text{ var } y + \sigma_u^2$$
$$= \frac{\sigma_u^2}{1 - (\lambda + \beta g_1)^2}. \qquad [15.13]$$

If the policymaker wishes to minimise the variance of y by choosing the optimal value for g_1 (g_0 does not appear in [15.13]), the way to do this is to maximise the denominator of [15.13], which means setting $(\lambda + \beta g_1)^2$ equal to zero, which means choosing g_1 so that

$$g_1 = -\lambda/\beta \qquad \qquad [15.14]$$

This then makes the denominator of the expression for $E(y)$ in [15.12] equal to 1, and choosing the optimal value for g_0 so as to set $E(y)$ equal to the target level y^* requires

$$\alpha + \beta g_0 = y^*,$$

hence

$$g_0 = \frac{y^* - \alpha}{\beta} \qquad [15.15]$$

Substituting these values for g_0 and g_1 into the monetary growth function [15.10] gives the optimal feedback rule as

$$\dot{m}_t = \frac{y^* - \alpha}{\beta} - \frac{\lambda}{\beta}y_{t-1} \qquad [15.16]$$

where the fact that the parameter on lagged output is non-zero indicates that a rule with feedback is superior to a rule without feedback (in which monetary growth is set equal to a constant). As a check [15.16] can be substituted into [15.9]; this shows that output is indeed equal on average to the target level, with a variance equal to that of the random disturbance term.

The above completes the proof of the 'Keynesian' proposition that, in the context of the economy given by [15.9] above, a rule with feedback is optimal. But suppose that [15.9], the way the policymaker believes output is determined, is misconceived; suppose the true structural model of the economy is as follows:

$$y_t = \phi_0 + \phi_1 y_{t-1} + \phi_2(\dot{m}_t - \dot{m}_t^e) + u_t \qquad [15.17]$$

$$\dot{m}_t = g_0 + g_1 y_{t-1} + v_t \qquad [15.18]$$

$$\dot{m}_t^e = g_0 + g_1 y_{t-1} \qquad [15.19]$$

where [15.17] shows the response of output to the difference between actual and expected monetary growth, which can be thought of as determining the difference between actual and expected inflation, as in the model of the previous section; [15.18] is the monetary growth function, here including a random variable v_t with mean zero and variance σ_v^2 to represent any 'slippage' between the monetary authority's intentions and the outcome; and [15.19] shows how the private sector makes a rational forecast of monetary growth on the basis of its knowledge of [15.18], again as in the previous model.

If this is the true model of the economy, then the true relationship between output on the one hand and monetary growth and lagged output on the other is that obtained by substituting from [15.19] into [15.17]:

$$y_t = \phi_0 + \phi_1 y_{t-1} + \phi_2 \dot{m}_t - \phi_2(g_0 + g_1 y_{t-1}) + u_t$$
$$= (\phi_0 - \phi_2 g_0) + (\phi_1 - \phi_2 g_1)y_{t-1} + \phi_2 \dot{m}_t + u_t \qquad [15.20]$$

Clearly the structure of this equation is the same as that of [15.9], with $(\phi_0 - \phi_2 g_0)$ corresponding to α, $(\phi_1 - \phi_2 g_1)$ to λ, and ϕ_2 to β. But if [15.17–15.19] is the true model, then substituting in [15.17] only for expected monetary growth from [15.19] but not for actual monetary growth from [15.18] is rather odd. If the latter substitution is made as well, [15.17] simplifies to:

$$y_t = \phi_0 + \phi_1 y_{t-1} + \phi_2 v_t + u_t \qquad [15.21]$$

where output no longer depends on the policy parameters g_0 and g_1: as in the previous model, policy is therefore ineffective. In addition, suppose the monetary authority was to try to set g_1 at the level which was previously found to be optimal; this implies

$$g_1 = -\frac{\lambda}{\beta} = -\frac{\phi_1 - \phi_2 g_1}{\phi_2} = g_1 - \frac{\phi_1}{\phi_2} \qquad [15.22]$$

This is now impossible: g_1 cannot be set equal to itself minus some other number. Thus equation [15.22] cannot be satisfied; or in other words, since different values of g_1 will leave equation [15.22] equally unsatisfied, the equation does not restrict the value of g_1 in any way. The reason is that the behaviour of the monetary authority is understood by the private sector and taken into account in its expectations of inflation; any variation in monetary growth simply causes a variation in the rate of inflation without any effect on output. Thus with rational expectations systematic monetary policy is ineffective, and nothing can be achieved by having non-zero feedback. Therefore g_1 might as well be set equal to zero as in Friedman's monetary rule; this will have the additional advantage (not directly visible in this model) that average inflation will be equal to g_0, which, in this non-growth setting, should according to Friedman's rule also be set equal to zero. The assumption of rational expectations thus provides a vindication of the monetary rule, though on the basis of a different sort of argument.

Finally, the above model can be used to explain what is called the Lucas Critique. If a policymaker who did not understand that the true model was that of [15.17–15.19] carried out standard econometric regressions on equation [15.9], he would obtain estimates for α, λ and β which were in fact estimates for $(\phi_0 - \phi_2 g_0)$, $(\phi_1 - \phi_2 g_1)$ and ϕ_2 respectively. But these estimates for α and λ would clearly depend on the values of g_0 and g_1 during the period of the data used for the regressions; they could not therefore be used to investigate how output would have behaved if, for example, the monetary authority had been pursuing a monetary rule (in which case g_0 and g_1 would have been different). More generally, the Lucas Critique states that the typical parameter estimates produced by non-rational expectations econometric models themselves reflect the way in which policy was being operated during the period concerned; it is not therefore legitimate to use such estimates to analyse how the outcome might have been different if policy had in fact been operated in a different way. Instead, it is necessary to estimate purely structural parameters (i.e. parameters corresponding to those in [15.17–15.19] rather than those in [15.9]) in order to be able to use the estimates for subsequent counterfactual simulations.

The perfect market clearing assumption

At first sight the policy ineffectiveness results in these models depend on the assumption of rational expectations, and when rational expectations were first introduced this was how the results were widely interpreted. Nowadays it is recognised that they depend also on an assumption that markets clear perfectly, which in this context means that the market automatically 'finds' and sets the equilibrium price; alternatively it is said that these models interpret the Phillips curve as an inverted supply curve. This point is worth investigating more carefully.

In New Classical Macroeconomics firms adjust their output in response to the market price, producing more output when the price is particularly advantageous to them and less output when it is less advantageous; similarly workers supply more labour when the real wage is particularly high (at least as they perceive it), and less labour when it is relatively low. In the market for goods and services, suppose that firms in aggregate produce more when the actual price level is higher than the price level they had expected because they interpret this as evidence of an increase in the demand for the good they produce, and vice-versa. Formally, this can be stated as follows:

$$Y_t = F(P_t/P_t^e), \quad F' > 0.$$

where Y_t is output, P_t/P_t^e is the actual price level relative to the expected price level, and F stands for the functional relationship between these two, which has a positive derivative ($F' > 0$) such that output is higher when actual prices are higher relative to expected prices. It is now convenient to recast this relationship in logarithmic terms, using lower-case letters to indicate log variables, assuming a log-linear form for the function F, and defining the units of output such that the natural rate of output Y_N is equal to 1 (hence y_N, the log of Y_N, is equal to zero, and y_t is > 0 or < 0 as output is above or below the natural rate):

$$y_t = h(p_t - p_t^e), \quad h > 0.$$

This says that output will be above or below the natural rate as prices are above or below the expected level. Adding and subtracting hp_{t-1} and rearranging gives

$$y_t = h(p_t - p_{t-1}) - h(p_t^e - p_{t-1}) = h\Delta p_t - h\Delta p_t^e.$$

Dividing through by h and rearranging gives

$$\Delta p_t = \frac{1}{h} y_t + \Delta p_t^e. \qquad [15.23]$$

This says that inflation is equal to some function of output plus expected inflation (Δp_t is the log of P_t/P_{t-1}, whereas elsewhere in this book the proportional rate of inflation has been defined as $(P_t - P_{t-1})/P_{t-1}$, so Δp_t measures the rate of inflation as the log of $1 +$ the proportional rate). Equation [15.23] has the form of an expectations-augmented Phillips curve (with inflation equal to expected inflation at the natural rate), but it is derived as an 'inverted supply curve', that is the underlying behaviour corresponds to that involved in a New Classical aggregate supply curve.

While this view can be traced back to Fisher (1911) and can be found in Lucas (e.g. 1972), there is an alternative account of the micro-underpinnings of the Phillips curve to be found in Phelps (1968), which is emphasised by Laidler (1982, Chapters 1 and 4). Here firms are seen as setting both prices and wages (but not quantities of goods or labour): they set wages to attract the labour they require, and they set prices to control their sales. In the goods and services market they set prices relative to what prices had been expected to be in order to expand or reduce their sales, and their objective for their sales depends on current sales relative to their capacity output: if they are selling more than they can produce in the long run they raise prices, to reduce sales into line with their capacity, and if they are selling less than they can produce they lower prices to increase sales. Formally, using logs and the conventions adopted above (and treating the natural rate of output as equivalent to firms' capacity output), this can be written as

$$p_t - p_t^e = gy_t, \ g > 0.$$

Adding and subtracting p_{t-1} and rearranging gives

$$p_t - p_{t-1} = p_t^e - p_{t-1} + gy_t$$
$$\Delta p_t = \Delta p_t^e + gy_t. \qquad [15.24]$$

Equation [15.24] has the same form as [15.23] with g corresponding to $1/h$. But it has been derived from a very different view of the world.

The key difference is that the Fisher–Lucas account of the micro-underpinnings of the Phillips curve has causation running from prices to output, via firms' response to prices (relative to expected prices); and implicitly the actual prices are set by some market mechanism (economists often say 'as if by some Walrasian auctioneer', since Walras used the fiction of an auction as a means to try and explain how the price mechanism works). The Phelps–Laidler account, on the other hand, has causation running from output/demand to prices, via the way in which firms set the prices, so that here the setting of prices is included in the model rather than assumed from outside. The Fisher–Lucas account is referred to as an 'equilibrium' and a 'perfect-market-clearing' one, because prices always move automatically to the level at which supply equals demand even though agents may sometimes have incorrect expectations. The Phelps–Laidler account is sometimes described as 'disequilibrium' or 'non-perfect-market-clearing' because prices, since they are set by agents with incomplete information, may move to levels that do not clear all markets. In addition, since in the Phelps–Laidler case firms make wage offers in order to influence the amount of labour supplied to them, it would be possible to modify the model so as to have firms making positive decisions on the quantity of labour they wish to employ as well as on the wage at which they will employ it, for example laying off workers in a recession instead of cutting the wage rate.

In many ways the distinction between these two views of the micro-underpinnings of the Phillips curve is the most fundamental divide between modern macroeconomists, though it is not always made explicit by the way in which they argue. The two models of the earlier sections of this chapter both incorporate the Fisher–Lucas view. The first (Gordon) model starts in equation [15.1] with a conventional Phillips curve but this is immediately rearranged in [15.2] to give unemployment (thought of as related to output) as a function of the difference between actual and expected inflation, and it is [15.2] which forms the basis for the subsequent argument. Moreover, the actual rate of inflation is directly determined by monetary growth (plus the demand shock). In the second (Sargent and Wallace) model prices do not appear explicitly but they lie behind the actual relative to expected monetary growth variables, and the structural equation for output [15.17] has output responding to the difference between these two in the same way as the first model. Thus the policy ineffectiveness result depends on the ability of prices to move to the new equilibrium: however the monetary authority behaves, prices move to clear the markets and because their behaviour is understood by the private sector its expectations move in the same way.

Suppose, however, that prices (or, more particularly, wages) are 'sticky' in some way. In that case price movements do not ensure that the market always clears and this introduces in the framework of the above models a further possibility for actual and expected prices to diverge and a possibility for the monetary authority to influence the divergence, in which case policy is no longer ineffective even though expectations are rational. If, as in Phelps and Taylor (1977) and Fischer (1977), workers enter wage contracts which will run for two periods then the government can take actions after the contract has been agreed which will influence nominal demand in the second period, but wages cannot adjust appropriately in that period so that there is some impact on real demand and output. And if such wage contracts are 'staggered', that is the contracts of different groups of workers are not synchronised but overlapping, in any period there will always be some workers who cannot adjust immediately to changes in demand and stabilisation policy therefore has some ability to influence real output and employment. More generally the introduction of price or wage stickiness in the form of non-instantaneous or incomplete adjustment of the actual level to the new equilibrium level will give some scope for stabilisation policy.

One useful way of thinking about these issues is to ask not 'do markets clear perfectly?' but 'what markets clear perfectly?'. Hicks (1974) distinguished between 'flexprice' and 'fixprice' markets. The former can be thought of as markets which are dominated by specialist traders or market-makers, that is agents who are continuously engaged in both buying and selling and therefore have an incentive to search out the information which will allow them to make profits by adjusting their prices as quickly as possible; typical examples are centralised specialist (professional or wholesale) financial markets, such as those for money (that is, Treasury bills or short-term bank deposits), foreign exchange, bonds and equity. Fixprice markets are those where prices are set on a decentralised basis, typically at discrete intervals, by agents who lack the incentive to invest in obtaining full information; the archetypal example is the labour market, but some economists (most obviously New Keynesians but also mainstream economists) would put many manufactured products, particularly those where there is some product differentiation and imperfect competition, in the same category.

Conclusions and qualifications

Simple models incorporating rational expectations have been presented in which stabilisation policy turns out to be ineffective. However, these models also incorporate the assumption of perfect market clearing, and this assumption is equally necessary for the policy ineffectiveness result. If markets do not clear perfectly, then even if expectations are rational there may be some scope for policy to influence real demand and output.

Any assumption of imperfect market clearing is open to the criticism that it assumes arbitrarily that agents agree to contracts which prevent them from maximising profits and/or utility. Indeed, as discussed in Chapter 19, New Classical economists are inclined to argue that, even if price stickiness existed (which they probably contest), it would be wrong to assume its existence unless a proper explanation of it, that is one based on rational/optimising behaviour, could be given.

It should also be noted that the two policy-ineffectiveness models examined here are not full New Classical rational expectations models (and the Sargent and Wallace (1976) model was put forward with an explicit warning to that effect). In these models the actual rate of inflation was determined by the rate of monetary growth plus some demand shock variable, but without reference to supply conditions. In a full model, by contrast, the equilibrium price level is determined by the interaction of supply and demand, that is the price level is determined endogenously as a solution to the model as a whole. Such models are mathematically difficult to solve, and for that reason have been eschewed here. The intuition, however, is straightforward: in terms of the AD/AS model of chapter 13 (Figure 13.10), the price level is always determined by the intersection of AD and AS, and rational expectations ensure that the private sector can anticipate both what the monetary authority is doing and how this interacts with the real economy to determine prices. The simpler models presented here, on the other hand, cannot be understood easily in AD/AS terms because they assume in effect a horizontal AD curve where the price level is fully determined by monetary policy and any shock variables without reference to supply, and AS then adjusts to the price level.

Exercises

(i)   Construct a variant of the Sargent and Wallace model in which output depends on lagged output and a composite macro policy variable, where that variable is the sum of monetary growth and the budget deficit d_t, with monetary policy following the reaction function [15.18] and the budget deficit determined as follows:

$$d_t = g_2 + g_3 y_{t-1} + g_4 T_t + w_t$$

where T_t is the number of years before the next election, and w_t is a random variable with mean zero representing the imprecision of budgetary control.

(ii) Show mathematically that policy is equally ineffective in this model (as in the model discussed in the chapter), and explain intuitively why this is so.

Further reading

A number of the papers mentioned in the text are well worth further study, in particular Gordon (1976), Sargent and Wallace (1976) and Laidler (1982, Chapters 1 and 4). More complete New Classical rational expectations models are given in Attfield *et al.* (1991, Chapter 4) and Cuthbertson and Taylor (1987, Chapter 3).

Chapter 16

Targets, rules, discretion and time-inconsistency

The last chapter discussed the proposition that systematic macroeconomic policy is ineffective in a world of rational expectations and perfect market clearing. This chapter examines a related but broader issue: should monetary policy be operated on the basis of a fixed rule or target, or should the monetary authorities be free to use their discretion in choosing what they think is the best setting for policy in each period? It starts by looking at the two main strands of literature that are relevant: the targets and instruments literature initiated by Poole (1970), and the rules versus discretion literature which goes back to Simons (1936). It then examines in detail the concept of time-inconsistency (or dynamic inconsistency) due to Kydland and Prescott (1977), which has transformed thinking on this question, and looks more briefly at some of the subsequent literature.

Targets and instruments

Poole (1970) set out to examine within the fixed-price IS–LM context the choice between setting interest rates and fixing the money supply. The former can be thought of, crudely, as a Keynesian policy in which monetary policy is secondary and accommodating, while the latter is the no-growth equivalent of a monetary rule.

In the IS–LM context setting the interest rate (and allowing the money supply to adjust to maintain the interest rate at the chosen level) generates in effect a horizontal LM curve, such as LM_A in Figure 16.1, whereas fixing the money supply implies the conventional upwards-sloping LM_B curve. Now suppose that there are random shocks to both expenditure and money demand, which the government cannot offset because it cannot predict them; instead the government wants to set its policy instruments so that the shocks when they occur have less deleterious effects on income and unemployment. These shocks cause the IS curve to shift leftwards and rightwards (for negative and positive shocks to expenditure), and the LM curve to shift rightwards and leftwards (for negative and positive shocks to money demand). If the IS shifts between

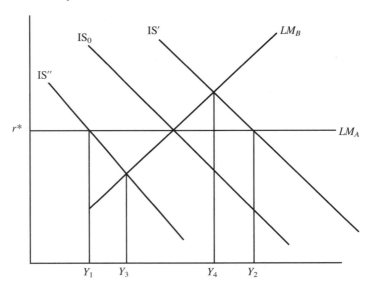

Figure 16.1

IS' and IS" as in Figure 16.1, with the LM unchanged, income varies between Y_1 and Y_2 if the interest rate is being set at r^*, but only between Y_3 and Y_4 if the money supply is being fixed. On the other hand, if money demand shocks cause LM_B to shift between LM' and LM" with the IS unchanged as in Figure 16.2, income varies between Y_1 and Y_2. But if the interest rate is being set horizontal shifts of LM_A have no effect on income: the money demand shocks are automatically absorbed through adjustments in the money supply designed to keep the interest rate constant. Thus setting the interest rate makes income

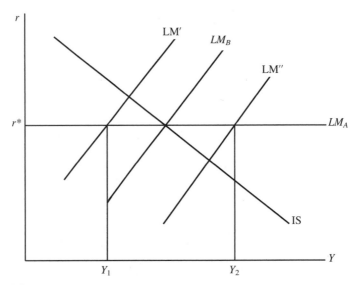

Figure 16.2

more susceptible to (that is, more affected by) expenditure shocks but insulates it from money demand shocks, while fixing the money supply makes income relatively less affected by expenditure shocks but vulnerable to money demand shocks. The implication is that if expenditure shocks are in some sense larger and more prevalent than money demand shocks it is better to fix the money supply, but if money demand shocks are larger and more prevalent than expenditure shocks it is better to set the interest rate.

The more complete analysis which Poole offered focuses on the implications of the two policies for the costs which the government faces under each kind of policy. This is formalised in terms of a quadratic 'loss function'

$$L = E[(Y - Y_f)^2] \hspace{4cm} [16.1]$$

according to which the government's loss (that is, its reduction in utility) is equal to the expected value of the square of the difference between actual income Y and the target (full employment) level of income Y_f. The squaring of the difference means, first, that the government finds deviations in either direction equally undesirable and, second, that it finds larger deviations relatively more undesirable. Here Poole considers, not just discrete shocks of a given size as in the graphical analysis of the previous paragraph, but shocks which are random variables with a mean of zero and a given variance. It turns out that the loss depends not just on the amplitude or variance of the two shocks but also on the correlation or covariance between them. If, for example, positive expenditure shocks are typically accompanied by positive money demand shocks of a comparable magnitude, then fixing the money supply will make the two shocks affect income in opposite directions (LM shifts left when IS shifts right, and vice-versa) and so reduce the fluctuation in income, compared to the interest rate setting policy which eliminates the money demand shock but exposes the economy to the full expenditure shock. But if positive expenditure shocks are accompanied by negative money demand shocks, fixing the money supply will exacerbate the fluctuation in income (LM shifts right when IS shifts right) by comparison with the interest rate setting case.

Within this framework it is also possible to consider the optimal form of monetary policy. Intuitively, the argument can be visualised in terms of a 'typical' shock in the form of an IS shift associated (to a greater or lesser degree) with an LM shift (in the same or the opposite direction). The effect on income will depend on (among other things) the slope of the LM curve, and there will be some optimal slope for the curve. The government can alter that slope so as to generate the optimal slope, by adopting an appropriate money supply policy which makes money supply depend on (vary systematically with) the interest rate, either positively or negatively. Thus the optimal form of monetary policy will in general be one which is a combination of setting the interest rate and fixing the money supply.

The conclusion that monetary policy should not take the form of a simple target for the money supply is strengthened by noting (with B. Friedman (1975)) that in practice the monetary authority does not 'fix the money supply'.

Instead, in the American institutional context of this discussion at least, it manipulates bank reserves and the interest rate. It can be thought of as first calculating, on the basis of some *ex ante* assumptions about the various likely shocks, the reserves and interest rate required to obtain the desired money supply (itself derived from some target level for overall income), and then setting reserves and the interest rate at those levels. But in that case the level which the money supply turns out to reach reflects the actual shocks affecting the economy in the period, which may be rather different *ex post* from those expected *ex ante*. The authority would do better to treat the actual money supply as an information variable conveying information about the actual shocks affecting the economy, and use that information to adjust the levels of reserves and the interest rate in order to improve the accuracy with which it can direct income towards the desired level.

Rules versus discretion

The second strand of the literature is concerned, not with the optimal form or structure of monetary policy, but with the question of whether policy should be determined by a rule or at the discretion of the monetary authority (which would take into account the state of the economy and, possibly, some other variables). The literature was initiated by Simons (1936), whose principal focus was on the misuse of discretionary power, particularly under the influence of political pressures: Simons wanted arrangements which would prevent 'discretionary (dictatorial, arbitrary) action by an independent monetary authority' (1936, p. 5) and would eliminate pressures from the government on the monetary authority. M. Friedman, on the other hand, in one of his earlier papers (1953) emphasised the technical difficulties of discretionary policy. The lags in the implementation, operation and effects of policy implied that the government needed to be able to make accurate forecasts; if it could not do so policy intended to stabilise might end up destabilising the economy.

Both elements can be found in Friedman's formal proposal of his 'monetary rule' (1960) (already referred to in Chapter 15). This specifies that the money supply should be made to grow, year in and year out, at a rate roughly equal to the underlying rate of productivity growth. On this basis monetary policy would ensure price stability over the medium term: it would be insulated from political pressures, and forecasting errors could not lead to destabilisation. At the same time policy would incorporate a minor countercyclical element, since the money supply would be growing more slowly than money income in booms, but more quickly in recessions.

Friedman's monetary rule proposal was a seminal idea frequently referred to in the discussion of these issues, but the proposal was not widely accepted in the 1960s. While it was obvious that policy could turn out to be destabilising if forecasts were seriously wrong, reasonable people could differ on the probability of large forecast errors. And it could be argued that governments should have the power to make mistakes subject only to the electoral process.

The acceptance of the natural rate hypothesis from the late 1960s and of the rational expectations hypothesis from the 1970s began to shift the argument in favour of the rule. The natural rate hypothesis implied that stabilisation policy could not affect the unemployment rate, or income, over the medium term since the economy would adjust to a stimulus via a rise in the inflation rate and a return to the natural rate of unemployment and output. If, in addition, expectations were rational then the government's ability to influence the real economy in the short term – at least by systematic, and therefore predictable, policies – disappeared as well (as discussed in Chapter 15). However, the most important change in attitudes followed Kydland and Prescott's (1977) exposition of the concept of the time-inconsistency of policy.

Time-inconsistency

Figure 16.3 provides a simple introduction to this concept. The vertical axis measures inflation (in price terms), and the horizontal axis measures the difference between the actual rate of unemployment and the natural rate. This means that the vertical axis indicates points where unemployment is at the natural rate and actual inflation equals expected inflation; it therefore depicts the long-run vertical Phillips curve. The short-run Phillips curves for particular levels of expected inflation are drawn here as straight lines, for simplicity.

Now suppose that the government (possibly though not necessarily reflecting overall social preferences) has some target for inflation and unemployment given by the point $\hat{u}$ which is on the horizontal axis but to the left of the vertical axis: the government would like inflation to be zero but it would also like unemployment to be below the natural rate. The latter could be high because,

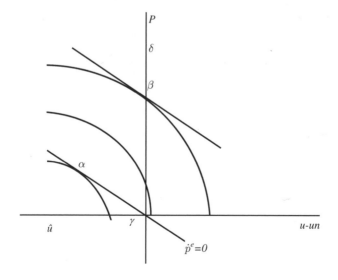

Figure 16.3

for example, of frictions and distortions of some kind in the labour market – such as restrictive practices of various kinds – or perhaps because of a mismatch in the supply and demand for skills, and the government may wish, for political and social reasons, to reduce unemployment to a lower level. If $\hat{u}$ is the government's preferred target, it will have a set of indifference curves such as those shown in the figure at successively larger distances from $\hat{u}$, indicating successively lower utility. Along any such curve, inflation and unemployment change together in ways that just keep the government's utility unchanged: in the north-west quadrant of the diagram, for example, a movement to the north-west along a given curve involves rising inflation being compensated by lower unemployment, and when unemployment dips below $\hat{u}$ the curve turns down as a reduction in inflation is now needed to compensate for unemployment going below the government's target. For reasons discussed below, these curves are homothetic, that is any ray from the point $\hat{u}$ will cut the various curves at points at which they have the same slope; and along the different rays the various curves will be at the same distance from each other.

If expected inflation was initially zero so that the economy was on the $\dot{p}^e = 0$ short-run Phillips curve, the government would attempt to maximise its own utility by getting on to the indifference curve nearest to the point $\hat{u}$. It would therefore stimulate the economy in order to move along the short-run curve to the point α. But in this model expectations are assumed to be rational, and rationality includes the understanding by the private sector of the government's preferences. The private sector therefore knows that if the economy was on the $\dot{p}^e = 0$ curve the government would move to α, at which inflation is positive rather than zero. But this means that expected inflation will never be zero, so that the economy cannot be on the $\dot{p}^e = 0$ curve.

What expectations are possible and what position for the economy is possible? Clearly the only long-run equilibrium will be (a) on the long-run vertical Phillips curve, i.e. at the natural rate of unemployment, and (b) at a point where the government has no incentive to stimulate (or contract) the economy and the private sector therefore believes that the economy will stay at that point. In Figure 16.3 this point is β, where the government's indifference curve is tangential to the short-run Phillips curve so that the government cannot reach a higher level of utility for the given level of expected inflation. But point β is clearly inferior for both the government and the private sector to, say, point γ, at which unemployment is also at the natural rate but inflation is lower.

The idea of time-inconsistency in policy relates to the optimal policy as chosen at different time periods. If, for example, the economy was initially at point δ in Figure 16.3, the government might choose to move to zero inflation at γ, which would increase its utility, but once it got to γ it would realise that – since inflation expectations were now down to zero – it could improve its position by stimulating the economy to get to α. More formally, time-inconsistency exists when the policy chosen by optimising in one time period is not the same as the policy chosen by optimising in the next period. In this form time-inconsistency is a phenomenon which exists in a range of other areas. A common example is patent law: here, *ex ante* a law which ensures that an inventor will reap the benefits of an invention will encourage inventions, but once something has been invented it would be more efficient to let all firms make use of the invention. Other cases can be found in social policy issues. *Ex ante*, for example, a prohibition on divorce may ensure (a) that people get married only when they are sure about the commitment involved and (b) that people try harder to maintain the relationship. Such a prohibition may therefore reduce the amount of marriage-related unhappiness. *Ex post*, however, if a given marriage has clearly broken down, allowing a divorce may substantially reduce the unhappiness experienced by at least one of the various parties involved. Thus the general phenomenon of time-inconsistency is a widespread one. In the context of macro models with rational expectations there is an added twist: time-inconsistency means that the private sector will not believe that the government will really do what it says in the first time period, and this affects the range of choices open to the government.

The diagrammatic analysis set out above can be usefully complemented by an algebraic exposition. One way of formulating the government's preferences is through a loss function (corresponding to that used in the targets and instruments literature above) as follows:

$$L = a\pi^2 + (y - ky^*)^2, \quad a > 0, \quad k > 1 \qquad [16.2]$$

The government's preferred target is assumed to be zero inflation and some level of output ky^* which is greater than the natural rate of output y^* (and thus implies unemployment below the natural rate of unemployment). Its loss is a quadratic function in inflation π and the difference between actual output y and ky^*, which means that it equally dislikes deviations from its preferred target in either direction and that its dislike increases as the deviations get larger. These are the properties that generate the homothetic preferences underlying the indifference curves in Figure 16.3.

Within the natural rate/rational expectations framework the only way in which output can exceed the natural rate y^* is if actual inflation π exceeds expected inflation π^e, and the government's loss function is sometimes written as:

$$L = a\pi^2 - b(\pi - \pi^e), \quad b > 0 \qquad [16.3]$$

An advantage of this formulation is that the two terms can be thought of as the costs of inflation and the benefits of surprise inflation respectively, where the latter may include – in addition to the reduction in unemployment already discussed – benefits in the form of an effective increase in tax revenue: surprise inflation lowers the real value of government debt whose nominal value is fixed (which covers most government debt for most industrial countries, although it excludes index-linked government securities which are important in some countries such as the UK).

However, in order to relate the algebra more closely to the diagrammatic analysis, version [16.2] of the loss function will be used here. It needs to be combined with a standard expectations-augmented Phillips curve relationship (written for output rather than unemployment)

$$y = y^* + b(\pi - \pi^e), \quad b > 0 \tag{16.4}$$

to give

$$L = a\pi^2 + [y^* + b(\pi - \pi^e) - ky^*]^2. \tag{16.5}$$

Suppose first that the government tries to minimises its losses, taking expected inflation as given. Differentiating [16.5] with respect to inflation (which is the variable the government is assumed to be able to choose), setting the derivative to zero to find a minimum (it is easy to check that the second order condition for a minimum is satisfied) and solving for the rate of inflation produces

$$\frac{\partial L}{\partial \pi} = 2a\pi + 2b[y^* + b(\pi - \pi^e) - ky^*] = 0$$

$$\Rightarrow \quad \pi = \frac{b}{a + b^2}[(k - 1)y^* + b\pi^e]. \tag{16.6}$$

But rational expectations implies that the private sector can solve the above problem for itself and will therefore expect inflation at this level. In that case substitution of π for π^e in [16.6] yields an equilibrium inflation rate of

$$\pi_d = \frac{b}{a}[(k - 1)y^*] \tag{16.7}$$

and the government's loss, from [16.5], turns out to be

$$L_d = a\left[\frac{b(k - 1)y^*}{a}\right]^2 + [y^* - ky^*]^2$$

$$= \frac{a + b^2}{a}[(k - 1)y^*]^2 \tag{16.8}$$

where the subscripts on π and L refer to the 'discretionary solution'. This solution corresponds to point β in Figure 16.3: the government is minimising its losses (trying to reach the indifference curve nearest to its preferred target) and the private sector understands this and forms its expectations accordingly. The discretionary solution inflation rate varies inversely with a, the weight on inflation in the government's loss function; positively with b which is the parameter in the expectations-augmented Phillips curve and corresponds to the absolute value of the slope of the short-run Phillips curve in Figure 16.3 (thus the flatter the Phillips curve the higher the rate of inflation); and positively with k which indicates how far the government's preferred target for output differs from the natural rate. The discretionary solution loss also varies with a, b and k in the same directions.

Suppose instead that the government announces it is going to reduce inflation to zero, the private sector believes this promise (so that expected inflation is zero), but the government then reneges on its promise and optimises, given $\pi^e = 0$:

$$\frac{\partial L}{\partial \pi} = 2a\pi + 2b[y^* + b\pi - ky^*] = 0$$

$$\Rightarrow \pi_f = \frac{b}{a + b^2}[(k-1)y^*], \tag{16.9}$$

$$L_f = \frac{a}{a + b^2}[(k-1)y^*]^2. \tag{16.10}$$

where the subscripts refer to the 'fooling solution'. It will be obvious that this fooling (or 'cheating') solution which corresponds to point α in Figure 16.3, involves lower inflation and lower losses for the government than the discretionary solution, but it is not a solution that is viable in the long run under rational expectations.

Suppose finally that the government can find some way of convincing the private sector that it will stick to a decision to reduce inflation to zero and that it does so. In this case actual and expected inflation are equal to zero, and the government's loss is given by

$$L_p = [(k-1)y^*]^2 \tag{16.11}$$

where the subscript refers to the 'pre-commitment solution' in which the government commits itself in advance to not exploiting the gains available to it when expected and actual inflation fall to zero.

Comparison of [16.8], [16.10] and [16.11] shows that

$$L_f < L_p < L_d \tag{16.12}$$

that is, from the government's point of view the fooling solution is preferable to the pre-commitment solution which in turn is preferable to the discretionary solution. Comparison of [16.7], [16.9] and the pre-commitment inflation rate shows that

$$0 = \pi_p < \pi_f < \pi_d. \tag{16.13}$$

Thus, since the fooling solution is not viable in the long run, the pre-commitment solution is preferable, both for the government and for the private sector (which is assumed to have the same preferences as the government or simply to prefer lower inflation). The problem of the time-inconsistency of policy is that in the absence of pre-commitment the economy ends up at the discretionary solution with a rate of inflation much higher than either the government or the private sector would like.

Further developments

The introduction and spread of the concept of time-inconsistency stimulated two main strands of further work. Rogoff (1985) argued that a better solution than the straightforward discretionary one could be obtained if monetary policy was placed in the hands of a central banker who was more 'conservative' than society as a whole, in the sense that he or she had a stronger aversion to inflation. Given expression [16.8] for the loss under discretion,

$$L_d = \frac{a+b^2}{a}[(k-1)y^*]^2 = \frac{a+b^2}{a}L_p$$

the preferences of a more conservative central banker will incorporate a higher value of a, and higher values of a make L_d smaller (the denominator a rises more proportionally than the numerator $a+b^2$) and closer to the pre-commitment loss. However, in a stochastic world where output is affected by a random shock variable ϵ so that equation [16.4] becomes

$$y = y^* + b(\pi - \pi^e) + \epsilon,$$

it can be shown that the more conservative central banker is also less responsive to external shocks so that output may become more variable: there is therefore a trade-off between the price-stability benefits of conservatism and the output-variability costs.

Barro and Gordon (1983) initiated a series of papers on the question of whether the desire to obtain the long-term benefits of a reputation for price stability could successfully constrain the government from opportunistic behaviour. The underlying idea is that a government is tempted to behave opportunistically (i.e. to exploit the existing level of expected inflation so as to reduce unemployment) by the difference between the loss it faces under the fooling and pre-commitment solutions. However, when it does so it is also 'punished' by an upward change in the private sector's expectations of inflation in the next period, which raises its future loss from the (no longer credible) pre-commitment level to the discretionary level. In the model set out above, the temptation is equal to

$$L_p - L_f = [(k-1)y^*]^2 - \frac{a}{a+b^2}[(k-1)y^*]^2 = \frac{\theta}{1+\theta}L_p \qquad [16.14]$$

where

$$L_p = [(k-1)y^*]^2, \quad \theta = \frac{b^2}{a} > 0.$$

Similarly the one period punishment is equal to

$$L_d - L_p = \frac{a+b^2}{a}[(k-1)y^*]^2 - [(k-1)y^*]^2 = \theta L_p \qquad [16.15]$$

Clearly the one period punishment is greater than the temptation. However, to find the net gain for the government from behaving opportunistically the punishment has to be discounted to compare its present value with the (present value of) the temptation. If the discount rate is δ and the punishment lasts for one period only, the net gain is

$$L_p \left[\frac{\theta}{1+\theta} - \frac{\theta}{1+\delta} \right] = L_p \left[\frac{\theta(\delta-\theta)}{(1+\theta)(1+\delta)} \right] \qquad [16.16]$$

This net gain can be positive or negative, depending on the relative magnitudes of δ and θ. If it is positive, the government would gain by reneging on a commitment to zero inflation, the private sector will therefore expect the discretionary solution inflation rate, and the government will accept that solution (it is the best position it can choose on the short-run Phillips curve given by the private sector's expectations). If it were negative, the government would not gain, the private sector will expect the government to keep to its commitment and the government will do so.

However, it is not obvious that the punishment involved will last for only one period. An alternative extreme assumption is that if the government once tries to cheat then the private sector will expect it to do so in all subsequent periods. That means that the punishment is equal to the difference between the discretionary loss and the pre-commitment loss in each subsequent period, discounted to obtain the present value:

$$\frac{\theta L_p}{1+\delta} + \frac{\theta L_p}{(1+\delta)^2} + \frac{\theta L_p}{(1+\delta)^3} + \cdots = \frac{\theta L_p}{\delta}$$

The net gain can then be expressed as

$$L_p \left[\frac{\theta}{1+\theta} - \frac{\theta}{\delta} \right] = L_p \left[\frac{\theta(\delta - 1 - \theta)}{\delta(1+\theta)} \right] \tag{16.17}$$

This expression is positive only if $\delta > \theta + 1$, a stronger condition than that required for [16.16] to be positive; if the punishment lasts for ever, then, it is less likely that the government will inflate.

Barro and Gordon (1983) used a slightly different model, in which the punishment lasts for one period and is the same as the temptation, so that (given the discounting of the punishment) there is always a net gain and zero inflation is never credible. Backus and Driffill (1985) developed the analysis further by examining the case where the private sector is not certain about the government's preferences – whether it is 'wet' or 'hard-nosed' – and tries to work these out from its actions. A wet government may then have an incentive to pretend that it is 'hard-nosed' in order at a later date to be able to move the economy from the equivalent of point γ to point α. Both of these papers, and those which succeeded them, have taken a game theory perspective on the issue, with the government 'playing' some rate of inflation and the private sector 'playing' some rate of expected inflation and each receiving various payoffs. There turns out to be scope for a variety of assumptions within this basic framework, and the results differ significantly. All that can be said by way of summary is that reputational effects may sometimes ensure that the government produces a low-inflation equilibrium but they do not guarantee a result as good as that offered by the pre-commitment solution. Attention has therefore turned increasingly, in policy discussion at least, towards methods of pre-commitment.

A pre-commitment is essentially some device by which the government can – visibly and convincingly – 'tie its hands'. One way of doing this is for the government to publicly assume some commitment such as an explicit target for the growth of the money supply or the growth of nominal income or the rate of inflation (or in an open economy the exchange rate against a stable-price currency), in such a way that it would suffer a serious loss of face if it failed to keep to that commitment. Of course, such a target would need to be met on a consistent basis for credibility to be established and maintained. It would also need to be visibly consistent with other elements of the government's economic policy. A monetary target accompanied by a runaway budget deficit may look unconvincing to the private sector, to the point where it assumes that the target will be allowed to be missed.

An alternative is for control of monetary policy to be given to an institution which is separate from the government and which is given the primary task of keeping prices stable, that is, an independent central bank of this sort. In recent years efforts have been devoted by economists to measuring the extent of central bank independence, by examining a range of factors from the government's influence over interest rates through the way in which central bank directors are appointed to the kind of credit facilities which central banks are obliged to provide to their governments. These measures have then been used to examine whether greater independence is associated with lower inflation and/or lower economic growth. Most analysts have found an inverse relationship beween independence and inflation but no relationship between independence and growth, which suggests that the price-stability benefits of central bank independence do not impose a cost in terms of growth (or unemployment). Attention then turned to investigations of the kind of arrangement or contract between government and central bank which would guarantee low inflation (e.g. Walsh, 1995).

Conclusions and qualifications

The first strand of thought examined here – the targets and instrument literature – did not provide a justification for the use of simple monetary rules. The second strand – the rules versus discretion literature – provided some arguments but not all economists found them convincing. The intellectual development (there was, of course, also the experience of higher inflation in the 1970s and 1980s) that led to a swing in opinion towards rules and targets was the introduction of the concept of time-inconsistency. Optimal policy is time-inconsistent if the actions which are optimal at one time are different from those that are optimal at another time, and that inconsistency will be understood by rational economic agents. Through this concept, economists have shown that governments cannot easily keep inflation low because the private sector will tend to believe, correctly, that governments have an incentive in some situations to inflate. These arguments establish a case for some additional measures to reinforce the credibility of monetary policy, such as the adoption of explicit monetary targets (or explicit targets for some other nominal magnitude such as the growth of nominal income, inflation or the exchange rate), or such as the granting of greater independence to central banks which – because they would be given the task of keeping prices stable and because they do not have to win elections – would not have the same incentive to inflate.

However, some additional remarks should be made here with regard to the experience of monetary policy over the last quarter-century. First, the widespread adoption of monetary targets in the mid-1970s should be understood more as the response to the end of the Bretton Woods period of fixed exchange rates than as the results of a new understanding among governments or central banks of the theories of rational expectations or time-inconsistency. Second, in the Anglo-Saxon countries in particular the period has seen major and continuing shocks to money demand which have exacerbated the problems of operating effective monetary policy (and have been largely responsible for the adoption of targets for nominal magnitudes other than the money supply). Third, the role of policy mistakes should never be underestimated: there have been a number of important occasions when policy makers brought about or acquiesced in higher or lower interest rates, faster or slower monetary growth, and/or higher or lower exchange rates than can be seen with hindsight to have been sensible, but in some cases they did these things not because they were trying to 'cheat' or to win elections by stimulating income and employment, but because they had not properly understood the likely effect of their actions.

Exercises

(i) Use the algebraic version of the IS–LM model set out in Chapter 7 to investigate the effect on equilibrium income of (a) a shift in autonomous expenditure and (b) a shift in autonomous money demand. Now modify the model so that the interest rate is always fixed at $\bar{r}$ and the money supply becomes endogenous, and rework (a) and (b).

(ii) In the diagrammatic exposition of time-inconsistency, what is the effect on points α and β of (a) a reduction in the difference between $\hat{u}$ and the natural rate of unemployment, and (b) an increase in the importance the government attaches to price stability?

(iii) In the algebraic exposition of time-inconsistency; (a) show what happens to the results if the government's target for output is equal to the natural rate (i.e. if $k = 1$); (b) derive the discretionary, fooling and pre-commitment inflation rates and losses for the Barro and Gordon model which uses equation [16.3] for the loss function, and show that the temptation here is equal to the one period (non-discounted) punishment.

Further reading

B. Friedman (1990) provides a survey of the targets and instruments literature, and Fischer (1990) a survey of the rules versus discretion literature, including time-inconsistency. A more detailed discussion of the Barro–Gordon and Backus–Driffill literature, with an appropriate emphasis on its game-theoretic elements, can be found in Blackburn and Christensen (1989). A range of other issues including central bank independence are reviewed in Fischer (1994), while Goodhart (1994) and Cukierman (1994) provide useful discussion on the optimal form of monetary policy.

Chapter 17

Deficits and debt

Chapter 14 shed some light on the interaction of monetary and fiscal policy within a fixed-price IS–LM model, and Chapters 15 and 16 discussed different aspects of macroeconomic policy within a flexible-price rational expectations model. This chapter looks at the interaction of monetary and fiscal policy within a model of the latter kind, emphasising the overall stock of government debt in addition to the deficits that cause changes in that stock. A simple 'monetarist arithmetic' model is set up, and informal analysis is used to explain the striking results obtained by Sargent and Wallace in their (1981) paper. The model is then used to examine the more recent European integration-inspired debate on the need for limits to debt and deficits.

Basic monetarist arithmetic

The idea here is to proceed from the government budget constraint, which says that the budget deficit must be financed by some combination of bond and money financing, to examine the relationship between the growth of the stock of debt (bonds), the extent to which the deficit is financed by bonds or by money, and the growth of the money stock. Consider first the following government budget constraint

$$G - T + rB = \frac{dB}{dt} + \frac{dM}{dt} \qquad [17.1]$$

where G and T are real government expenditure and tax revenue, B and M are the stocks of outstanding government bonds (debt) and the monetary base respectively, r is the real interest rate payable on existing debt, and dX/dt is the growth over time of X. Now divide both sides by income Y and use lowercase letters to indicate the ratio of the variable to income:

$$g - t + rb = \frac{1}{Y} \cdot \frac{dB}{dt} + \frac{1}{Y} \cdot \frac{dM}{dt} \qquad [17.2]$$

Next differentiate the debt to income ratio $b = B/Y$ with respect to time t:

$$\frac{db}{dt} = \frac{Y \cdot dB/dt - B \cdot dY/dt}{Y^2} = \frac{1}{Y}\frac{dB}{dt} - \frac{1}{Y}\frac{B}{Y}\frac{dY}{dt}$$

This can be rearranged, with the notation $\dot{h} = dh/dt$, to give

$$\frac{1}{Y} \cdot \frac{dB}{dt} = \frac{1}{Y}\cdot\frac{B}{Y}\frac{dY}{dt} + \frac{db}{dt} = \frac{b\dot{Y}}{Y} + \dot{b}$$

which can be substituted in [17.2] to give

$$(g - t) + rb = \frac{b\dot{Y}}{Y} + \dot{b} + \frac{1}{Y}\frac{dM}{dt} = bx + \dot{b} + \dot{m}$$ [17.3]

where x is the proportional growth rate of income $\dot{Y}/Y$ and $\dot{m}$ is the growth of the monetary base as a proportion of income $1/Y \cdot dM/dt$.

Equation [17.3] is a modified government budget constraint. The left-hand side is the overall budget deficit, consisting of two elements: the primary deficit $(g - t)$ is the difference between the government's expenditure on goods and services and its receipts from taxation, while rb is the government's expenditure on debt service (i.e. the interest payable on the government debt), each element being considered as a proportion of income. On the right-hand side bx should be understood as the additional amount of government debt that can be issued while the debt to income ratio remains the same: if, for example, income were growing at 5% a year and the initial stock of debt was equal to 50% of income, then the stock of debt could grow by 2.5% a year with the ratio unchanged. The second element is the growth of the debt to income ratio $\dot{b}$. The third is the monetary financing of the deficit (in relation to income) $\dot{m}$.

Unpleasant implications

Sargent and Wallace (1981) use a version of the above relationship embedded in a simple macroeconomic model to examine the effect of lack of coordination of monetary and fiscal policy. Their implicit institutional context is the US, where fiscal policy (expenditure and taxes) are decided by Congress in an often tortuous and highly lagged political process while monetary policy is set by a largely independent central bank, the Federal Reserve Board, which has much more ability than Congress to react promptly to domestic and international economic developments. Sargent and Wallace assume that fiscal policy involves a predetermined stream of (significant) budget deficits, and investigate the consequences of different responses by the monetary authority. Although from the east of the Atlantic this may seem a strange starting point, it can be regarded as a not entirely inaccurate stylisation of the Reagan era in the US (which was just beginning as their paper was first published). Their macro model is a simple monetarist one in which real income growth is constant and the price level is set purely by the interaction of money demand, which incorporates a constant income velocity, and money supply, which is driven by the government budget constraint.

To understand their argument it is convenient to rearrange equation [17.3] to yield:

$$\dot{m} = (g - t) + (r - x)\,b - \dot{b}. \tag{17.4}$$

Sargent and Wallace take the primary deficit as positive and given (determined by the fiscal authority), and they assume that the real interest rate payable on government debt r is greater than the economy's growth rate x. This assumption may not have been valid for some periods in the inflationary 1960s and 1970s, but it has been generally true of the 1980s and 1990s, and Sargent and Wallace argue that it is highly plausible for the situations of high fiscal deficits which they are considering. The second element on the right-hand side of [17.4] is therefore positive, which means that total debt service costs exceed the amount of debt finance which can be issued without raising the debt to income ratio. The third element, the growth of the debt to income ratio, enters with a negative sign: the higher this growth the lower – other things being equal – the rate of monetary growth.

Next, and most fundamentally, Sargent and Wallace assume that there is a limit to the growth of the debt to income ratio b. They argue that the ratio can grow for a while but surely not forever. The stock of government debt could obviously not exceed the total stock of savings, and it would probably hit an effective ceiling well before that. Formally, this can be modelled in two ways. The more intuitive way is to specify a maximum level to the ratio, such that when the actual ratio reaches this maximum at, say, time τ, it can rise no further. But the more tractable way (emphasised by Sargent and Wallace) is to assume that the debt to income ratio hits a ceiling at a specified time τ, and after that point can grow no further. Either way, once the ceiling is reached the growth of the debt to income $\dot{b}$ falls to zero, equation [17.4] reduces to

$$\dot{m} = (g - t) + (r - x)b \tag{17.5}$$

and monetary growth takes off: the primary deficit and that part of the debt service costs which cannot be covered by new debt issues must be 'monetised'.

The interesting question relates to the effect of alternative monetary growth rates in the period before τ, when monetary growth can be held down by the issue of large amounts of debt. If the monetary authority keeps monetary policy in this period tighter in order to keep inflation lower, then either the specified ceiling is reached more quickly, or the actual debt to income ratio will be higher when time τ is reached. After time τ, however, monetary growth and therefore inflation must accelerate. So in the first case, tighter monetary policy in the pre-τ period results in the acceleration of inflation occurring sooner than it would have done otherwise. In the second case, tighter monetary policy in the pre-τ period results in the actual ratio being higher when time τ is reached, so that the acceleration of inflation when it comes will be greater (because in [17.5] b is now larger).

However, these striking results – 'tighter monetary policy now leads to higher inflation later' – do not exhaust the possibilities of the model. So far it has been assumed that the demand for money is related purely to income, but theory and evidence suggests that the demand for money should also vary inversely with expected inflation. In this case, as Sargent and Wallace show formally, it is possible that tighter monetary policy in the pre-τ period can lead to higher inflation in that period, as well as later. It turns out that there are two forces affecting inflation under this scenario. Tighter monetary policy reduces the growth of the money supply and this tends to lower the rate of inflation. But tighter monetary policy also implies higher inflation later which leads to higher expectations of inflation now, and the rise in expected inflation reduces the (growth of the) demand for money, which, for given money supply growth, tends to raise inflation. For some plausible configurations of the parameters it is therefore possible that tighter monetary policy now can lead to higher inflation now. While those configurations may not always hold, and while the results depend in particular on an extreme assumption about profligate fiscal policy not being coordinated with monetary policy, the moral that such a lack of coordination is potentially damaging is an important one. Indeed, it is one of the few strong arguments against central bank independence.

Non-apocalyptic implications

If it were true that there is a ceiling to the debt to income ratio, it would surely be possible to find empirical evidence of ratios tending to some level, with the monetary financing of deficits increasing as they come closer. In fact, however, the empirical evidence shows very wide variations in debt to income ratios both across countries and over time. In the UK, for example, the ratio (specifically the OECD's data on general government gross financial liabilities as a percentage of nominal GDP) fell from 54% in 1979 to a trough of 39% in 1990, before rising to 60% in 1996. In that year other major countries' ratios varied from 61% in France, 62% in Germany and 63% in the US through 81% in Japan and 101% in Canada to 125% in Italy. Thus the fundamental assumption of the Sargent and Wallace argument – that there is a set limit to the ratio, after which it cannot rise further – appears on the surface at least to be unjustified by the empirical evidence. Moreover, that evidence can be rationalised easily enough, by suggesting that the ratio can vary over a wide range as the result of variations in the relative rate of return on government debt as opposed to other financial assets.

However, the basic framework outlined above can be used in other, possibly more revealing ways. First, it highlights in a useful way the extent to which fiscal deficits in one period affect the debt service costs that have to be paid in later periods: a rise in b leads to a higher overall fiscal deficit which has to be financed in one way or another; if monetary financing of the deficit is restricted for other reasons, the deficits may become unsustainable. This suggests that there is a trade-off between the use of fiscal policy in different periods: more use now reduces the scope for later use. While this point was widely ignored in the 1960s and 1970s, many of the countries that allowed their debt to rise significantly in the 1980s and early 1990s found that fiscal policy was in effect no longer available to them.

Second, instead of using equation [17.5] to investigate the consequences for monetary growth of a ceiling to the debt to income ratio, equation [17.3] can be rearranged so as to consider the consequences of fiscal deficits for the debt to income ratio:

$$\dot{b} = (g - t) + (r - x)b - \dot{m}$$ [17.6]

This says that the growth of the ratio will be determined by the primary deficit, the existing stock of debt multiplied by the difference between the rates of interest and growth, and (with a negative sign) the rate of monetary growth. It is now widely taken for granted that inflation should be kept low, and that fiscal deficits should be financed in non-inflationary, and therefore mainly in non-monetary, ways. For example, these conditions have been adopted in the plan for a European monetary union (EMU): the explicit aim of the new institutional arrangements will be to ensure price stability, and neither the national central banks nor the new union-level European Central Bank will be allowed to provide credit to national governments (or to the European Union itself). This means that in equation [17.6] the monetary financing term $\dot{m}$ (monetary financing of the fiscal deficit as a proportion of income) will be zero, which in turn means that there will be greater upward pressure on the debt to income ratio.

In the discussions on EMU that culminated in the Maastricht Treaty of December 1991, there was concern that in this situation some national governments might run large fiscal deficits that could cause problems for other countries or for the union as a whole, by absorbing a disproportionate share of new union-wide savings or by leading to a situation where overall fiscal policy in the union (set by individual national governments without much regard to the 'spillover' effects of fiscal policy in one country on aggregate demand in other countries) was in conflict with the monetary policy of the central bank. It was therefore decided that individual national governments should keep their debt to income ratios no higher than 60% (on a definition which yields slightly lower figures than those given above) and their fiscal deficits no higher than 3% of national income. These particular numbers have been widely criticised and cannot be defended with any precision, and the need for specified limits has been contested. Nevertheless, the argument that unsustainable national budget deficits would create major problems for the European Union under EMU would find considerable, though not universal, support from economists. The framework offered by equation [17.6] can then be used to examine the implications of, for example, stabilising the debt to income ratio for the primary deficit: given zero monetary financing, the existing stock of debt and some assumptions about the interest rate and the real growth rate, a constant ratio $(\dot{b} = 0)$ implies a particular (typically negative) level for the primary deficit. It was also possible on this basis to calculate the primary deficits (or surpluses) which European countries should run before EMU starts in order to be able to enter EMU with their deficits and debts within the specified limits (which were part of the entry criteria as well as part of the behaviour required after entry).

Conclusions and qualifications

Fiscal deficits increase the stock of government debt outstanding, which in turn increases the interest payments which the government has to make on its debt in subsequent periods. If there is a natural limit to the debt to income ratio then a separation of powers and lack of coordination between the fiscal and monetary authorities may lead, if the fiscal authority runs continuing large deficits, to a situation where the deficits and part of the debt service cost on the existing debt are necessarily monetised. In that case monetary growth will accelerate, and inflation with it.

This doomsday scenario is unlikely to be realised, in particular because it is far from clear empirically or theoretically that such a limit exists. However, the basic relationships underline the effect of fiscal deficits in one period on the interest payments and therefore the deficit itself in the next period, and suggest that major recourse to fiscal deficits in one period is likely to make fiscal policy largely unusable for some time afterwards. These relationships can also be used to analyse the implications for the primary deficit of restrictions on the monetary financing of deficits and the debt to income ratio, such as were involved in the Maastricht plans for EMU.

An important qualification, or rather complication, to the analysis should be noted, however. All of the formal analysis conducted above has been in real terms, with real government expenditure and tax revenues and the real interest rate on government debt. In the context of a zero-inflation EMU or in the context of Sargent and Wallace's assumptions (rational expectations so that nominal interest rates rise to include expected inflation) there is no problem. But in a world in which inflation is positive and expectations at least sometimes seriously mistaken, it is important to recognise that the real value of outstanding conventional (non-indexed-linked) bonds is reduced by unexpected inflation – that is, inflation which was not expected at the time of issue and is therefore not compensated by higher nominal coupon payments. Indeed, this phenomenon may be one reason why governments are sometimes prone to inflation: it decreases their real liabilities and in that sense constitutes an 'inflation tax' which supplements or takes the place of other forms of tax revenue. It is also the reason why, for example, the UK's debt to income ratio fell during the 1970s despite continuing large budget deficits. The formal analysis set out above needs to be implemented in this case with considerable care, for example, by 'inflation-adjusting' the fiscal deficit to take account of the revenue from this inflation tax (there are a number of slightly different ways in which such adjustments can be made).

Exercises

(i)   What happens to the main Sargent and Wallace results if the real interest rate is less than the rate of economic growth?

(ii)   On the Maastricht definition the debt to income ratios of France, the Netherlands and Belgium in 1996 were 56.5%, 78.5% and 130.1% respectively. If the growth rates for each country were assumed to be 3% and the rate of interest was assumed to be 4%, how large should the primary budget surplus be in each country in order to stabilise its debt to income ratio without resorting to monetary financing of the government deficit?

Further reading

The original Sargent and Wallace (1981) paper is technically difficult (and its appendices more so), but an easily accessible introduction to 'debt dynamics' with some discussion of the EMU issues can be found in De Grauwe (1997, section 9.2). An alternative treatment of both debt dynamics and the inflation-adjustment of the fiscal deficit can be found in Leslie (1993, Chapter 1). Begg (1987) includes an attempt to make sense of official UK data, building on the key work by Miller (e.g. 1985). The source for both sets of data in the chapter on countries' debt to income ratios is the statistical annex of the OECD's *Economic Outlook* for June 1997.

Chapter 18

Modelling the exchange rate

Chapter 12 contained a brief discussion of how (flexible) exchange rates are determined. This chapter sets out one model, the asset market model sometimes referred to as the Dornbusch overshooting model, in some detail, and then discusses less formally some of the insights provided by portfolio balance models.

The Dornbusch overshooting model

This model was first developed in part as an attempt to explain why flexible exchange rates turned out to be so volatile. In the debates over fixed versus flexible exchange rates in the 1950s and 1960s proponents of the latter (and some of the former) had assumed that flexible exchange rates would move relatively slowly and smoothly. But within a few years of the disintegration of the Bretton Woods arrangements, under which most major currencies had been fixed to the dollar from the mid-1940s to the early 1970s, that assumption had been shown to be misplaced: there were large and sometimes rapid changes in exchange rates, and currency crises turned out to be at least as common under flexible as under fixed rates.

The Dornbusch model is a complicated one (although it requires no arcane mathematical techniques), but it is worth working through with some care. In the algebraic exposition which follows, all variables are in natural logarithms and asterisks indicate variables pertaining to the 'world' economy, which is assumed to be large relative to the domestic economy. The key intuition to bear in mind is that it is assumed that goods prices are 'sticky' (they cannot adjust quickly) whereas financial or asset prices (interest rates and exchange rates) adjust quickly to clear the markets.

Suppose first that equilibrium in financial markets requires that the yield on domestic bonds given by the domestic interest rate r minus the expected depreciation of the domestic currency $\dot{e}^e$ (where the exchange rate is defined as the domestic currency value of a unit of foreign exchange, so that a rise in e is a depreciation) is equal to the yield on foreign bonds r^*.

$$r - \dot{e}^e = r^* \qquad [18.1]$$

It is assumed here that domestic and foreign bonds are perfect substitutes, that is there are no reasons other than the expected yield which affect the relative demands for them; and that capital mobility is perfect, that is capital flows respond strongly to incipient yield differentials so as to ensure that [18.1] always holds. Equation [18.1], which is the same as equation [12.13], is called the uncovered interest parity condition.

Next, consider the expectations term $\dot{e}^e$. In this rational expectations model private sector agents correctly calculate the long-run equilibrium exchange rate $\bar{e}$ and they assume correctly that the exchange rate adjusts towards that long-run equilibrium by some proportion θ of the difference between it and the current exchange rate:

$$\dot{e}^e = \theta(\bar{e} - e), \quad 0 < \theta < 1. \qquad [18.2]$$

Next, suppose that equilibrium in the money market requires the real money supply $m - p$ to equal real money demand (which depends positively on real income – here assumed to be constant at the natural rate of output $\bar{y}$ – and negatively on the interest rate):

$$m - p = \phi\bar{y} - \eta r, \quad \phi, \eta > 0. \qquad [18.3]$$

Next, consider domestic aggregate demand, which is assumed to be a function of the real exchange rate $e + p^* - p$ (in non-log terms this amounts to EP*/P, that is the ratio of foreign prices in domestic currency to domestic prices, so it is a measure of the international competitiveness of domestic output affecting net exports); the foreign level of income y^* (which also affects exports); domestic income (a consumption-type effect); the domestic interest rate (an investment-type effect); and a domestic autonomous expenditure term g:

$$d = \alpha(e + p^* - p) + \beta y^* + \gamma\bar{y} - \delta r + g, \quad \alpha, \beta, \gamma, \delta > 0 \qquad [18.4]$$

Finally, assume that domestic output is fixed at some natural level $\bar{y}$ and inflation is a function of excess demand, that is the difference between aggregate demand and aggregate output:

$$\Delta p = \psi(d - \bar{y}) = \psi[\alpha(e + p^* - p) + \beta\bar{y} = \gamma y^* - \delta r + g - \bar{y}], \quad \psi > 0. \qquad [18.5]$$

Notice that the price level does not move to clear the market, it just responds to excess demand by rising and to excess supply by falling, and there is no expected inflation term.

These equations provide the starting points for the model. It is convenient to consider the long-run equilibrium position first, and then relate the short run equilibrium to it. In long-run equilibrium the exchange rate e is at its long run level $\bar{e}$, expectations of exchange rate change are therefore equal to zero (equation [18.2]), and the domestic interest rate is equal to the foreign interest rate (equation [18.1]); at the same time income is as always in this model at the natural level $\bar{y}$. Substituting in equation [18.3] produces

$$m - p = \phi\bar{y} - \eta r^* \qquad\qquad [18.6]$$

The right-hand side of equation [18.6] is now given, so that the (exogenous) domestic money supply must determine the equilibrium price level $\bar{p}$:

$$\bar{p} = m - \phi\bar{y} + \eta r^* \qquad\qquad [18.7]$$

Long-run equilibrium also requires that aggregate demand is equal to output, i.e. (using also the long-run equality of domestic and foreign interest rates)

$$\alpha(\bar{e} + p^* - \bar{p}) + \beta y^* + \gamma\bar{y} - \delta r^* + g = \bar{y}$$

$$=> \bar{e} = \bar{p} - p^* - \frac{1}{\alpha}[\beta y^* - (1 - \gamma)\bar{y} - \delta r^* + g] \qquad\qquad [18.8]$$

The foreign price level and the terms in brackets on the right-hand side of [18.8] are all exogenous, so that once $\bar{p}$ is determined from [18.7] $\bar{e}$ is determined as well. In addition, the long-run equilibrium levels of the exchange rate and the price level must be proportionally related (for given values of the exogenous variables the difference between their logarithmic values is always the· same, in other words the quotient of their non-logarithmic values is always the same, so they must each rise or fall in the same proportion). The model therefore incorporates what is called relative purchasing power parity (which refers to changes rather than levels) in the long run.

Short run equilibrium in asset markets requires that uncovered interest parity holds and that the money market clears. It can be found by substituting from [18.1] and [18.2] in [18.3]:

$$m - p = \phi\bar{y} - \eta[r^* + \theta(\bar{e} - e)] = \phi\bar{y} - \eta r^* - \eta\theta(\bar{e} - e) \qquad\qquad [18.9]$$

Rearranging equation [18.7] for the long-run equilibrium as

$$m - \bar{p} = \phi\bar{y} - \eta r^*$$

and subtracting it from [18.9] gives the relationship between the short-run price level and the exchange rate in terms only of the long-run levels:

$$\bar{p} - p = -\eta\theta(\bar{e} - e)$$

$$=> p = \bar{p} + \eta\theta(\bar{e} - e) \qquad\qquad [18.10]$$

or alternatively

$$e = \bar{e} + \frac{1}{\eta\theta}(\bar{p} - p) \qquad\qquad [18.11]$$

Equations [18.10] and [18.11] make clear two things: there is an inverse relationship between the actual price level and the actual exchange rate; and when either of these two prices is at its long-run equilibrium level the other must be at its long-run equilibrium too.

It is now convenient to consider short-run goods market equilibrium by constructing a schedule along which inflation is equal to zero. From equation [18.5] zero inflation requires that aggregate demand is equal to output:

$$\alpha(e + p^* - p) + \beta y^* + \gamma \bar{y} - \delta r + g = \bar{y} \qquad [18.12]$$

In the short run the domestic interest rate is not equal to the foreign rate but is determined from equation [18.3]. Substituting from there and rearranging gives

$$\alpha(e + p^* - p) + \beta y^* + \gamma \bar{y} - \delta \cdot \frac{(\phi \bar{y} - m + p)}{\eta} + g = \bar{y}$$

$$\Rightarrow p = \frac{\alpha\eta}{\alpha\eta + \delta} \cdot (e + p^*) + \frac{\eta\beta}{\alpha\eta + \delta} \cdot y^* - \frac{\eta(1 - \gamma) + \delta\phi}{\alpha\eta + \delta} \cdot \bar{y}$$

$$+ \frac{\eta}{\alpha\eta + \delta} \cdot g + \frac{\delta}{\alpha\eta + \delta} \cdot m \qquad [18.13]$$

The long-run equilibrium of equation [18.13] is

$$\bar{p} = \frac{\alpha\eta}{\alpha\eta + \delta} \cdot (\bar{e} + p^*) + \frac{\eta\beta}{\alpha\eta + \delta} \cdot y^* - \frac{\eta(1 - \gamma) + \delta\phi}{\alpha\eta + \delta} \cdot \bar{y}$$

$$+ \frac{\eta}{\alpha\eta + \delta} \cdot g + \frac{\delta}{\alpha\eta + \delta} \cdot m$$

and this can be subtracted from equation [18.13] to express the relationship between price level and exchange rate more simply in terms of deviations from the long-run equilibrium:

$$p - \bar{p} = \frac{\alpha\eta}{\alpha\eta + \delta} \cdot (e - \bar{e}) \qquad [18.14]$$

Equation [18.14] shows that when the exchange rate is at its long-run equilibrium level so also is the price level. Given what was said above about equation [18.10], this shows that long-run equilibrium in both asset and goods markets occurs at the point $(\bar{p}, \bar{e})$. Equation [18.14] can also be differentiated to find the relationship between p and e:

$$\frac{\partial p}{\partial e} = \frac{\alpha\eta}{\alpha\eta + \delta} > 0, \; < 1.$$

Short-run goods market equilibrium therefore requires that for a higher (depreciated) exchange rate the price level must be higher, but not as much. The underlying relationship can be seen in terms of equation [18.4]: a rise in e improves competitiveness (the first term on the right-hand side) and therefore raises aggregate demand, while a rise in p reduces competitiveness (the first term) and therefore reduces aggregate demand, but via the money market equation [18.3] it also raises the interest rate and therefore reduces aggregate demand (via the fourth term on the right-hand side). Thus, for aggregate demand to remain equal to output, a rise in e must be accompanied by a smaller rise in p, hence $\partial p / \partial e$ is positive but less than 1.

The relationships derived so far can be presented diagrammatically as in Figure 18.1. Here the 45° line shows the relationship between the long-run equilibrium price level (on the vertical axis) and the long-run equilibrium exchange rate (on the horizontal axis) given by equation [18.8].

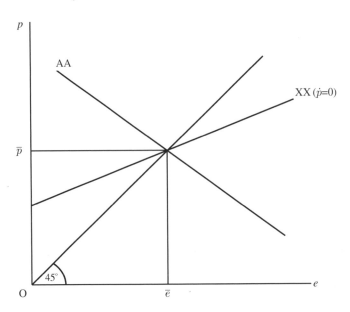

Figure 18.1

It should be noted that the vertical intercept may be positive or negative; here for simplicity it is drawn as zero. The AA curve plots the short-run asset market equilibrium relationship given by equation [18.11]. And the XX curve plots the short-run goods market equilibrium relationship given by equation [18.14]. The AA and XX curves intersect on the 45° line at the long-run equilibrium levels $\bar{e}$ and $\bar{p}$.

This analysis has proceeded by working out the equations underlying the three curves in Figure 18.1, but it is worth noting that an alternative route can be taken which uses the techniques more normally used to solve full rational expectations models. Equation [18.7] gives a horizontal line from $\bar{p}$ which can be thought of as the schedule along which the exchange rate is not changing (because it is at its long-run equilibrium – see the derivation of [18.7] above). The XX curve is the schedule along which inflation is zero. It is then possible to work out in what direction the price level and the exchange rate are changing at any point on Figure 18.2 by reference to these two schedules. Above the $\dot{e}=0$ schedule the price level is above its long-run equilibrium, the interest rate is therefore above the foreign interest rate, expected depreciation is therefore positive and the exchange rate must actually be depreciating; while below the schedule by the same logic the exchange rate must be appreciating. These movements are indicated by the horizontal arrows in Figure 18.2. To the left (north-west) of the $\dot{p}=0$ schedule the exchange rate is below (appreciated relative to) the level at which aggregate demand equals output, therefore there is excess supply and the price level must be falling; while to the right (south-east) the exchange rate is depreciated relative to the level that equates aggregate demand and output, so there must be excess demand and the price level must be rising. These movements are indicated by the vertical arrows in Figure 18.2. The AA schedule can then be seen as the locus of the only points at which the left–right and up–down movements combine to bring about a movement towards the full equilibrium point ζ. This is what is referred to as a 'saddlepath'; in rational expectations models the saddlepath is the unique stable path along which full equilibrium can be approached, and it is assumed that the economy 'jumps' on to such a path.

Monetary expansion in the Dornbusch model

Now consider the effect of an increase in the domestic money supply. By equation [18.13] this shifts the XX schedule up to X'X' as in Figure 18.3, by equation [18.7] the long-run equilibrium price level is increased, and by equation [18.8] the long-run equilibrium exchange rate is also increased (by the same amount). The AA schedule therefore shifts out to the right so that it intersects the new XX schedule at ξ on the 45° line. In the short run the price level is fixed at $\bar{p}_0$ so the exchange rate jumps from $\bar{e}_0$ to e_1, on the new A'A' schedule. From there the economy gradually moves north-west along AA' until it reaches the new long-run equilibrium point ξ with the price level and the exchange rate at $\bar{p}_1$, and $\bar{e}_1$, respectively.

What this means is that the monetary expansion brings about a higher domestic price level and a depreciated exchange rate in the long run, but in the

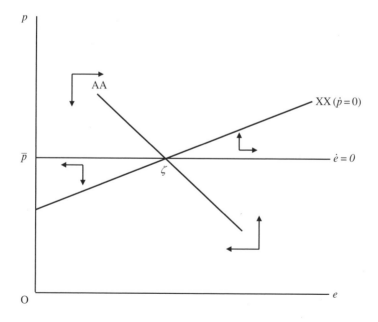

Figure 18.2

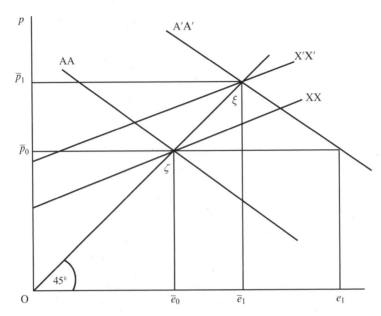

Figure 18.3

short run because prices are sticky the interest rate falls below the foreign
interest rate and this requires (for equilibrium in financial markets – equation
[18.1]) an expectation of appreciation; however, this can occur – given the
nature of the expectations in the model (equation [18.2]) – only if there is a
prior depreciation which goes beyond what is required in the long run. In the
subsequent adjustment period there is excess demand (the economy is below
X'X') so that prices rise; and this in turn means that the domestic interest rate
gradually falls back towards the world level and the exchange rate gradually
appreciates towards its long-run level.

Fiscal expansion in the Dornbusch model

Fiscal expansion can be analysed in this model in terms of an increase in the
domestic autonomous expenditure term g. From equation [18.13] an increase in
g shifts the XX schedule upwards to X'X' in Figure 18.4. It does not affect the
equilibrium price level since g does not appear in equation [18.7]. However, it
also shifts upwards the 45° line (as can be seen from a rearrangement of
equation [18.8]). Since the new long-run equilibrium is at point ξ, the AA
schedule shifts down to A'A' and the exchange rate moves directly to $\bar{e}_1$,
without any overshooting and without any change in the price level.

The underlying behaviour here is as follows: the larger fiscal deficit boosts
aggregate demand but this has to be offset in the long run by a decline in some
other element of aggregate demand, and in this case the appreciation of the
nominal and (with the price level unchanged because the money supply has not

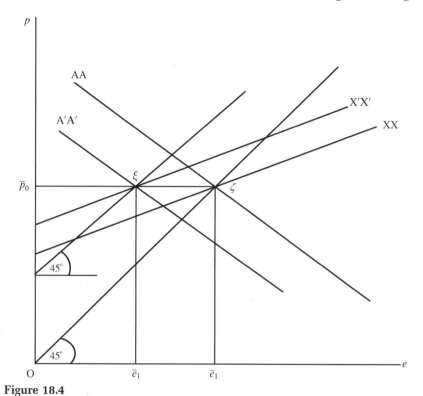

Figure 18.4

changed) real exchange rate provides the required decline via reduced international competitiveness. Since the price level does not have to change, so that its stickiness does not slow down the adjustment, the economy moves to the new full equilibrium at once.

The Dornbusch model: alternative diagrammatic exposition

A useful alternative way of understanding the model, which also makes it easy to introduce variations in the assumptions, is through the diagrammatic presentation of Figure 18.5. Here the movements of key variables are shown over time, for a somewhat different case. Suppose there is zero inflation in the world economy, but the domestic economy has been inflating at a certain rate for some time (both economies are assumed to be static, i.e. not growing). Moreover, this has been well understood so that the exchange rate has been continuously depreciating in line with inflation and the domestic interest rate has been standing above the foreign interest rate by a margin consistent with expectations of both inflation and depreciation. Then suppose that the domestic monetary authority decides to turn over a new leaf and to replace its inflationary policy by a zero rate of monetary growth in order to produce price

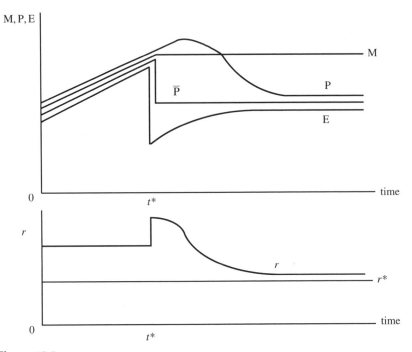

Figure 18.5

stability. Again this is known to and understood by private sector agents, whose expectations of inflation and of long-run depreciation fall to zero.

In this situation the short-run impact of the tightening of monetary policy must fall entirely on the interest rate: neither prices nor output can adjust so the only way in which money demand can adjust to money supply is via a rise in the interest rate. But a rise in the interest rate is consistent with equilibrium in financial markets (the uncovered interest parity condition) only if it is accompanied by an increased expectation of depreciation. And the latter can occur only if there is an immediate appreciation of the exchange rate to beyond its long-run equilibrium level.

These developments are illustrated in Figure 18.5. In the initial period domestic money, domestic prices (both actual and the long-run equilibrium level), and the exchange rate are all rising at the same rate. Then at time t^* monetary policy changes and the money supply ceases to rise. The domestic interest rate (in the lower part of the figure), which had been constant at a margin above the foreign interest rate, rises sharply. Domestic inflation continues to rise for a while, due to the inertia or stickiness in the goods market, but then slows and turns negative, with domestic prices falling towards the long-run equilibrium price level given by $\bar{P}$. That level is actually below the level reached at time t^*, because the fall in expected inflation leads to an increase in the demand for money (as in the Sargent and Wallace model discussed in Chapter 17) and therefore a lower price level in relation to the money supply. As prices fall, equilibrium in the money market allows a fall in the interest rate towards its long-run equilibrium level, which is that given by the world interest rate (since the world economy also has zero inflation). Meanwhile the exchange rate drops sharply (i.e. appreciates) at time t^*, and then rises (depreciates) gradually towards its new long-run equilibrium level at which point it will be back in line with domestic prices because purchasing power parity is assumed to hold in the long run.

Portfolio balance models

The Dornbusch overshooting model is usually identified as a 'monetary' model of the exchange rate, mainly because of its emphasis on the money supply and its summary treatment of other financial assets. The other main strand of work in this area is the portfolio balance literature, which can be thought of as developing out of the portfolio analysis pioneered by Tobin's work on the demand for money discussed in Chapter 5.

The first key point about the portfolio balance models is that they treat domestic bonds and foreign bonds as different assets which are not perfect substitutes for each other. In other words, investors are not concerned only about the relative rates of return on the two kinds of bond. One possible difference is that bonds from one country may be traded in a larger and deeper market so that the bonds are easier to sell and their price is less volatile; in other words the market is more liquid. Other possible differences relate to the risk of default or to 'political risk', that is the risk that the government concerned may take some action which adversely affects bondholders – risks which may be much higher, for example, on the bonds of some developing or transition economies than on those from the main industrial countries.

The implication of imperfect substitutability is that the demand for each asset has to be modelled separately. Portfolio balance models typically include demand equations for each of money, domestic bonds and foreign bonds in which the proportion of overall financial wealth held in each form is a function of the return on each asset (that on money being assumed to be zero). With (nominal) wealth W defined as the sum of money M, domestic bonds B and the domestic currency value of foreign bonds eF, i.e.

$$W = M + B + eF \qquad [18.15]$$

the demand for each asset can be written as follows (with the various first derivatives of the functions written as M_r and so on):

$$\frac{M}{W} = M(r, r^*), \ M_r < 0, \ M_{r^*} < 0$$

$$\frac{B}{W} = B(r, r^*), \ B_r > 0, \ B_{r^*} < 0$$

$$\frac{eF}{W} = F(r, r^*), \ F_r < 0, \ F_{r^*} > 0$$

where r^* should be thought of as the overall return on the foreign bond, including the expected depreciation of the domestic currency. Thus a rise in the return on domestic bonds leads investors to hold less money, more domestic bonds and less foreign bonds; while a rise in the return on foreign bonds leads them to hold less money, less domestic bonds and more foreign bonds. However, as in Tobin's analysis, investors will not ordinarily hold all their assets in one form of wealth whatever the configuration of interest rates, because the second derivatives of the above expressions will be of the opposite sign to the first derivatives (e.g. a 1% rise in the return on the domestic bond leads investors to increase their demand for domestic bonds by a certain amount, but further 1% rises lead to smaller and smaller increases in the demand). In addition, the overall wealth constraint of equation [18.15] implies that the responses of the demand for each asset to a change in the domestic (or the foreign) interest rate must be related in a particular way: a rise in the domestic interest rate, for example, leads to a rise in the demand for domestic bonds, a fall in the demand for money and a fall in the demand for foreign bonds, but overall wealth holdings must remain the same, so that

$$M_r + B_r + F_r = 0,$$

and

$$M_{r^*} + B_{r^*} + F_{r^*} = 0.$$

These relationships can then be used to examine the effect of increases in the supply of or demand for different assets.

One implication of this analysis is that uncovered interest parity does not hold in portfolio balance models: investors are not concerned only with the relative rates of return on domestic and foreign bonds, so that equality between rates of return may not occur and cannot be used as an equilibrium condition in a formal model. Instead the relationship between domestic and foreign interest rates can be expressed most simply as

$$r = r^* + \dot{e}^e + \rho$$

where as well as expected depreciation a separate term ρ has now been included for the 'risk premium' on domestic bonds, which may be positive or negative and indicates the risk investors believe to be involved in holding domestic as opposed to foreign bonds (in terms of the increased or decreased return required to compensate them for that risk). The risk premium can in turn be modelled as depending on, for example, the amount of domestic bonds outstanding (on the grounds that default is more likely so ρ is higher when that stock is larger).

The second key point about the portfolio balance models is that their formulation of wealth allows a different role for the current account. In the overshooting monetary model all bonds are perfect substitutes, there is no emphasis on the ownership of each type of bond, and there is no analysis of current as opposed to capital account disequilibria. But in the portfolio balance models the imperfect substitutability of domestic and foreign bonds leads to a concern with their accumulation or decumulation in the hands of residents and non-residents, and that depends on the state of the current account. Under flexible exchange rates the overall balance of payments is zero, so that a current account deficit is offset by a capital account surplus. But a capital account surplus involves non-residents accumulating stocks of domestic bonds and/or residents reducing their holdings of foreign bonds). This in turn means that a full long-run equilibrium can occur only when the current account is in balance (otherwise stocks of financial assets are changing which will affect behaviour). It also means that current account and capital account imbalances affect the international flow of interest payments, and hence affect the real rate of exchange required for the current account to balance: the larger the net debt service costs a country has to pay the higher net exports of goods and services need to be for the current account to balance, and therefore the more competitive the real exchange rate needs to be. This condition therefore provides an alternative to purchasing power parity as a long-run equilibrium condition.

Finally, it should be noted that portfolio relationships of this kind can exist within a variety of models of the real economy (more or less Keynesian) and of expectations (rational or other), and can therefore generate a variety of results, and it is for this reason that no complete portfolio balance model has been expounded here. In recent years portfolio relationships have been increasingly embedded in models with rational expectations and strong self-equilibrating tendencies, and in some respects at least they then generate results such as overshooting which have much in common with the 'monetary' models, while retaining features such as the condition for the current account to balance in the long run.

Conclusions and qualifications

This chapter has presented a full formal model of the Dornbusch overshooting model, in which exchange rates overshoot in response to monetary, but not fiscal, policy changes. The key reason for this result is the assumption that financial markets clear quickly but goods markets slowly. Research which has relaxed this assumption – for example, by introducing lags in the adjustment of portfolios – or altered the assumptions of the model in other ways – by allowing income to vary, or making capital less than perfectly mobile – does not always produce overshooting and sometimes generates undershooting. The empirical evidence on the Dornbusch model is also mixed. However, it is a neat model with assumptions generally regarded as not implausible, and it remains a popular benchmark in work on the determination of exchange rates.

The portfolio balance literature allows a richer and more differentiated menu of financial assets, takes account of international interest payments and introduces wealth effects from the current account. It thereby yields a range of additional insights, but it also generates a wider range of results depending in particular on the specific features of the wider models used. The empirical evidence here too is somewhat mixed.

A flurry of research in the 1980s put the emphasis on 'news' – the idea that exchange rates change in response to new information becoming available to the markets. But it is not obvious what constitutes 'news' or how to measure it, and empirical work has been largely unconvincing. Thus, although the analytical models used are considerably more sophisticated than those used at the beginning of the flexible exchange rate period (the early 1970s), our understanding of the determinants of exchange rates remains seriously incomplete.

Exercises

(i)   Trace through the effects of (a) a monetary contraction and (b) a rise in the foreign price level, in the full Dornbusch model.

(ii)   What happens to the workings of the Dornbusch model if the demand for money is a buffer-stock demand as in Chapter 5?

(iii)   The unification of Germany in 1990 led to a large rise in the German government's budget deficit (to finance unemployment and reconstruction in the east), and this in turn led to a rise in the German interest rate. What light can the portfolio balance approach shed on the likely long-run effects of these developments?

Further reading

The Dornbusch model is presented in his original paper (Dornbusch, 1976) and, in a more accessible form, in his (1980) text on open economy macroeconomics, which includes some discussion of the rationality of the expectations assumed and of the relationship between θ and the speed of adjustment of the price level. The seminal paper in the portfolio balance literature is by Branson (1977); it is applied to the German unification case in Branson (1994). Useful surveys of theoretical and empirical work on exchange rate determination can be found in Gibson (1996), MacDonald and Taylor (1992).

Chapter 19

New Keynesian and New Classical economics

This chapter provides a brief survey of some further developments in macroeconomics. It looks first at some of the key ideas now referred to as New Keynesian economics, and then at the business cycle theory which has arisen within and out of New Classical macroeconomics. It ends with a discussion of some of the methodological issues which have arisen in these controversies.

New Keynesian economics

The term New Keynesian has been used since the early 1980s to refer to a range of economists who share with older Keynesians a concern with unemployment and an assumption that market economies are not perfectly self-equilibrating, but differ from them in focusing their research primarily on the microeconomic foundations of macroeconomics. To some extent New Keynesian economics is a response to a New Classical critique that was common in the late 1970s and 1980s: the claim that Keynesian macro theory is not good economics because it illegitimately assumes that prices and wages are sticky or rigid, when it cannot explain why they should be (and it can be demonstrated that in general such stickiness implies that economic agents must be forgoing opportunities to increase their profits or their utility). Thus New Keynesian economics puts a heavy emphasis on microeconomic issues, and much of it is devoted to the exposition of models of how and why firms may not adjust their prices when demand changes, models of credit markets in which there is rationing (demand for loans exceeds supply yet interest rates do not rise), and models of why the wage rate does not move to clear the labour market. This emphasis comes at the expense of attention to the policy issues with which macroeconomics has traditionally been concerned.

It should be noted that when the term 'New Keynesian' was introduced it was applied retrospectively to a number of mainstream macroeconomists who had not conceived of their work in quite that way. Moreover, the concept of a New Keynesian school has been promoted by two different sets of economists belonging to two different strands of thought: the price rigidity/imperfect competition strand exemplified by economists such as Mankiw and Romer (e.g. Mankiw, 1985; Ball, Mankiw and Romer, 1988); and the imperfect information strand exemplified by Stiglitz (e.g. Stiglitz and Weiss, 1981; Greenwald and Stiglitz, 1988). Both of these strands also draw on models of the labour market.

Price rigidity and imperfect competition

One of the best-known models of this strand of thinking is the 'menu cost' model (Mankiw, 1985). This focuses on a monopolist who (as price-setter rather than price-taker) has to choose whether to change his price when demand shifts. It is assumed that there are certain costs involved in adjusting price, referred to as menu costs – i.e. the costs of printing new menus with different prices – but generally understood to refer to a wider set of costs which includes other forms of publicity and effects such as dissatisfaction caused to established customers by price changes. A rational monopolist will therefore balance these costs of price adjustment against the benefits from adjusting his price in the form of increased profits. Under some circumstances, notably where marginal revenue falls but marginal cost is unaffected, the former will outweigh the latter, and the monopolist will choose not to adjust his price.

Those circumstances typically involve what are called 'real rigidities', that is inflexibilities of some kind in real variables such as marginal cost. When the economy is characterised by such real rigidities, particularly if labour costs do not fall sharply in recessions or rise sharply in booms, then menu costs which prevent prompt or complete price adjustment can cause demand shifts to be reflected in large fluctuations in aggregate output and employment. This occurs partly because of the 'aggregate demand externality' by which firms which do not lower their prices in a recession cause real aggregate demand to be lower, for a given level of nominal aggregate demand, than it would be otherwise; if all firms were to lower their prices together real balances would rise and real demand for all firms' output would increase.

For these economists, price stickiness can be explained as the product of imperfect (typically monopolistic) competition combined with costly price adjustment and real rigidities of some kind. They see themselves, therefore, as answering the New Classical critique by providing proper microfoundations for the assumption of price stickiness.

Imperfect information

The effects of imperfect information on market exchange have been explored in a variety of contexts by Akerlof (in particular, his 1970 paper on the secondhand car market) and by Stiglitz and his various collaborators (e.g. Rothschild and Stiglitz, 1976; Grossman and Stiglitz, 1980; Stiglitz and Weiss,

1981; Greenwald and Stiglitz, 1988). In Akerlof's market for 'lemons' the sellers of cars have more information on the quality of the cars than the buyers. The buyers therefore estimate the likely quality of any car they are offered on the basis of the range of qualities of cars which sellers would be willing to sell at the existing price. In such a situation no trade may take place, even though under conditions of full information there are buyers who would be willing to pay the prices at which sellers are willing to sell their cars. At any hypothetical price buyers believe there will be a lot of dud cars as well as good cars on sale and they will therefore be willing to pay only a lower price, but at that lower price sellers are not willing to sell the better cars so the average quality of cars on sale is lower and buyers are willing only to pay a lower price still, and so the market implodes.

The Stiglitz and Weiss paper presents an explanation of credit rationing, in the context of a market for bank loans where the borrower has better information on the likely success of his investment project than the bank. When the bank raises the interest rate on its loans, adverse selection effects mean that the average quality of its customers and its loan portfolio deteriorates (less risky customers drop out but riskier ones continue to demand loans). At the same time moral hazard effects mean that the bank's customers have incentives to undertake riskier projects. Both of these effects reduce the return to the bank's lending activities, and the bank therefore prefers to lend at a lower interest rate (where less risky borrowers are still borrowing and where borrowers undertake less risky projects) even though this means that it has to refuse loans to some of its potential customers.

The general thrust of these papers (and the others referred to above) is that where the two sides to a putative exchange have access to different information, the market mechanism may result in an equilibrium which is Pareto-inefficient and where less trade takes place than would in fact be beneficial to both the parties concerned. The most general implication for macroeconomic analysis is that prices may be imperfectly flexible and may not always adjust so as to clear the markets, but there are also a number of more specific implications such as the possibility that monetary policy may work in part through quantity effects on the degree of credit rationing as well as through the price (interest rate) effects conventionally analysed, for example, in the discussion of the transmission mechanism in Chapter 7.

Models of the labour market

Before the term 'New Keynesian' came into existence some macroeconomists (e.g. Fischer, 1977) had presented rational expectations models in which wages were set in advance and could not be adjusted as rapidly as monetary policy. Such long-term wage contracts make the nominal wage sticky and thereby allow monetary policy to influence real aggregate demand. Taylor (e.g. 1979) went beyond this to formulate a model in which wages are 'staggered', that is to say wages in different firms are set at different times, so that any moment part of the labour force is on a fixed, long term, contract but another part is in the process of agreeing a new contract. If these are nominal contracts which are not automatically adjusted in line with inflation or other factors, then wages again become sticky, with the average wage rate adjusting only gradually over a number of periods, and monetary policy has some real stabilising effect. This work was open to the criticism that it simply assumed that wage contracts were long term and staggered. Economists who can more properly be described as New Keynesian then tried to explain the staggering, for example in terms of firms' desires to see what their competitors are doing before they make final decisions.

However, the bulk of New Keynesian work on the labour market has focused on two related but slightly different issues. First, can involuntary unemployment exist, that is a situation where the supply of labour exceeds the demand for it at the existing wage rate? Secondly, why do wages move over the cycle in the way they do (they appear to be either acyclical or mildly procyclical)?

The strongest answers appear to be those given by 'efficiency wage' theories. These argue that – for a number of reasons – workers work more efficiently when better rewarded. The idea was originally developed in the context of developing countries, where higher wages were seen as ensuring better nutrition and fitness in the workforce and hence greater productivity. Since then attention has switched to models in which firms set wages above the market-clearing level in order to create an incentive for workers to work harder, to avoid absenteeism or to stay with the firm: in each case the higher wages make the worker value the particular job more highly (since the alternative is a job at a lower wage or unemployment). The effect is that wages do not move to clear the labour market, the real wage is inflexible, and there is equilibrium unemployment.

New Keynesian thinking also includes 'insider–outsider' models, where a firm's existing employees (the insiders) have already acquired firm-specific knowledge which makes them more valuable to the firm than untrained outsiders. This increases the bargaining power of the insiders; it tends to raise their wages and make them less responsive to aggregate demand shocks. More generally, bargaining models of the labour market predict wage and employment results that differ from those of competitive models. Thus New Keynesian economics provides a number of partial equilibrium micro models which can in some cases be put together or placed in a wider context in such a way as to generate macro predictions concerning price and wage stickiness, unemployment and cyclical fluctuations.

New Classical macroeconomics and business cycles

The policy-ineffectiveness proposition discussed in Chapter 15 depends on the inverted supply curve interpretation of the Phillips curve, according to which output (employment) deviates from the natural rate only in response to prices turning out to be different from expected. And with rational expectations agents are assumed to correct mistakes in their expectations promptly. Early work by New Classical macroeconomists tried to develop equilibrium models of the business cycle within this framework. Lucas (1975), for example, modelled the cycle as initiated by shocks to the money stock, in a context of imperfect information (of a kind somewhat different from that highlighted in New Keynesian models). When the money stock rises and with it the prices of specific products, economic agents face what is called a 'signal-extraction problem': they have to work out the extent to which the rise in the price of their product is a rise in demand for that product (e.g. as the result of a change in tastes) to which they should respond by increasing output, and the extent to which it reflects an economy-wide rise in the overall price level (for which an increase in their output would be inappropriate). Lucas assumes that agents work largely on the basis of their past experience, in the sense that if prices have been very variable before they will expect the bulk of the price rise to be a general phenomenon, but if prices have been constant for a long period they will interpret the rise as specific to their product.

Under these circumstances a monetary shock causes output to deviate from its natural rate in the period concerned. However, fluctuations in output are generally thought to have a cyclical component; that is, if output is above (below) trend in one period it is likely to be above (below) trend in the following period as well. In order to explain this kind of fluctuation, Lucas assumed that monetary shocks are serially correlated (i.e. the shock in one period is systematically related to the shock in the next). In this case agents can use the shock in one period to help them to predict the shock in the next period, so that in later periods they will correctly interpret a higher proportion of the shock as general rather than particular, and the response of output will become smaller over time. At the same time in his model the shocks are spread through the economy and through time – 'propagated' – by the inability of the fixed capital stock to adjust to a new desired level within one period: positive monetary shocks, which are understood as implying some increase in real demand, lead to increased investment which cannot then be 'undone' when it becomes clear that the shocks were purely monetary; negative monetary shocks lead to a desire to reduce the capital stock, which can be achieved only gradually (since gross investment cannot be negative).

Models of this kind, however, were soon felt to be unsatisfactory; in particular, there is little convincing justification for the assumption that monetary shocks are serially correlated. Instead, economists from this school moved on to modelling business cycles as resulting, not from monetary, but from real shocks such as shocks to technology (e.g. inventions or innovations). In doing this they drew on the neoclassical economic growth models of the 1950s, and they set out to build their models on the basis of fully specified microfoundations of an essentially Walrasian kind, that is where prices adjusted flexibly to equilibrate demand and supply. From the first paper by Kydland and Prescott (1982) there has developed a large literature on real business cycles. The analytical models concerned are equilibrium ones like Lucas's monetary model, the propagation mechanisms in many but not all of the models also emphasise lags in the adjustment of the capital stock, and the technology shocks are often assumed to be serially correlated. But the initiating source of disturbances is now real not monetary. Indeed, in many of these models the money stock becomes endogenous, determined by (expected) increases in output, which brings real business cycle theorists into a rather surprising alliance with traditional Keynesians. A second key propagation mechanism in these models is intertemporal substitution in labour supply: the idea is that the supply of labour is highly responsive to small variations between periods in the wage rate, so that more labour is supplied in booms when the real wage is higher because workers find it optimal to do more work then, while reductions in the wage in recessions cause workers to choose to take time off work in such periods. Finally, empirical analysis has shown that cyclical fluctuations do exist but are rather less regular than economists may previously have believed.

An important feature of many real business cycle models is that their authors aim to provide empirical support for them not by econometric testing but by simulations of 'calibrated' models. The calibration of a model involves the choosing of plausible magnitudes for the parameters of an analytical model, on the basis of research conducted elsewhere (much of it at the micro level), and then the simulation of the calibrated model to see if it can produce fluctuations in income and other variables which are comparable to those observed in existing economies. This technique has proved highly controversial, for a number of reasons. Critics claim that the testing involved is very weak, and the scope for experimentation designed to improve the results is alarmingly wide. At the same time it is difficult to believe that technology shocks can be as large as is necessary for the models to 'fit', and many studies of labour supply suggest that the intertemporal elasticity is much lower than required.

Methodological issues

A number of the issues that have arisen in debates between and about New Keynesians and New Classicals are questions of what constitutes good economics and how economics should proceed, and some discussion of these issues may be useful.

First, New Classical economists have argued strongly that macroeconomic models ought to have proper microfoundations. For a long time (since at least the 1960s) it has been generally accepted that this is highly desirable, but it has also been seen as difficult. Thus the question is more, what sort of microfoundations can reasonably be provided for macro models? And the problem is that complete macro models based on fully specified microfoundations are bound to be very complex, too complex to allow easy treatment of the kind of issues with which macroeconomics has traditionally been concerned.

The New Classical answer to the problem is to use what are called 'representative agent' models in which all consumers are identical and all producers are identical, so that only a single representative agent needs to be considered in each case. While this kind of simplification has a powerful effect in making macro models more tractable, it means that an important set of problems cannot be considered at all: those problems which depend on the differences between agents, such as information asymmetries and credit constraints, and those problems which concern the coordination of the actions of different agents. Some New Classical models also preclude discussion of the labour market by assuming that all agents other than the government are identical consumer-producers who each work on their own account, selling their produce in the market and buying other products from it, but not employing or being employed by anyone else.

The New Keynesian approach, on the other hand, is to concentrate on getting the micro right, with all its complexities. Accordingly, New Keynesians have been able to present plausible partial equilibrium accounts of price and wage stickiness and other phenomena, but have not been able to integrate them into a complete macro model.

By contrast the older Keynesians and monetarists and others who now fall into the category of mainstream macroeconomists tend to use macro models with inadequately specified microfoundations, because they consider that is the only basis on which they can address the macro questions that concern them. They then justify their assumptions partly with reference to the empirical evidence and partly by reference to the micro models which New Keynesians and others have developed.

A good illustration is provided by the phenomenon of price and wage stickiness. The New Classicals have rejected the assumption of stickiness in a macro model. They have not for the most part claimed that prices and wages are perfectly flexible, or that stickiness is an empirically incorrect assumption. Rather they have argued that it is wrong to make such an assumption unless you can explain, on the basis of 'first principles' of utility- and profit-maximisation, why stickiness should exist; surely agents who failed to adjust their prices and wages to market-clearing levels must be forgoing realisable gains, and it would be wrong to assume they would do so. Against this methodological principle it has been argued, by mainstream as well as New Keynesian economists, that the inability to explain a fact or regularity which has been recognised by economists almost from the beginning of the subject does not require the scientist to deny its existence, and such a denial would unnecessarily reduce our knowledge. Moreover, there are now enough partial equilibrium explanations of price and wage stickiness to justify the assumption.

A rather different example of the difficulty of building proper microfoundations concerns agents' expectations. New Classical and real business-cycle models assume not merely that expectations are rational but that economic agents know the model concerned. It is easy to identify situations in which this assumption is defensible – for example, in an economy which has not been subject to either significant structural change or significant change in the aims and techniques of economic policy for a long period. However, when these qualifications do not hold (and the Lucas critique has done more than anything else to underline the possible non-constancy of government policy), agents may not know the full model and may need to 'learn' about how policy is being operated. But in that case it is necessary to be very careful in applying rational expectations assumptions. An unsatisfactory example is Barro's (1978) study of the US over the period 1945–76 which assumed that in those periods agents operated on the basis of their understanding of a New Classical model in which (anticipated) changes in the money stock affect prices rather than real income. But throughout that period the conventional wisdom, based largely on an unaugmented version of the Phillips curve in which aggregate demand stimulus has effects (in the long as well as the short run) on both income and inflation, was quite different, and presumably it is this conventional wisdom which must have governed the way agents formed their expectations in that period.

Concluding comments

New Keynesian economics has produced a large number of interesting insights, mainly incorporated in partial equilibrium micro models, which provide at least partial rationales for some of the assumptions commonly made in mainstream macroeconomics and hence defences of those assumptions against New Classical criticisms. On the other hand, New Keynesian economics as such has not yet developed macro models comparable to those of mainstream economists, or models which can be used to address the policy issues on which those economists focus.

The price rigidity strand has given at least partial rationales for price and wage stickiness, though these involve in part the replacement of one not fully justified assumption by another, that of imperfect competition. But that then raises the question, would the economy be a perfect market-clearing one if only there were perfect competition? The imperfect information strand of New Keynesian economics tries to model the workings of the market mechanism more directly, drawing on some of the latest developments in microeconomics. The corresponding question which that raises is, would the economy be a perfect market-clearing one if only there was perfect information? Most mainstream economists and many old Keynesians would give a no to the former question, but perhaps a qualified yes to the latter. It should also be noted that Tobin, as a representative of the older Keynesians, has rejected the view that Keynesian economics hinges on price rigidity (a view which recalls the earlier Keynesian–neoclassical synthesis) and insisted that his vision is one in which markets clear, but not instantaneously and continuously (Tobin, 1993, p. 46). The imperfect information strand of New Keynesian economics seems therefore to have more continuity with old Keynesianism, old monetarism and modern mainstream economics (and also with the way in which Keynes himself has been interpreted since the reappraisal presented by Clower (1965) and Leijonhufvud (1968)), while the price rigidity strand appears to stand a little apart, perhaps precisely because its development has been more clearly a response to New Classical arguments. That says nothing, of course, about the correctness of either strand.

New Classical macroeconomics set out to build an equilibrium model of business cycles in which the source or cause of cycles was monetary shocks. When this failed to be convincing, economists from that school tried to model business cycles as the equilibrium result not of monetary but of real (largely technological) shocks. That attempt has raised a great deal of controversy, whose outcome is still unclear, but it has at least forced economists to look much more closely at the nature of the fluctuations concerned. At the same time the New Classical emphasis on microfoundations, however vulnerable its own microfoundations to methodological and other criticisms, has forced economists to confront questions that were largely left aside in the 1950s and 1960s. In doing so it contributed to the development of the price rigidity strand of New Keynesian economics. It also provided a stimulus to the development by economists such as Woodford (1992) and Farmer (1993) of equilibrium models in which there are multiple equilibria, each consistent with a different set of expectations or beliefs held by economic agents; such work sometimes has a much more Keynesian flavour in terms of its welfare implications. Thus, just as the neoclassicals of the 1930s and 1940s used the Keynesian framework to generate non-Keynesian conclusions, the new 'sunspot' theorists are using the New Classical framework to generate Keynesian implications.

In conclusion, then, while neither of the schools considered in this chapter is likely, in the present writer's view, to end up as the dominating paradigm of macroeconomics, both of them have pushed the borders of the subject outwards and will be seen by later historians of economics to have made net contributions which are strictly positive.

Further reading

The 1993 symposium on New Keynesian economics in the *Journal of Economic Perspectives* contains useful papers by Romer (1993) and Greenwald and Stiglitz (1993), representing the two strands, and Tobin (1993) as an old Keynesian. The Mankiw and Romer (1991) volumes contain many of the key papers from both strands, and Stiglitz (1992) is also worth reading partly for his methodological comments. Laidler (1990, Chapter 4) and Brunner (1989) contain methodological as well as wider comments on New Classical macroeconomics by monetarist-mainstream economists. Hoover (1988) discusses equilibrium business cycles, both monetary and real, as well as other aspects of New Classical macroeconomics. A more sympathetic treatment of New Classical ideas can be found in Barro (1990, part 6). Useful but more difficult treatments can be found in McCallum (1992) and Romer (1996).

Bibliography

Akerlof, G. 1970. The market for 'lemons', qualitative uncertainty and the market mechanism, *Quarterly Journal of Economics*, **84**, 488–500.

Artis, M. 1979. Recent developments in the theory of fiscal policy, in Cook and Jackson (1979).

Artis, M.J., Leslie, D. and Smith, G.W. 1982. Wage inflation: a survey, in Artis, M.J., Green, C.J., Leslie, D. and Smith, G.W. (eds), *Demand Management, Supply Constraints and Inflation*, Manchester University Press.

Artis, M.J. and Lewis, M.K. 1976. The demand for money in the United Kingdom, 1963–73, *Manchester School*, **44**, 147–81.

Artis, M.J. and Lewis, M.K. 1991. *Money in Britain: Monetary Policy, Innovation and Europe*, Hemel Hempstead: Philip Allan.

Artis, M.J. and Miller, M.H. 1979. Inflation, real wages and the terms of trade, in Bowers, J.K. (ed.), *Inflation, Development and Integration*, Leeds: Leeds University Press.

Attfield, C.L.F., Demery, D. and Duck, N.W. 1991. *Rational Expectations in Macroeconomics*, 2nd edition, Oxford: Blackwell.

Backus, D. and Driffill, J. 1985. Inflation and reputation, *American Economic Review*, **75**, 530–8.

Ball, L., Mankiw, N. and Romer, D. 1988. The New Keynesian economics and the output-inflation trade-off, *Brookings Papers on Economic Activity*, no. 1, 1–65.

Barro, R. 1974. Are government bonds net wealth?, *Journal of Political Economy*, **82**, 1095–117.

Barro, R. 1978. Unanticipated money, output and the price level in the United States, *Journal of Political Economy*, **86**, 549–81.

Barro, R. 1990. *Macroeconomics, 3rd edition*, New York: Wiley.

Barro, R. and Gordon, D. 1983. Rules, discretion and reputation in a model of monetary policy, *Journal of Monetary Economics,* **12**, 101–21.

Baumol, W. 1952. The transactions demand for cash: an inventory theoretic approach, *Quarterly Journal of Economics*, **66**, 545–56.

Begg, D. 1987. Fiscal policy, in R. Dornbusch and R. Layard (eds), *The Performance of the British Economy*, Oxford: Oxford University Press.

Blackburn, K. and Christensen, M. 1989. Monetary policy and policy credibility: theories and evidence, *Journal of Economic Literature*, **27**, 1–45.

Blinder, A. and Solow, R. 1973. Does fiscal policy matter?, *Journal of Public Economics*, **2**, 319–37.

Branson, W. 1977. Asset markets and relative prices in exchange rate determination, *Sozialwissenschaftliche Annalen*, **1**, 69–89.

Branson, W. 1994. German reunification, the breakdown of the EMS and the path to Stage Three, in D. Cobham (ed.), *European Monetary Upheavals*, Manchester University Press.

Brunner, K. 1989. The disarray in macroeconomics, in F. Capie and G. Wood (eds), *Monetary Economics in the 1980s*, London: Macmillan.

Buiter, W. 1985. A guide to public sector debt and deficits, *Economic Policy*, **1**, 13–78.

Cagan, P. 1965. *Determinants and Effects of Changes in the Stock of Money*. New York: National Bureau of Economic Research.

Carlin, W. and Soskice, D. 1990. *Macroeconomics and the Wage Bargain*, Oxford: Oxford University Press.

Carline, D. 1985. Trade unions and wages, in Carline, D., Pissarides, C.A., Siebert, W.S. and Sloane, P.J., *Labour Economics*, Harlow: Longman.

Chick, V. 1995. Is there a case for Post-Keynesian economics?, *Scottish Journal of Political Economy*, **42**, 20–36.

Chirinko, R. 1993. Business fixed investment spending: modeling strategies, empirical results, and policy implications, *Journal of Economic Literature*, **31**, 1875–911.

Christ, C. 1968. A simple macroeconomic model with a government budget restraint, *Journal of Political Economy*, **76**, 53–67.

Clower, R. 1965. The Keynesian counterrevolution: a theoretical appraisal, in F. Hahn and F. Brechling (eds), *The Theory of Interest Rates*, London: Macmillan.

Cobham, D. 1984. Convergence, divergence and realignment in British macroeconomics, *Banca Nazionale del Lavoro Quarterly Review*, no. 146, 159–76.

Cobham, D. 1991. The money supply process, in C. Green and D. Llewellyn (eds), *Financial Markets and Institutions*, Oxford: Blackwell.

Coddington, A. 1983. *Keynesian Economics: The Search for First Principles*, London: Allen & Unwin.

Cook, S. and Jackson, P. 1979. *Current Issues in Fiscal Policy*, Oxford: Martin Robertson.

Cross, R. (ed.) 1993. *The NAIRU*, special issue of the *Journal of Economic Studies*, **20**, 1–140.

Cukierman, A. 1994. Central bank independence and monetary control, *Economic Journal*, **104**, 1437–48.

Currie, D. 1976. Macroeconomic policy and government financing, in M. Artis and A. Nobay (eds), *Contemporary Economic Analysis*, London: Croom Helm.

Currie, D. 1981. Monetary and fiscal policy and the crowding-out issue, in M. Artis and M. Miller (eds), *Essays in Fiscal and Monetary Policy*, Oxford: Oxford University Press.

Cuthbertson, K. and Taylor, M. 1987. *Macroeconomic Systems*, Oxford: Blackwell.

De Grauwe, P. 1997. *The Economics of Monetary Integration*, 3rd edition, Oxford University Press.

Dornbusch, R. 1976. Expectations and exchange rate dynamics, *Journal of Political Economy*, **84**, 1161–76.

Dornbusch, R. 1980. *Open Economy Macroeconomics*, New York: Basic Books.

Economic Journal 1997. Controversy: microfoundations and the demand for money, *Economic Journal*, **107**, 1169–223.

Estrin, S. and Laidler, D. 1995. *Introduction to Microeconomics*, 4th edition, Hemel Hempstead: Harvester Wheatsheaf.

Farmer, R. 1993. *The Macroeconomics of Self-Fulfilling Prophecies*, Cambridge, MA: MIT Press.

Fischer, S. 1977. Long-term contracts, rational expectations and the optimal money supply, *Journal of Political Economy*, **85**, 187–209.

Fischer, S. 1990. Rules versus discretion in monetary policy, in B. Friedman and F. Hahn (eds), *A Handbook of Monetary Economics*, vol. 2, Amsterdam: North Holland.

Fischer, S. 1994. Modern central banking, in F. Capie, C. Goodhart, S. Fischer and N. Schnadt, *The Future of Central Banking*, Cambridge: Cambridge University Press.

Fisher, I. 1911. *The Purchasing Power of Money*, New York: Macmillan.

Friedman, B. 1975. Targets, instruments and indicators of monetary policy, *Journal of Monetary Economics*, **1**, 443–73.

Friedman, B. 1990. Targets and instruments of monetary policy, in B. Friedman and F. Hahn (eds), *A Handbook of Monetary Economics*, vol. 2, Amsterdam: North Holland.

Friedman, M. 1953. The effects of full-employment policy on economic stability: a formal analysis, in M. Friedman, *Essays in Positive Economics*, Chicago: University of Chicago Press.

Friedman, M. 1956. The quantity theory of money: a restatement, in Friedman, M. (ed), *Studies in the Quantity Theory of Money*, Chicago: University of Chicago Press.

Friedman, M. 1957. *A Theory of the Consumption Function*, Princeton: Princeton University Press.

Friedman, M. 1960. *A Program for Monetary Stability*, New York: Fordham University Press.

Friedman, M. 1968. The role of monetary policy, *American Economic Review*, **58**, 1–17.

Friedman, M. and Schwartz, A. 1963. *A Monetary History of the United States, 1867–1960*, Princeton: Princeton University Press for National Bureau of Economic Research.

Gibson, H. 1996. *International Finance*, Harlow: Longman.

Goldfeld, S. 1976. The case of the missing money, *Brookings Papers on Economic Activity*, no. 3, 577–638.

Goodhart, C.A.E. 1973. Analysis of the determination of the stock of money, in Parkin, J.M. and Nobay, A.R. (eds), *Essays in Modern Economics*, Harlow: Longman.

Goodhart, C. 1989. *Money, Information and Uncertainty*, 2nd edition, London: Macmillan.

Goodhart, C. 1994. What should central banks do? What should be their macroeconomic objectives and operations?, *Economic Journal*, **104**, 1424–36.

Gordon, R. 1976. Recent developments in the theory of inflation and unemployment, *Journal of Monetary Economics*, **2**, 185–219.

Greenwald, B. and Stiglitz, J. 1988. Examining alternative macroeconomic theories, *Brookings Papers on Economic Activity*, no. 1, 207–60.

Greenwald, B. and Stiglitz, J. 1993. New and old Keynesians, *Journal of Economic Perspectives*, **7**, 23–44.

Grossman, S. and Stiglitz, J. 1980. On the impossibility of informationally efficient markets, *American Economic Review*, **70**, 393–408.

Harris, L. 1981. *Monetary Theory*, New York: McGraw-Hill.

Hicks, J.R. 1937. Mr. Keynes and the 'Classics': a suggested interpretation, *Econometrica*, **5**, 147–59.

Hicks, J.R. 1973. Recollections and documents, *Economica*, **40**, 2–11.

Hicks, J. 1974 *The Crisis in Keynesian Economics*, Oxford: Blackwell.

Hoover, K. 1988. *The New Classical Macroeconomics: A Sceptical Inquiry*, Oxford: Blackwell.

Johnson, H.G. 1972. The monetary approach to balance-of-payments theory, in Johnson, H.G., *Further Essays in Monetary Economics*, London: Allen & Unwin.

Journal of Economic Perspectives 1997. Symposium on the natural rate of unemployment, **11**, Winter, 3–108.

Judd, J. and Scadding, J. 1982. The search for a stable demand for money: a survey of the post-1973 literature, *Journal of Economic Literature*, **20**, 993–1023.

Keynes, J.M. 1936. *The General Theory of Employment, Interest and Money*, London: Macmillan.

Klamer, A. 1984. *The New Classical Macroeconomics*, Brighton: Wheatsheaf.

Kydland, F. and Prescott, E. 1977. Rules rather than discretion: the inconsistency of optimal plans, *Journal of Political Economy*, **85**, 473–91.

Kydland, F. and Prescott, E. 1982. Time to build and aggregate fluctuations, *Econometrica*, **50**, 1345–70.

Laidler, D. 1982. *Monetarist Perspectives*, Oxford: Philip Allan.

Laidler, D. 1990. *Taking Money Seriously*, Hemel Hempstead: Philip Allan.

Laidler, D. 1992. Issues in contemporary macroeconomics, in Vercelli and Dimitri (1992).

Laidler, D. 1993. *The Demand for Money: Theories, Evidence and Problems*, 4th edition, New York: HarperCollins.

Leijonhufvud, A. 1968. *On Keynesian Economics and the Economics of Keynes*, Oxford: Oxford University Press.

Leijonhufvud, A. 1981. *Information and Coordination*, Oxford: Oxford University Press.

Leijonhufvud, A. 1992. Keynesian economics: past confusions, future prospects, in Vercelli and Dimitri (1992).

Leslie, D. 1993. *Advanced Macroeconomics: Beyond IS/LM*, London: McGraw-Hill.

Lipsey, R.G. 1960. The relationship between unemployment and the rate of change of money wage rates in the UK, 1862–1957: a further analysis, *Economica*, NS **27**, 1–31.

Lucas, R. 1972. Expectations and the neutrality of money, *Journal of Economic Theory*, **4**, 103–24.

Lucas, R. 1975. An equilibrium model of the business cycle, *Journal of Political Economy*, **83**, 1113–44.

McCallum, B. 1992. Real business cycle theories, in Vercelli and Dimitri (1992).

MacDonald, R. and Taylor, M. 1992. Exchange-rate economics: a survey, *IMF Staff Papers*, **39**, 1–57.

Mankiw, N. 1985. Small menu costs and large business cycles: a macroeconomic model of monopoly, *Quarterly Journal of Economics*, **100**, 529–39.

Mankiw, N. and Romer, D. (eds), 1991. *New Keynesian Economics*, 2 volumes, Cambridge, MA: MIT Press.

Miller, M. 1985. Measuring the stance of fiscal policy, *Oxford Review of Economic Policy*, **1**, 44–57.

Miller, M. and Orr, D. 1966. A model of the demand for money by firms, *Quarterly Journal of Economics*, **80**, 413–35.

Muth, J. 1961. Rational expectations and the theory of price movements, *Econometrica*, **29**, 315–35.

Nickell, S. 1997. Unemployment and labour market rigidities: Europe versus North America, *Journal of Economic Perspectives*, **11**, Summer, 55–74.

Ott, D. and Ott, A. 1965. Budget balance and equilibrium income, *Journal of Finance*, **20**, 71–7.

Phelps, E.S. 1967. Phillips curves, expectations of inflation and optimal unemployment over time, *Economica*, NS **34**, 254–81.

Phelps, E. 1968. Money wage dynamics and labour market equilibrium, *Journal of Political Economy*, **76**, 678–711.

Phelps, E. 1992. Expectations in macroeconomics and the rational expectations debate, in Vercelli and Dimitri (1992).

Phelps, E. and Taylor, J. 1977. The stabilizing powers of monetary policy under rational expectations, *Journal of Political Economy*, **85**, 163–90.

Phillips, A.W. 1958. The relation between unemployment and the rate of change of money wage rates in the United Kingdom, 1861–1957, *Economica*, NS **25**, 283–99.

Poole, W. 1970. Optimal choice of monetary policy instruments in a simple stochastic macro model, *Quarterly Journal of Economics*, **84**, 197–216.

Rogoff, K. 1985. The optimal degree of commitment to an intermediate monetary target, *Quarterly Journal of Economics*, **100**, 1169–89.

Romer, D. 1993. The New Keynesian synthesis, *Journal of Economic Perspectives*, **7**, 5–22.

Romer, D. 1996. *Advanced Macroeconomics*, New York: McGraw-Hill.

Rothschild, K. and Stiglitz, J. 1976. Equilibrium in competitive insurance markets: an essay on the economics of imperfect information, *Quarterly Journal of Economics*, **90**, 629–49.

Sargent, T.J. 1986. *Rational Expectations and Inflation*, New York: Harper & Row.

Sargent, T. and Wallace, N. 1976. Rational expectations and the theory of economic policy, *Journal of Monetary Economics*, **2**, 168–83.

Sargent, T. and Wallace, N. 1981. Some unpleasant monetarist arithmetic, *Federal Reserve Bank of Minneapolis Quarterly Review*, Fall, 1–17.

Siebert, H. 1997. Labour market rigidities: at the root of unemployment in Europe, *Journal of Economic Perspectives*, **11**, Summer, 37–54.

Simons, H. 1936. Rules versus authorities in monetary policy, *Journal of Political Economy*, **44**, 1–30.

Stiglitz, J. 1992. Methodological issues and the New Keynesian economics, in Vercelli and Dimitri (1992).

Stiglitz, J. and Weiss, A. 1981. Credit rationing in markets with imperfect information, *American Economic Review*, **71**, 393–410.

Sumner, M.T. 1984. The history and significance of the Phillips curve, in Demery, D., Duck N.W., Sumner, M.T., Thomas, R.L. and Thompson, W.N., *Macroeconomics*, Harlow: Longman.

Surrey, M.J.C. (ed.) 1976. *Macroeconomic Themes*, Oxford: Oxford University Press.

Taylor, J. 1979. Staggered wage setting in a macro model, *American Economic Review*, **69**, 108–13.

Thomas, R.L. 1993. *Introductory Econometrics,* 2nd edition, Harlow: Longman.

Tobin, J. 1956. The interest elasticity of transactions demand for cash, *Review of Economics and Statistics*, **38**, 241–7.

Tobin, J. 1958. Liquidity preference as behaviour towards risk, *Review of Economic Studies*, **25**, 65–86.

Tobin, J. 1963. Commercial banks as creators of 'money', in D. Carson (ed.), *Banking and Monetary Studies*, Homewood: Irwin.

Tobin, J. 1969. A general equilibrium approach to monetary theory, *Journal of Money, Credit and Banking*, **1**, 15–29.

Tobin, J. 1993. Price flexibility and output stabilisation: an old Keynesian view, *Journal of Economic Perspectives*, **7**, 45–66.

Tobin, J. and Buiter, W. 1976. Long run effects of fiscal and monetary policy on aggregate demand, in J. Stein (ed.), *Monetarism*, Amsterdam: North Holland.

Varian, H. 1993. *Intermediate Microeconomics*, 3rd edition, New York: Norton.

Vercelli, A. and Dimitri, N. 1992. *Macroeconomics: A Survey of Research Strategies*, Oxford: Oxford University Press.

Walsh, C. 1995. Optimal contracts for central bankers, *American Economic Review*, **85**, 150–67.

Williamson, J. and Milner, C. 1991. *The World Economy*, Hemel Hempstead: Harvester Wheatsheaf.

Woodford, M. 1992. Equilibrium endogenous fluctuations: an introduction, in Vercelli and Dimitri (1992).

Index